WOUNDED
WINGS

WOUNDED WINGS

ONE MAN'S SECRET STRUGGLE

BY

JEANNE DONOVAN AND **RONALD I. JOHNSON**

TCU
Press

FORT WORTH, TEXAS

Library of Congress Control Number: 2025002061

TCU
Press

TCU Box 298300
Fort Worth, Texas 76129
www.tcupress.com

Design by Julie Rushing

DEDICATION

Milian,

Thank you for loving, supporting, and sharing your life with our brother. Your memories of him have helped us tell his unique story.

CONTENTS

NOTE TO THE READER

This book has two authors, half-siblings Ronald Johnson and Jeanne Donovan. The voice of the storyteller varies depending on who had the best vantage point at the time salient events happened to the book's primary subject, Gilbert Johnson. In those portions written in first person, the author is identified.

ACKNOWLEDGMENTS

A book is only an idea until the authors find support for their endeavor. We wish to thank Dan Williams, director of TCU Press, for having faith in our initiative and helping us focus our efforts in the right direction. Over twenty years ago, and years after Gil's death, Milian France sent her unpublished original screenplay titled *The Mystery of Loving Men* to our father, Marlin Johnson, who later sent it to Jeanne for safekeeping. Milian said, "I wanted to show him how good and honorable Gil had been as a man, and how tragic it was that he had life changing things in childhood, and yet created himself to be an honorable and exemplary man." She wrote a screenplay of their time together as a therapeutic release. She had loved Gil for well over a decade (1973–88), even though he found it impossible to form a monogamous, permanent relationship with her because of his past. We lost contact with Milian years ago but finally located her again. We are grateful that she opened her heart once more, this time to help us piece together parts of Gil's adult life that were unknown to us.

Our brothers, David and Daniel Johnson, were always patient and complied with many requests for recollections of family lore. You two wrote the manual on how to be good brothers.

Linda Lee Cadwell, Diana Lee Inosanto, and Chris Kent deserve special mention. These three opened up a treasure trove of priceless insights surrounding a special period in Gil's personal and professional life. Long live the *Tao of Jeet Kune Do.*

It took a long time for all the puzzle pieces of Gil's life to be discovered and put together, so our spouses deserve very special thanks for their love and patience while we chased a dream. Jeanne's husband, Nowell, fully supported our project and never complained about her seemingly endless hours of sequestration. She loves him dearly for his patience and for being a marvelous sounding board as she recalled painful memories. Ron's wife,

Suparaht, was extremely supportive of the project and realized its value before Ronald did.

INTRODUCTION

(As told by Ronald)

January 1998 was another dry and cold winter month in Albuquerque, New Mexico. My sister Jeanne Johnson Donovan came from her home in Fort Worth, Texas, for an extended stay because our father, Marlin Eugene Johnson, was undergoing another round of chemotherapy. My wife, Raht, and I were preoccupied with two small children, and mom appreciated Jeanne's assistance caring for dad. During this period, Raht, Jeanne, and I took a day trip up to Santa Fe to sightsee and get better acquainted. Jeanne was the oldest child of dad's first marriage, and I was the youngest child of his second. Up to the age of thirty-five I had spoken to Jeanne perhaps twice. We were amiable strangers with a common father. I have no recollection of what we did in Santa Fe that winter day, but I do recall telling and hearing numerous stories of our common father and sharing memories from our own very different childhoods. That day a door cracked opened and gave us a peek into a large, unexplored archive of Johnson history.

Over the next twenty-two years Jeanne and Nowell continued their distinguished association with Texas Christian University in Fort Worth while raising their two adorable daughters. Raht and I, providentially not long after my father's passing, moved to Denton, Texas, began a new job, and raised our own two children. The relative closeness of our homes, only an hour's drive from each other, gave Jeanne and me ample opportunities to nurture familial bonds thirty-five years overdue.

Several years ago Jeanne showed me the beginnings of a biography she was attempting to write about Gil, her full brother and my half-brother. However, the painful weight of Gil's story and other pressing family commitments hindered Jeanne from completing a draft. So, her draft was returned to its dusty box along with all her collected research files and put in a closet. Neither Jeanne nor I was satisfied with that decision. Time passed. The Donovan girls left home and started their own lives. The Johnson children grew up and left home, too. It was now time to remove that old box from Jeanne's closet and decide either to tape the box shut and never discuss the contents again or muster the courage to reopen some old, personal wounds, ask some uncomfortable questions about a topic we both found repugnant, and tell Gil's story to anyone willing to listen. We chose the latter. What follows is the true tale of a young man who gallantly pursued a full life and almost overcame the enormous odds stacked high against him until the demons within became too heavy to carry.

We humbly submit to you the story of our beloved brother Gilbert Lee Johnson. It is our sincerest hope that the story behind the story will be of service to those individuals and family members battling the effects of long-term sexual trauma inflicted on children.

CHAPTER 1

FINAL DAYS

Los Angeles County General Hospital was once a grand lady. It was proudly built atop a hill overlooking the Boyle Heights district of east Los Angeles during the darkest period of the Great Depression. Its nineteen stories and eight hundred beds were a beacon of hope that provided modern medical care for the growing city and facilitated the training of generations of medical professionals. Massive limestone carvings of ancient, toga-clad physicians standing on either side of an angel with her spread wings, administering aid to the sick, looked down upon the hospital's main entrance. On the arching ceiling of the lobby was painted a beautiful fresco depicting the Greek god of medicine, Asclepius, giving aid to a mother's infant child. The hospital's exterior art deco architecture used repeating geometric blocking patterns to elegantly join the various building wings. The design also incorporated strong, vertical, and horizontal lines to emphasize the window's overall importance to the structure. Ambient light was necessary for a patient's healing and recovery. She was a sight to behold, but, unfortunately, the grandeur would not last forever.

Father Time was not kind to this grand lady. A population explosion following World War II, urban sprawl, strained county budgets, and conflicting city priorities all worked to bring about County General Hospital's downfall. Since the institution was a city-owned and -managed facility, it also was the first-line medical care center for Los Angeles's expanding homeless community, substance abuse victims, and shooting and stab victims. The attendant sights and smells drove the more well-to-do citizens to newer or private hospitals. By the 1980s the place was a shadow of itself. And to add insult to injury, County General Hospital, being a focal point of an emerging national health epidemic, was being publicly criticized for not providing better patient care to counter the threat. Not since the great influenza epidemic of 1918 had the American public been exposed to a health threat like this. The new threat was called AIDS, acquired immune deficiency syndrome. In the winter of 1987, Los Angeles County had 4,437 AIDS cases, resulting in 2,768 deaths. Similar numbers were seen in San Francisco and New York City. County General Hospital was treating an average of fifty to sixty inpatients per day with AIDS or AIDS-related complex. Our thirty-eight-year-old brother, Gilbert Lee Johnson, was one of those statistics. A statistic becomes something altogether different when it involves your own brother.

The US Centers for Disease Control (CDC) whispered into the public's ear in June of 1981 when they published a "Morbidity and Mortality Weekly Report" (MMWR) describing cases of a rare lung infection, Pneumocystis carinii pneumonia, in five young, previously healthy gay men in Los Angeles. All the men had other unusual infections as well, indicating that their immune systems were not working; two men died by the time the report was published. In September 1982, the CDC used the term "AIDS" for the first time and released the first case definition of it as a disease at least moderately predictive of a defect in cell-mediated immunity, occurring in a person with no known case for diminished resistance to that disease. That same year, the CDC reported cases of AIDS in infants who had received blood transfusions. The whisper became a shout when the CDC noted in their March 1983 edition of the MMWR that most cases of AIDS had been reported among homosexual men with multiple partners, people who inject drugs, Haitians, and hemophiliacs. The report "suggested" that AIDS may be caused by an infectious agent that is transmitted sexually or through exposure to blood or blood products. However, in a later report the same year they changed the "may be caused by" language to rule out transmission by casual contact, food, water, air, or environmental surfaces. The American public conveniently chose to disregard the report's statement about actual modes of infection transmission and began to build barriers, invisible and tangible, between themselves and anyone they construed to be in the infected population. Notably, in the spring of 1985, Ryan White, an Indiana teenager who contracted AIDS through contaminated blood products used to treat his hemophilia, was refused entry to his middle school. His family's protracted legal battles brought AIDS awareness to the forefront of the American consciousness. And to be entirely transparent, in 1985, all of us in Gilbert's immediate family sided with the general public's uneducated fears to one degree or another. That all changed in a matter of minutes in the spring of 1986 when Gilbert sat in his North Hollywood apartment, picked up the phone, and in succession first called his mother in Antlers, Oklahoma, because she was the easiest to tell, then Jeanne in Fort Worth, then our brother David in Colorado Springs, and divulged his AIDS diagnosis. Finally, the most difficult call came last, to our father in Albuquerque, New Mexico. The shame and trepidation Gilbert felt making that last call must have been unbearable. The rest of us found out after the fact. The weight of Gilbert's news was so immense that no one even asked him how he contracted the disease. We all drew our own conclusions.

Ronald Remembers

I was in my final year at the University of New Mexico and was living in an apartment that was closer to the campus than my parent's westside home. One Tuesday mother invited me over for dinner, as she frequently did. I gladly accepted the offer and made my way out to Paradise Hills after my last class. After dinner dad took me into the living room and told me the news about Gilbert. Mother was not in the room. As the word "AIDS" left his mouth, my father's entire body slumped and broke into uncontrollable sobs and tears. I almost came out of my own skin. I had never seen my father shed a tear, much less break into near hysteria in my presence in my twenty-three-year-old life. In hindsight, I was more distraught over my father's emotional display than what he told me. On the drive back to my apartment, I recall feeling sincere pity for Gilbert but also feeling slightly perturbed that our family name may be tarnished due to his actions. It was not my proudest moment.

Jeanne Remembers

Our phone rang midmorning on February 12, 1988. My preschool-age daughters were squealing nearby, playing a game. Susan French, a friend of my brother, was on the other end. She got straight to the point. Gil had passed away in the middle of the night. Even though all the family knew he didn't have long to live, the finality of her words stabbed my heart like a dagger.

Susan told me that Bo, a close friend of Gil's, had become his caretaker in the final days of his life. When Bo woke in the morning around 8:00 a.m., he immediately realized that Gil must have died in his sleep, because Gil always woke in the night and needed help, alerting Bo by clanging a brass mortar inside its foot-tall brass pestle. The mortar and pestle were one of Gil's souvenirs from his travels to Saudi Arabia. His most prized possession, though, was a graceful Arabian Saluki dog. Her name was Dasmah. She slept beside Gil's bed.

Susan also called our father to relay the news. As I had traveled from Fort Worth to Los Angeles only six weeks prior to visit with Gil, we all agreed that Dad, along with our brothers Darrell, Danny, and David, would drive from Albuquerque to Hollywood to handle funeral arrangements, clear out his apartment, and find a home for Dasmah.

As I put the phone down, I recalled the last time I saw Gil alive. He and I had been talking by phone over the previous year, beginning when he rang me with the news that he had acquired AIDS. He didn't say how. I had my own thoughts, but I had no reason to believe he was homosexual, especially since he had several girlfriends over the years. To say this news was a shock is putting it mildly. The AIDS epidemic was killing people around the world, so stories were on all the networks, just like COVID-19 is today. Everyone was scared because we didn't fully understand how it was transmitted. We knew doctors were trying to find a cure, or at least a treatment for AIDS, but the process was painfully slow and full of failures. At that time, one thing was certain: AIDS was a death sentence.

As Gil's health deteriorated, he had to periodically go to the hospital for platelet transfusions. Before he reached that stage of his illness, though, he participated in a clinical study. Half the patients were given the drug AZT, while the control group was given a placebo. Gil prayed he was getting the AZT, but he eventually learned he was in the control group. Following that discovery, his decline became quite rapid.

Six weeks before Gil died, he let me know he was back in the hospital again for another transfusion; he held little hope and thought his end was near. He wasn't angry, nor bitter, and he had forgiven the trespassers who had led him to this awful place. He had resigned himself to his fate.

I packed my bags, left my little girls with their father, and flew to Los Angeles.

Susan picked me up at the airport. After dropping my bags at Gil's apartment, she drove me along the tortuous Los Angeles freeway to the hospital. Near the hospital we stopped for gas. Before I could put my fingers on my car door handle, a homeless man yanked the door open and begged me for money. I was already feeling sick to my stomach; now I felt intimidated as well. As I looked around the area, I saw homeless people scattered everywhere. This was not a happy, clean place. Inside the hospital, it was the same. In fact, along the hallways patients were lying in hospital beds pushed against the dreary, marred walls. The place was overcrowded and felt dirty. I thought, "This is a horrible place for my brother to die. It shouldn't be like this."

When I walked into Gil's room, I was first disappointed to find that he shared his room with several other patients. Like the hallways, privacy was not possible. More importantly, I was shocked when I saw his emaciated state. Where once Gil had possessed an athletic body attained through years of rigorous karate training, now he looked anorexic, nearly bald, and his face and body was peppered with blotchy bruises, a definitive sign that he was suffering from thrombocytopenia, a bleeding disorder that prevents blood from clotting. AIDS patients were treated with platelet transfusions to help the blood clot, but all transfusions could do was extend the life of the patient for a brief period. Gil's time was rapidly running out.

What do you say to a man who is dying other than "I miss you, I'm sorry, and I love you"? He told me about the procedures doctors were using to give him some relief, but there was resignation in his voice. Then we moved on to mundane conversations to change the subject. After about an hour Susan said we needed to get back on the road soon or we would be traveling during rush hour. She planned to bring me back in the morning.

I spent the evening alone in Gil's apartment, walking through the rooms, touching things I knew he loved, and going through stacks of photos from his karate days and his travels to Iran during the 1979 revolution. None of the faces in the photos were familiar to me, but I knew these people had been important to him. At the same time, I felt fear. I had heard all kinds of rumors about how easy it was to catch AIDS. Could we catch it from hugging, drinking from the same glass, or sharing a razor? Tonight, I would be sleeping in his bed. Would I catch it from lying on the sheets? Those concerns sound ridiculous now, but at that time, we didn't have answers to all our questions. The internet as we know it today did not exist in the 1980s; there was no Wikipedia. Our main sources for news were three network television stations and newspapers, so information we can find in seconds today took days or weeks to make the rounds across the country. In the interim, our imaginations ran wild.

Susan picked me up in the morning for one last trip to the hospital. All was the same as before, but Gil had another visitor while I was there. He was the actor John Saxon. We were introduced, and then he spoke softly to Gil. John had performed in many movies, most notably costarring with Bruce Lee in *Enter the Dragon*. John and Gil's friendship began when Gil became the editor of Bruce Lee's memoirs, *Tao of Jeet Kune Do*—the most famous karate book ever published. John squeezed Gil's hand and left the room.

The dreaded moment came for me to say goodbye to my brother for the last time. I had to return to my children and needed to get to the airport in time for my flight. After sharing our feelings for each other, and expressing regrets, I finally turned away from him with a lump in my throat and left the room. Tears stained my face, but I didn't want Gil to see them. My parting thought was "Dear God, why did this have to happen?"

Returning to the present, Gil's life was finally over, but so was his pain—not just the physical devastation to his body but also the ache in his heart from all he had endured growing up. His mind was now at rest; no more demons or doubts could cloud his thoughts. Mental confusion led him to this moment in time with predictable results, but events in the beginning of his life sealed this fate, because when the first domino fell during his formative years, a chain reaction was set in motion that no one stopped in its tracks. Nowhere along that chain reaction did anyone put up a *meaningful* protective blockade to help him; instead, his trauma was kept secret. The question is, why?

We will reveal the reasons in this book.

CHAPTER 2

A HOUSE BUILT ON SAND

The parenting we experienced continues to influence us into adulthood and in our own parenting. It gets even more interesting when we blend our attachment history with our partner's.

Lisa Qualls, The Connected Parent

The Johnson Family

Ira Johnson's father, Owen, was of German stock. German immigrants tended to be industrious, thrifty, punctual, stoic, and talented craftsmen. Owen worked as an itinerant farm laborer who, over a period of twenty years, migrated across the United States, starting in Bedford, Indiana, then on to Arkansas, finally settling in Paducah, Texas. Along the way, two of his children were born in Indiana, five were born in Arkansas, and his last child, Ira, was born in Texas in 1896.

A few years after Ira was born, the Johnsons finally put down roots. Owen and his son-in-law Buck Creamer pooled their funds and bought property south of Chalk, which they planned to farm. Ira remained in this same area his entire life. He did not inherit his father's wanderlust. Ira had found his green fields, and he enjoyed raising crops on them.

Ira married Deedy Moffitt in 1915, and in the next twenty-two years they raised a houseful of six children, all of them born in Paducah. There were three girls and three boys. The Johnson family was profoundly religious, although Ira and Deedy attended different churches their entire married life. Ira and the children attended the Church of Christ, while Deedy attended the Baptist Church. Nevertheless, they had a happy and fulfilling marriage and raised children whose lives mirrored their parents'.

Two of Ira's brothers, Tolbert and Vora, also lived in Texas, although they drifted to different cities from time to time, finally ending up in Borger. In

1926, the town became the oil-boom capital of the Panhandle, and as word spread, Borger attracted oilmen, panhandlers, card sharks, bootleggers, drug dealers, and prostitutes. Ira's brothers fit right in with the boomers. One had already served time in jail for bootlegging, and both were in a vehicle with their father, Owen, when the car overturned. The men were drunk. Owen died. The corruption in Borger had become so serious that in 1927 Texas governor Dan Moody called in the Texas Rangers to clear the scum out of town. Ace Borger and his partner had hired a husband-and-wife team who put sixteen hundred prostitutes on their payroll, so the line of "ladies" leaving Borger was astounding, and that was only part of the corruption the Rangers had to expel from the city. That same year Vora and his second wife, Abbie, visited family in Paducah. They brought their six daughters with them. Vora's family lodged in the home of Deedy's parents; their home was close to Ira's house. During this visit, one of Vora's daughters confessed to her mother that her father had been molesting her for quite some time. Furious, Abbie grabbed their .38 revolver and shot Vora three times. Ira raced Vora to the hospital. Outside the hospital, a local mob gathered in front; they were debating whether to lynch Vora. Ira faced them off with a revolver tucked into his pants. He told them justice would have to wait until Vora was out of the hospital. Vora recovered, but he was never legally held accountable. About five years later, Vora was accepted at Ira Johnson's family dinner table. During dinner Vora made the mistake of making a lewd remark about Thelma, Ira's fifteen-year-old daughter. After Thelma slapped him, Ira glared at Vora with steel in his eyes and told him in no uncertain terms that Thelma was never to be touched under any circumstances. Vora was a bad soul who needed to be kept at bay, but kin were kin, through thick and thin.

Arguably the 1930s was the most difficult period for all the early settlers of Cottle County, Texas. Two massive events coalesced in this decade, leaving lasting scars on the hearts and minds of the entire community. First, after years of unchecked financial speculation on the New York Stock Market Exchange, grossly overvalued stocks of publicly traded companies became worthless overnight. The economic depression eventually fell on West Texas in early 1933. Banks closed. Money in the form of cash was withdrawn at alarming rates by frightened citizens nationwide. Fear of economic collapse permeated all of society. Financial institutions did not have sufficient cash reserves to meet their clients' needs. Their response was to close the doors until new federal legislation was in place to stimulate cash reserves. The newly elected president, Franklin D. Roosevelt, addressed the nation on this topic on March 12, 1933. Ira and Deedy were assuredly sitting in front of their radio to hear their new president's plan of action. Ira was not a Democrat before the Roosevelt administration, but he reconsidered his political loyalties. The president had effectively explained a complex situation in a manner even a dryland farmer with a third-grade education understood. The road to financial recovery would take years, but at least the Johnsons had hope.

The eldest of Ira and Deedy's children, Thelma, Hughel, and Mildred, all handled chores around the house and in the fields. Thelma was vivacious and dreamed of life beyond West Texas. Hughel was a large child who was not averse to using brute force when he thought it was needed. Mildred, on the other hand, was a kind and shy child but very dependable with her assigned chores. Ira was known to say, regarding his children, *Some of our kids didn't talk, and some talked too much.* Mildred considered herself in the former group. Marlin was in the latter. Ira and Deedy were in their early forties when they added again to the household; Betty Lou was born in 1936 and Waylon in 1938.

Ira was a natural worrier, and during the Depression there was good reason to be worried. He had a family to feed and clothe, but even before the Depression, he did not know year to year whether the cotton crop would fail or succeed because of weather and insects. During the Depression, the price of cotton dropped dramatically, significantly affecting the family budget. Deedy and Ira did their best to tighten their belts. Ira became his own blacksmith and did all the repairs to farm equipment, as well as fixing cars and trucks. Deedy used cotton flour sacks to make wash cloths, curtains, and even clothing. They churned their own butter. Ira also made wood furnishings for the house rather than buying them. They fed their children by raising their own chickens and pigs; beef was too expensive. They also grew their own vegetables. Ira was not only a deft hand at fixing things; he had the mind of an engineer, inventing electromechanical contraptions. The Johnson's AM radio was battery powered, but the rechargeable batteries were cumbersome. Rather than purchase an expensive wind-powered recharger, Ira made one from a reclaimed alternator taken from a Model T car. He formed propeller blades from scrap lumber, which he attached to the alternator. Then he affixed the whole thing to the windmill tower at the back of the house. Thereafter, wind powered the battery recharger, while also pumping water up from the well. His son, Marlin, inherited his father's skills.

The second shattering event of the 1930s was the Dust Bowl. A drought of almost biblical proportions fell upon the Texas-Oklahoma Panhandle from 1933 to 1936. Prior to this, droughts had regularly occurred on an eight-to-eleven-year cycle. A bad drought period was historically two consecutive years of subpar amounts of rainfall. This time, however, the rainless period lasted three miserable years. The massive drought resulted from years of over-farming and gross land mismanagement. This, combined with months of rainless weather, created an ecological disaster. The effects were so costly they eventually set in motion sweeping farming reform still in place today. The epicenter of the drought was two hundred miles to the northwest of Cottle County, but its ill effects reached down and touched the western counties on the Rolling Plains.

The conditions were at their hellish worst in the spring of 1935. Those who lived through that time never forgot it. Relentless, high winds and dust saturated the air. During the months of March and April, high winds blew for forty-seven days. During most of these dust storms, visibility was limited to a mile or less, and during six of these dust storms, visibility was less than five hundred feet. One of Ira's neighbors noted in his diary on April 9th, "I started in to set the forms around the milk house I am building, but the wind and sand began to blow so hard I quit and came in the house and have been in all day. This sand and dust are getting awful. The dirt is sure blowing in the orchard. Looks to me like the stock would get so much sand it would kill them." Then came the sandstorm of April 14, 1935. Newspapers called it Black Sunday. One historian wrote, "The day dawned clear and fresh. By noon the blue skies and balmy temperature were too tempting to resist, and people rushed outdoors to do all the things they postponed during the first three dust-ridden months of the year." About 6 p.m. that evening the menacing great granddaddy of all Panhandle dust storms engulfed the area. After it struck, visibility was reduced to zero. In Dalhart one man was within forty-five feet of his barn when the dust struck, and it took him more than an hour to find his way to the structure. Automobiles and trains had to stop where the storm struck them. People feared for their lives, and this fear did not quickly fade. Ira and Deedy's resolve and faith were stretched to the brink. By the grace of God, they endured and pushed on.

The Purtha Family

The Purtha family, along its paternal line, was Polish, and as such it belonged to a very mobile population. Our great grandfather and grandmother were both immigrants from Poland, a country that has been partitioned and repartitioned repeatedly by surrounding countries for centuries. When they were born, and certainly up until they immigrated in the 1890s, the country's boundaries as we know them today did not exist. John Leo Purta was born in Warsaw at a time when Russia controlled the territory. His wife, Frances Zameslewski, was born in a part of Poland controlled by Germany. Her birth city is unknown. Each rightly said they were born in Russia or in Germany, but nevertheless they were still Polish. Family lore claimed that when John was seventeen, he stowed away on a ship headed to Ellis Island, New York. John and Frances met in Illinois after immigrating to the United States.

Chicago and its surrounding suburbs were a magnet for Polish immigrants. Michigan City, Indiana, was considered an extended part of the Chicago metroplex, where many Polish immigrants and their descendants settled. The Purthas were part of those communities for many years. Indeed, Chicago bills itself as the largest Polish city outside of Poland, and Polish is the third most spoken language in the city. Most immigrants preferred urban cities to agrarian towns and were highly mobile. Like their compatriots, the Purthas uprooted their lives and moved many times; occasionally, however, they returned on a temporary basis to Michigan City or the Chicago area. In this they were not unusual: as historian John Bukowczyk said, between 40 to 60 percent of Polish immigrants would move from one urban area to another within ten years. Leo Purtha was mechanically skilled, so he always sought jobs in urban towns. Bukowczyk's theory was that "many immigrants with agricultural backgrounds were eager to migrate because they were finally freed from local plots of land as they had been in Poland. . . . Others ventured into business and entrepreneurship, and the majority of them opened small retail shops such as bakeries, butcher shops, saloons, and print shops". Socially, Polish weddings typically occurred on Saturdays and were all-day events. Polka bands were comprised of drums, trumpets, accordions, and singers. Guests danced to waltzes and their all-time favorite, the Polish Hop. The Purthas' son Jack would later enjoy such a lively Polish wedding.

Poland is described as one of the most religious countries in Europe, which was as true if not more in the nineteenth century. The largest percentage of the population was, and still is, Roman Catholic, so it is not surprising that John and Frances were practicing Catholics. They raised seven children with a religious hand, practicing Proverbs 13:24, "He that spareth his rod hateth his son; but he that loveth him chasteneth him betimes." In other words, "He who spares the rod spoils the child." As adults, the Purta siblings eventually dispersed to different cities and states, including California. The original Purta name morphed to Purtha, apparently because people kept misspelling it, although some of Leo's siblings managed to hold on to the original spelling.

Leo Purtha met May Thompson in Indiana. They married in South Bend in 1928 at St. Joseph Catholic Church. Over a period of ten years, they were gifted with three children, Jack, Elsye, and Neil. According to Elsye, Leo continued the family tradition of corporal punishment. When one of the children needed to be chastised, Leo told the miscreant to pull a switch off a tree and deliver it to him. Elsye said Leo whipped the back of her bare legs so hard they bled. On other occasions, she was told to kneel with bare knees in a corner where he had strewn hard corn kernels. Sometimes he whipped them with a belt. Oddly, by the time his grandchildren, Jeanne and Gilbert, arrived, Leo seemed a different man than their mother described. By then, Leo was subdued and quiet, but his word was final on any issue. Some have even described him as gentle. As long as anyone remembered him, Leo preferred his family's company to socializing outside the home. His jobs included working in a metal plating factory and as a laborer for the Pullman Standard Car Company. At home he planted large vegetable gardens and handled repairs around the house.

Without giving a reason, Elsye recalled that Leo despised the Catholic Church. In all the years Leo and May were married, he refused to attend services. Since May never learned to drive, she was dependent on him for transportation her entire life, and so her days of attending Mass were over. However, May never lost her religious zeal. If she wasn't canning home-grown vegetables or cooking or cleaning house, she was either reading the Bible or writing religious poems and prayers, which she referred to as witnessing for God. She also copied her writings and sent them to her siblings and friends. She was a prolific writer, which brought her many letters of thanks. She always kept a picture of Jesus hanging on the wall as her witness. Occasionally, with Leo acting as her driver, May worked as a nurse's aide for a retirement home, where she gathered lots of new friends to write prayers for and about. Many of her letters to and from family were also written to collect family genealogical histories.

The Purthas' son Jack married in 1953, five years after his engagement, but he and Anna had no natural children. In the 1960s they adopted or fostered two young boys, but there were some difficulties with them. Jeanne thinks the boys may have been removed from their home. Elsye did not explain what went wrong. The Purthas' youngest son, Neil, was a troubled boy. He did not finish school, instead enlisting in the marines. He lacked the discipline to stick it out, so twice he went missing without leave. As a result, he was court-martialed and sent back home. He did odd jobs after that, but he was always sponging off his parents. He was also involved in a tragic accident that killed a woman. The accident occurred at night when Neil was driving with a passenger in the front seat of his car. Neil's car plowed into the rear of a parked car sitting at the side of the road with no lights on. That vehicle burst into flames with a woman inside. For reasons never explained to little ears listening in on this conversation, Neil and the passenger swapped places before the police arrived. It is hard to imagine anyone other than a family member being willing to take the blame. Jeanne believes Leo was the passenger. In terms of his personal life, Neil married at the age of twenty. He and his wife, Edna, had five children, but Neil was always running around on her. During one of their separations, he visited his folks in Oklahoma, and while there he stole money and possessions. After Leo's death, he showed up again to see his mother. He managed to find a job in a nearby town repairing refrigerators. For reasons only known to Neil, he became an alcoholic. Months after getting the job, he was found dead of a heart attack at the age of forty-two.

Marlin's Dreams

Marlin Johnson was proud to be the son of a dryland farmer, but he had no desire to follow in his father's footsteps. He was gifted with mechanical skills, so after he graduated from high school in Paducah in 1945, he asked his father if he would be willing to financially support him so he could attend Texas Technical College (later Texas Tech University). He wanted to study engineering. Ira's immediate answer was "No!" Ira previously had said no to his daughter Thelma when she asked for support to study nursing. (Ira never changed his mind about Thelma's dreams, because he believed women belonged at home.) Not to be defeated, Marlin searched for an alternative means to achieve his dream. He learned that if he enrolled in the ROTC program at TTC, paid for the first two years of tuition himself, and maintained a minimum GPA, tuition for the final two years would be free. In return, Marlin would be required to enlist in the army for a minimum of six years as a commissioned officer. Because Ira believed that men must find jobs, Marlin's arguments finally won him over, and he agreed to financially support his son. He also expected Marlin to find a part-time job. Sadly, Marlin's dream fell apart after only two semesters on campus; he did not have enough money to meet his needs. He returned to Paducah in 1946 with his pride deflated, but he was undeterred in his desire to become an engineer. World War II had recently ended, and the GI Bill was signed into law to help veterans with tuition assistance and low-interest rate mortgages, as well as by establishing veterans' hospitals. Marlin's next idea was hatched. In June 1946 he enlisted in the US Navy for two years. His plan was to use the GI Bill to pay his tuition at TTC once he was discharged from the navy. After enlisting, Marlin wrote Ira to say,

"Daddy, I sure thank you for the money, although I kinda hated to take it. One of the reasons I am in the Navy now is to keep from costing you any more money. I got to feeling like a parasite living off you and borrowing money that I didn't know when I could pay back. You will never know how I appreciated it."

The best laid plans of mice and farm boys often go awry, especially when two people are drawn together by a common interest.

As a boy, Marlin cherished his moments alone in the evening listening to the radio. He listened to big band performances, but he particularly enjoyed symphonic concerts. The music brought tears to his eyes. Marlin also loved singing and taught himself to play the guitar.

Elsye's Dreams

In 1946, when Elsie Purtha was a skinny pubescent girl of thirteen, her life took an exciting turn. Not only did she have a pretty heart-shaped face, pale aquamarine eyes, wavy dark brown hair, and an outgoing personality, she had the precocious voice of an angel. This talent brought accolades from family and friends, which encouraged her to continue developing it because she loved being the center of attention. Her dreams and ambitions took flight. She wanted to be an opera star, and what better place to begin her career than in Hollywood? Also, what better way to escape from serious issues at home? The Purthas lived in Compton, California, situated south of downtown Los Angeles, so Hollywood was only an hour's drive away.

Elsie's parents also enjoyed music. Singer Kate Smith was their all-time favorite star on the radio in the '30s and '40s and later on television. Smith's songs inspired patriotic Americans to buy war bonds to support the war effort. Her marathon broadcasts raised more revenue for the war effort than any other star in show business. She is especially known for her rendition of Irving Berlin's "God Bless America." Elsie listened to the broadcasts as well; her dreams to become a singer became reality when she spotted an advertisement in the *Daily News of Los Angeles* in November 1945:

> *Non-professional men and women at ONCE, to be auditioned for*
> *training in microphone singing, acting, and announcing. Commercial*

shows now in production for prospective sponsors. Call Hollywood
3636 for appointment between 1 and 9 p.m. any day.

Elsie convinced her father to make the call. The audition was a success. Carter Wright Studios hired Elsie and put her on the payroll in 1946. Elsie quit school and began contributing money to the family coffers. She worked nearly two years for the studio, collaborating with other performers on stations KXLA, KLAC, and KFVD and joining the American Federation of Radio Artists. One of her coperformers was Betty White, who would go on to become Hollywood's longest-living legend. These were very exciting days for such a young girl as Elsie.

With her newfound career, Elsie decided she must change her name—not once, but twice. As with many Hollywood performers, Elsie needed a stage name and so became Suzanne Morre. Unlike the hard sounding vowels in Elsie Purtha, the softer vowels in Suzanne Morre fell off the tongue with the grace of a conductor's wand. Also, in those days the Borden Dairy Company used a mascot on their products called Elsie the Cow. Elsie Purtha did not want to be teased by association, and so in her nonstage life began to write her name as "Elsye," a choice she maintained for the rest of her life.

Destiny

In the same month that Elsye began her stint in Hollywood, her eldest brother, Jack, enlisted in the navy at the age of seventeen. Jack's tour of duty was cut short nine months later when he developed a lung condition that required hospitalization. The navy sent him to the US Naval Hospital in Long Beach for treatment. Unfortunately, the doctors had to remove one of his lungs. Consequently, the remainder of Jack's tour of duty was spent convalescing in the hospital until his discharge in 1948. By June 1947 Jack had a new roommate from Paducah, Texas, who was suffering from pleurisy. His name was Marlin Johnson, but he said family called him "Mo." The two sailors developed a strong friendship as they passed many months together in the ward. Jack and Mo were the same age and even resembled each other. They both were very slender, were about the same height, and had dark brown wavy hair. Jack's eyes were blue, like those of his parents and siblings; Mo's were brown. However, when they put on their uniforms to take weekend leave together, they looked like brothers. On Mo's first visit with Jack's family at their home, he was introduced to Jack's parents, Leo and May, to Elsye, and to their youngest brother, Neil. On one of those visits Jack announced to his parents that he had fallen for a nurse in the hospital named Anna and that they were talking about marriage. After several more visits with the Purthas, it became clear that Mo and Elsye were drawn to each other, in part because they both loved music. Mo also liked Elsye's thoughtful ways, but he was especially impressed with her singing. Youthful love was in the air, so Elsye helped Mo set up a recording session for him and another friend.

August 5, 1947

Dear Folks,

I spent last weekend again with my friend from L.A. His folks have really been nice to me. I am going to be best man at my buddy's wedding as soon as they decide on a date. I am going to their engagement party next weekend.

I have really been having fun playing the guitar. I found a guy who plays the violin, and we entertain the bed patients. We are going to make some records tomorrow.

Love, Marlin

On another occasion, Mo visited the KXLA studio to watch Elsye perform. Afterwards Mo asked the technicians if they would record Elsye singing two songs that he liked: "I Wish I Didn't Love You So" and "What Are You Doing New Year's Eve?" Mo mailed the 33 rpm record to his parents in Texas.

August 11, 1947

Dear Folks,

I spent another weekend with my buddy who lives in LA. I can't remember ever having a better time . . . I might mention my buddy has a sister and I am going with her. You will probably be hearing a lot about her so I will tell you what she's like. Her name is Elsye

Purtha, and she is a singer on the radio. She is rather short, has dark brown hair and is as pretty as they come. In all my running around I have never before met a girl as nice. When I was in bed, she came out here on visitor's day and kept me company. That really helped me a lot, especially since I didn't know anyone else around here.

Love to all, Marlin

A month later, Marlin and Elsye were making plans for their future together. He was only eighteen; she was barely fifteen. Marlin wrote his parents with the big news:

September 8, 1947

Dear Folks,

As usual I spent the weekend at the Purthas. Sunday, we went to Griffith Park, and then to the museum. I certainly enjoyed myself. I always do enjoy myself though when I am with Elsye and her folks. I suppose you think I talk about them a lot, but you may as well get used to it, because you will hear a lot more from now on. I may as well tell you now that Elsye and I have begun to make a lot of plans for the future. When I say future, that's just what I mean. I intend to get out of the navy and finish school before I do anything. I know I am looking ahead a lot, but if you knew Elsye, you would know why. Just knowing her has given me something to work for and look forward to. She comes from a wonderful family too. Since the first time I saw them, they have treated me like one of the family. They even came to see me when I was sick. . . . Oh yes, they're not Jews, they're Polish.

Love, Marlin

Mo's last remark reflected the biases of the era. Our generation has shed such thoughts.

It didn't take long for Marlin to have qualms about his previous letter home, so he wrote again to reassure his parents that he and Elsye were not going to rush their plans.

September 15, 1947

Dear Folks,

I guess you thought by the way I wrote that we were planning to get married soon, but I want you to understand that we're not. We are informally engaged, but we intend to leave it that way for a long time. I couldn't think of marriage until I have something to offer Elsye, and that will take two years at the least. I have talked the whole thing over with Elsye's parents, and they gave me the same advice that you did. I just wish that you could meet these people, because I know you would like them. As for Elsye, well, I don't think there's another girl like her anywhere. I have met just about every kind of girl there is since I came in the navy, and I know she is all right. Up until I met her, I had been rather undecided just exactly what I was going to do when I got out of the navy, but now I have something to work for and look forward to.

Love, Marlin

Less than two weeks later, the doctors discharged Mo from the hospital. The navy returned him to duty on the USS *Washburn* in San Diego—the last place he wanted to be. A few days later he turned nineteen. Elsye continued her singing career in his absence, but she pined away for Mo. After ten long months at sea, Mo was honorably discharged from the navy and headed straight to Compton to see Elsye.

Their separation had been unbearable, in addition to Elsye being very keen to get away from her parents, with good cause. After much planning, and giving Elsye time to complete her singing commitments, their wedding took place November 6, 1948. The ceremony was held in Los Angeles and was attended by sixty-five family members and friends. The bride wore a white

Marlin Johnson weds Elsye Purtha, November 1948.
Courtesy of the Author's Collection.

velvet gown. Many Purtha family lived in the area and joined in the happy occasion. Mo was only twenty; Elsye was just sixteen. After the holidays were over, Mo and Elsye booked their train ride to Texas to begin their married life together.

They boarded the Santa Fe Super Chief, which claimed to be "The Train of the Stars" because it was famous for transporting Hollywood stars from Los Angeles to Chicago. This time, one of Hollywood's budding stars was going to permanently disembark in Texas. As the train slipped out of Union Station, the Pacific Ocean and Santa Monica Mountains lay behind them. Further along their journey, the train passed south of the Los Angeles National Forest, headed north through the San Bernardino National Forest to Barstow, and crossed the California border at Needles. Northward lay the Mojave Desert. The desert terrain continued along the route to Kingman, Arizona. Eventually the train climbed to seven thousand feet as it passed through Flagstaff, a beautifully situated town surrounded by the largest contiguous ponderosa pine forest in the United States. Further stops along the Super Chief route included Winslow, Arizona, Gallup, New Mexico, and Albuquerque. Elsye and Mo changed trains at Albuquerque to continue their journey to Amarillo, Texas, where Ira and Deedy would pick them up.

Amarillo is part of the High Plains, with flat land lying in every direction. The city is in the middle of the grasslands of the Texas Panhandle. An old tale from the nineteenth century claimed that "a squirrel could start at the Atlantic Ocean and go from tree branch to tree branch all the way to the Mississippi River. When the squirrel got to the Great Plains it stopped. It stopped because there were no more trees." Dense, grass-covered rolling prairies continued southward to Paducah. Apart from the dramatic change in landscape, Elsye realized she had exchanged a vibrant complex of cities with a population of about 1.7 million people for a quiet, remote town with less than three thousand residents. It was like traveling backward in time.

From the moment Mo and Elsye arrived in Texas, they were dependent on Ira's support to help them set up home. Mo may have done some farming for his father in return, which he would not have enjoyed. He also found work as a truck driver; this may have been his only transportation because they couldn't afford to buy a car. Money was extremely tight. The Johnson family owned 161 acres of farmland, on which they raised wheat and cotton, as well as some cattle. Over several decades the Johnson family, as well as other extended family, had built more than one homestead on their lands with their bare hands. One of the homes was in Chalk, a small community of fewer than one hundred residents about fifteen miles south of Paducah. The house had been abandoned decades before. Mo and Elsye were allowed to make this dilapidated, rustic house their home at no charge. There was no running water, only a well set away from the house. Elsye had to fetch pails of water to meet basic needs, but on at least one occasion, when she was six months pregnant with their first child, a bull chased her right up to the front door. On a different day, she woke in the morning to find a cow hanging its head through her bedroom window. Spring thunderstorms were very frightening. During a particularly bad storm, all they could do to protect themselves from a potential tornado was pull a door in front of them, adjacent to the corner of a room, to act as a barrier. Deedy, a fine seamstress all her life, helped clothe Elsye by making dresses for her from cotton flour sacks. Nothing was wasted by the Johnsons.

A new financial burden arrived November 16, 1949, one year and ten days after their marriage. Jeanne Marie was a healthy baby girl, but disappointingly, not the boy Mo was hoping for to continue the Johnson name. Immediately after giving birth, young Elsye told the doctor she was ready to have another baby.

April 5, 1950, about five months after Jeanne's birth, Cottle and King Counties were planning their first livestock show. To attract farmers in nearby counties, the organizers arranged for three days of booster trips to advertise the coming event. On the first day the caravan traveled from Paducah to Childress, Quanah, Chillicothe, Vernon, and Crowell. On the second they also began in Paducah, stopped in Matador, Turkey, Quitaque, Plainview, Lockney, and Floydada. The third trip left Paducah for Aspermont, Stamford, Haskell, Seymour, and Benjamin. The program included Bill Carroll, his five-piece band the Paducah Ramblers, and Mike Smith and his band from Matador. At each stop locals were entertained by two square dance performances. The dancers wore costumes, and the other caravan participants were asked to dress in cowboy regalia. Locals were encouraged to join the fun at each stop. Most importantly for Mo, Elsye was asked to sing with the traveling band. Even though she had a young baby, she was very keen to be part of the excitement and finally use her talent again. Arrangements were made for Mo's sister Betty to take care of Jeanne. Because Mo had to work to support them, he was not able to follow Elsye and the caravan. This was a turning point in their marriage. Elsye was thrilled. She could both have fun and earn a little money. Mo was jealous and unhappy about Elsye leaving their daughter in the care of someone else. She was supposed to stay at home.

Mo's cousin Sherrill may have played some role in the caravan, because Elsye and Sherrill struck up a close friendship. When Mo got wind of this, he became very angry. He thought Sherrill was trying to interfere in his marriage, although years later he told his father he trusted Elsye. When the event was over, like father like son, Mo told Elsye that her singing career was finished. Her job was at home. Elsye conceived another baby that same month. Once her tummy started to grow, small town gossipers added fuel to the rumors about Sherrill.

Mo was having trouble making ends meet, was in debt to his father, and was upset by rumors about his wife. To solve these problems, and to get Elsye away from Paducah, he reenlisted in the navy during the Korean War. His ship, the USS *Grasp*, was based in San Diego, but it soon shipped off for Korea. Elsye had rented an unfurnished house in Lynwood, only ten minutes away from her parents' home in Compton. She gave birth to Gilbert Lee on January 10, 1951, while Mo was at sea. One year later, Mo wanted out of the service on a hardship basis, claiming he was very worried about Elsye's ability to support herself and the children, especially as the Purthas were planning to return to Michigan City.

January 13, 1951, at sea

Daddy, when I left for the Navy this time, I said to myself that I wasn't going to ask any more favors of you, but I have a problem that is about to worry me to death. I am fairly well satisfied with my work here in the navy, but they just don't pay me enough money to support my family. It doesn't take much for me to get by, but Elsye is absolutely in a hard shape back there with the kids. She has made an awful good stand, but when you don't have you can't do. I have been trying everything to get out of the navy, but I find it can't be done without help, and that's the favor I'm asking. I can get money any time I need it from the navy relief, and I've done it, but that like any other debt has to be paid back.

The reason why I'm so desperate is because Elsye's folks are moving back to Indiana soon, and I just don't know what she will do there after they go. Now here's what I have to do to get a hardship discharge. There has to be a letter from some employer saying that he would hire me for more money than I am making in the navy. (With what I get and Elsye's allotment, the total is $177.50 a month.) Also, I have to have a letter from three reputable people not related to me saying why they think I should be discharged. If you could write a letter saying that you would hire me or rent to me, you wouldn't be obligated in the least way. All the navy wants is proof that I could get work if they let me out.

Now I don't want you to go to any trouble or put yourself out in any way to do these things. I wouldn't have asked, but I'm desperate. I know you're going to say, "I told you so," and I have it coming, but the needs of my family have made me swallow my pride and every- thing else. I want you to know I'm awfully proud of Elsye. I never believed she would pinch pennies and cut corners like she has been doing. There is no need to tell you what a load she has on her hands. Well, anyway, if you can do these things for me, it will be greatly appreciated, and I will add that if I do get out, I plan to get a defense job somewhere. I don't have any doubts but what I can make some money. In case you're wondering, I think I can truthfully say that this experience has taken all the foolishness out of me. This shows what happens when children are smarter than their parents.

Love to all, Marlin

Mo's letter set in motion a flurry of letters between himself, Ira, and Elsye over the next ten months. The three strategized on how best to meet the requirements to receive a hardship discharge. Both Ira and Elsye filed numerous affidavits with navy officials, only to have Mo's request turned down twice. As a last desperate measure, Ira wrote to Texas representative

Walter Rogers to seek his support. In response, Mr. Rogers paid a personal visit to Ira's home to discuss the matter and later wrote a letter to the navy in support of Mo's need to return to his struggling wife and children. All they could do was wait for news.

While all this was happening in the background, Mo, Ira, and Elsye were also writing each other about the pros and cons of Elsye returning to Paducah if Mo wasn't going to be released from duty. Her parents were going to move to Michigan City in April, leaving her totally alone. This suggestion reignited old rumors, but preceding those discussions, Mo wrote his father expressing his unfavorable opinions about the war in Korea. In the letter, he talked about the children and Elsye, saying,

March 20, 1951

Dear Folks,

Elsye sure has her hands full with both of them. I think she has done mighty well though considering what she has to do with. Elsye may be funny turned and high tempered, but she has proved herself in many ways to be a good wife and mother and that's what counts. I don't guess I need to tell you that our marriage was beginning to sag when I came back in the navy, but I believe this experience has straightened things out once and for all. If only young people could realize what a serious thing marriage is. Anybody can get married, but it takes lots of backbone to make it last.

Love, Marlin

In the following letters, Elsye and Mo discuss how the problems started in their marriage.

May 16, 1951, Los Angeles

Dear Mom & Dad,

I received your letter this morning, and I don't know exactly what to say. I knew when you phoned that something was wrong. I could tell right away. No, Dad, I didn't get mad when I read your letter. I'll never be able to thank you enough for being so understanding.

I don't know what was said back there, or how the situation is now, but I will say this much, Sherrill will <u>never</u> break up our home no matter what he says or does. Marlin and I have both made mistakes, and our marriage has been thru nearly everything possible. It took us a long time to realize how much we meant to each other, but the only thing that could make us part, is if Marlin wanted it that way. I just hope Sherrill does come to see me; I'll make him wish he had never met me.

At one time Marlin and I almost separated. If it hadn't been for Jeanne, it might have been that way, but we talked the matter over, and after a while, things just seemed to work out for us. Dad, I'm going on like nothing ever happened, and I hope whatever was told, won't make you think any less of me. I have come to love you and mama, as much as my own parents, in some ways moreso [sic]. I just hope you won't ever repeat that to my folks, naturally they would be hurt. Try to believe me when I say someone is making a mountain out of a molehill, for Marlin already knows that Sherrill cared a great deal for me. Sometime in everyone's life they say things they don't mean, when you feel you have no one who really cares, but that's all in the past, and that's where it's going to stay.

I don't know what Marlin plans to do after he gets out, but I hope he can find something that he will hold an interest in. It's been so long since he was home, and now it seems as if the days just drag by. I love him so much, dad, more than I ever thought it possible. It will be so good to start over again, and really try to make something of our marriage.

All our love, Elsye & babies

May 24, 1951, Sasebo, Japan

Dear Folks,

I got your letters and one from Elsye today. If I had known that it would cause so much trouble, I would never have mentioned about Sherrill. I suppose I didn't explain very well, so I will try to do that now. I won't go into details but will just say that he tried to come between Elsye and I and failed. I feel that you got the wrong impression as to what part

Elsye had in this. All I can say is, she handled him like a woman and a lady and that's as far as it went. Someday I will settle with him person- ally, but otherwise I hope the whole thing will be forgotten.

Just one more thing. I want you to know that there is nothing wrong between Elsye and I and hasn't been since I came back in the navy. We have both learned just how much we mean to each other. I worry about her all the time, but maybe not the way you think. It just scares me to think of her being there in that big city with no one around to help if something happened. Besides, she hardly ever gets to stick her head out of the house as the only way she has of getting around is walk. If something happened that she couldn't pay her rent on time, those people would throw her out in the street and never blink an eye. Just write to her and encourage her and show her you love her as I know you do. That's what she wants more than anything else. She keeps remembering the things that happened when we were in Texas, but she has grown up a lot and I think you will find her to be a changed person now.

Love to all, Marlin

Meanwhile, the efforts to obtain a hardship discharge for Marlin bore fruit.

October 18, 1951
Congress of the United States
House of Representatives
Washington, DC

Dear Mr. Johnson:

The Navy Department has just notified me that your application for a hardship discharge has been approved today at this Headquarters and a dispatch will be sent to your immediate Commanding Officer to that effect. After that, it will only be a matter of processing you for the return trip home and a discharge at some Base here in the States. It is a pleasure to be of this service to you.

With best wishes, I am
Very sincerely yours,
Walter Rogers

Marlin Johnson with Gilbert, David, and Jeanne, Easter 1955. *Courtesy of the Author's Collection.*

After Mo, Elsye, and their two children reunited, they returned to Texas. Rather than going back to Paducah, they settled in Plainview, where Mo found a job with Green Machinery. His natural mechanical abilities, enhanced by his training in the engine room of his ship, made him a good candidate for the job. The company manufactured and repaired irrigation pumps, which were sold across many counties. The job was a positive development, particularly as a third child, David Eugene, was born November 26, 1952. At last, Mo earned enough money for the family to buy a small home in Plainview, as well as a 1948 Ford DeLuxe Tudor two-door sedan.

Financially, their lives were on the upswing, but Marlin and Elsye's relationship fell apart again, reasons unknown. They separated after Easter

1955 and were divorced March 6, 1956. Marlin remarried four days later. Mutually, Elyse and Marlin agreed she would keep Jeanne and Gilbert, while David would stay with his father. In divorcing Elsye, Marlin essentially also divorced Jeanne and Gil, because he never offered them his financial or emotional support. It also seems he did little to dissuade others from believing that Gilbert was not his natural son, because rumors to that effect lingered for many years, even though photos of Marlin and Gilbert attest otherwise.

When Marlin remarried, his bride Flora brought two children from another marriage, Darrell and Nancy. Thus, Marlin immediately began his newly wedded life with Flora's children plus his son David to support. In following years, he and Flora had two more children: Daniel and finally Ronald.

Marlin Johnson, 1948.
Courtesy of the Author's Collection.

Gilbert Johnson.
Courtesy of the Author's Collection.

CHAPTER 3
IT'S A MAD, MAD WORLD

(Looking back in time, as remembered by Jeanne)

Like two sticks in a game of pickup, my younger brother Gil and I find our home life teetering on collapse again, only this time the law is on our heels. I'm sixteen, Gil is fourteen. We have only been at our new school in Roanoke, Illinois, for about a month. We haven't even made friends with anyone yet.

Today we got off the school bus in front of our rural farmhouse. It had been a beautiful crisp day, but now the sun is low in the sky. The moment we walk inside the house mom says, "We're leaving Illinois tonight and heading to Arizona." "But mom, we've only just moved here," we wail. She says that Bill is in trouble with the police, and if we don't leave the state immediately, both she and Bill will be in serious trouble. Gil and I are clueless as to why, and she isn't offering any more details. Bill is our *third* stepfather. They give us and themselves enough time to pack whatever we want to keep. We only have one car, a 1963 Ford coupe with bench seats in the back and bucket seats in the front, so we are limited to what we can take with us. I was sobbing earlier when mom said I couldn't take my kitten Missy with me, telling me to put her in the barn. Mom brushed off my concerns by saying, "She's a cat. She'll be fine!"

Darkness has descended, and the four of us are now settled into our cramped seats. Gil and I are in the backseat and will be using our bags as pillows for the long trip. Hulking Bill is in the driver's seat and is tightly gripping the wheel. He's been nervously jerking his head left and right, probably looking for cop cars. Mom was the last person to get into the car, with the poodle under her arm. Parents have all the privileges! She gives the signal that we're ready, and Bill jams hard on the gas pedal. We're off. At least we know we are going to end up at her brother Jack's home in Prescott. The roads surrounding our house are dirt and gravel and will be for the next nine miles, so gravel is pummeling the underside of the car and a huge cloud of dust is billowing up behind us. With no streetlamps to light our way, the car's headlights seem inadequate, especially at this speed. It's too dark to see outside and my eyes are tearing up again thinking about Missy being alone, so I close them and crawl inside my head to remember our history up to this point. So much has happened in sixteen years.

From the very earliest days, we have lived our lives as if on a stomach-churning roller coaster, but it has not been a fun park. There's been nothing but Sturm und Drang. I've thought for some time that Mom's middle name should be Melodrama, not Marie, because her infatuations with different men who end up hurting her have resulted in dozens of episodes of anger, tears, upheaval, and finally divorce. She's also frequently angry with me, some of which I earned, because I have a strong independent streak. In fact, Mom has said to me, "You're too independent for your own good!" Gil, on the other hand, is her sweet baby boy. She always keeps him under her protective wings. He never gets into trouble, so he can do no wrong. Where he gets the hugs and kisses, I get a scowl. I love Gil, but I'm hurt by her different attitudes toward us.

And speaking of Gil, he and I both have our own crosses to bear, and Mom knows the reason, yet she keeps putting us within reach of her father. Between the ages of two and a half and about fourteen, Gil was sexually traumatized by our maternal grandfather, Leo. I was also molested by him between the ages of three and a half and seven. Between Mom's marriages, Grandad was the only "father figure" in our lives. He preyed on our accessibility and fatherless vulnerabilities. I can still visualize the first time he molested us.

Dad, Mom, Gil, me, and six-month-old David had taken the train from Texas to Michigan City, Indiana, to stay at Leo and May Purtha's house on the dunes next to Lake Michigan. We made the trip because Uncle Jack was finally getting married. Jack and Dad became friends in 1947 when, as sailors, they both were hospitalized because of lung issues. In fact, that's when Dad met Mom. Anyway, Dad had promised to be Jack's best man, but it wasn't until 1953 that Jack's marriage finally took place. That trip probably cost my financially strapped parents a lot of money, which they

Leo Purtha with Jeanne, Gilbert, and David Johnson, 1953. *Courtesy of the Author's Collection.*

likely borrowed from Dad's father, Ira. In any case, Mom, Dad, and Gran, with little David in tow, left me and Gil in Granddad's care while they went out to handle wedding arrangements. Before leaving, Mom put us down for a nap on the floor and covered us with a blanket. The next thing I recall was waking up and feeling Granddad's hands on me, and then I noticed he was also touching Gil. Neither of us understood what he was doing. That was the only time he molested us when we were together. After that, we each were alone when he violated us, but many years passed before either Gil or I realized he was doing the same thing to both of us.

Mom has always been a very outgoing woman who loves being the center of attention. She also does not like being alone and needs financial support because she cannot support us on her own. I know she has tried her best; she's a hard worker and has managed the household budget very well, but she doesn't seem to be good at choosing husbands, including our natural father, although in his case, they were simply too young to marry. They were married when she was my age and divorced a couple years after Uncle Jack's wedding and Leo's first molestations. At the time of the divorce, Mom was still not aware of what had happened to Gil and me at Leo's house because we were too young to mention it. Nevertheless, the memories resurfaced for both of us years later.

I'm counting in my mind the number of houses we have lived in before today. There have been at least thirteen, three fewer than my age. That's a lot of moving. The number of schools we've attended is a blur, and because of that we never got involved with extracurricular activities or sports. We learned quickly there was little use in getting attached to anything or anyone. The names of our classmates are totally forgotten. Neither Gil nor I have stayed anywhere long enough to bond with friends our age. We don't know what it means to have a best friend. I guess Gil and I are each other's only friends, even though we are always arguing about petty things. With so much tension in the house, maybe this behavior can be excused.

What a day it's been for us! I've got to get some sleep and try to stop worrying. We should cross the Illinois state line in a couple more hours. Indeed, Bill doesn't stop driving after leaving Illinois. Instead, he carries on driving until we get to Kansas City, Missouri, where we find a cheap motel. It took us nearly six hours to get here, so we arrive in the early hours of the morning. I have a fitful night in a dreary room that Gil and I embarrassingly share. And now we're back on the road again, and once more my mind has nothing better to do than drift back in time, this time starting at the very beginning of our childhoods.

My memories of our natural father are very dim, because mom and Marlin divorced when we were about six and four. David, our youngest brother, was only two. At that age we were just little kids, yet one memory of our last day with Dad haunts me. I can see myself sitting on the bed in their bedroom while playing with mom's lipstick. Dad approaches and gives me a hug. He has tears in his eyes as he says, "Darlin', I'm going away. I just want you to know that I love you." I don't understand what he's saying, but it upsets me to see him crying.

Whatever it was that brought about their separation, Mom took her anxiety out on us three kids. One time Mom accused Gil of lying, so she made him eat soap and then go to bed. I was sometimes spanked with the bristles of a hairbrush or a belt for some childish misbehavior. I also watched her hold a match under David's fingers. Worst of all, she hit David hard on his back and left bruises. Years later Mom told me she wanted to teach David a lesson because she found him playing with matches. Not long after these incidents, and Dad's farewell, Mom packed a few necessities and put all of us, except for David, on a train headed again for Michigan City to stay with her parents. Mom felt remorseful about hurting David, so she chose to leave him with our father. Separation from David was hard for Gil and me to understand and was probably puzzling for David, but in hindsight I'm glad he didn't come with us, because I wouldn't wish our transient lifestyle on anyone, especially our little brother. And I wouldn't wish him to suffer at the hands of our grandfather. Nevertheless, we still wistfully talk about David.

The train ride to Indiana is not memorable, but the events that followed when we reached Michigan City laid the wobbly foundation of our homelife with Mom. Mom was just twenty-three when she and Dad separated. With no savings to speak of, no financial support from Dad, and with two young children in tow, she had no choice but to run home to her parents. When we arrived, Leo and May were still living in the beach house we had visited for Uncle Jack's wedding. At first Gil and I had some fun, like when we took turns jumping off the high porch, holding an umbrella to see if we could fly to the bottom. Fortunately, we landed in squishy sand. For some reason, Granddad gave Gil a small whip as a toy. Gil talked me into letting him practice wrapping the whip around my wrist and waist. I was gullible enough to say yes, but after a few sharp stings I refused to play his game anymore. Now that I think about it, giving a four-year-old boy a whip seems a little odd. I wonder if Leo was trying to keep Gil happy and quiet with gifts; he never gave toys to me. While still at the beach house, whenever Granddad tried to sit close to us when we posed for family pictures, Gil and I would either try to wriggle away from him or cry. There are a bunch of photos from those days where you can see Gil and me trying to avoid him, but in one, where I'm sitting by myself, I'm smiling. On the back Mom wrote, "See, Jeanne isn't *always* crying."

Our grandparents moved house not too long after we arrived, so we moved with them. We were now in the city of Michigan City rather than near the beach. By that time Gil and I were about five and seven. The big old house was painted a blah shade of tan, and inside it had very high ceilings and lots of large rooms. There were no table lamps; only a single light bulb glaring down on us from the ceiling of each room. The backyard was a good size and was shaded by many big trees. When it snowed, the drifts in the backyard were well over our heads, but we enjoyed building snowmen and making snow angels. In the spring, the trees were alive with nesting birds. Gil especially liked birds, maybe because Gran always had canaries or parakeets in the house. He was delighted whenever he found blue eggshells on the ground. One day, though, he discovered a young robin that had fallen, or been pushed, from its nest. Gil ran to Mom for help, wanting to save the fledgling. Fortunately, Gran had a spare cage, so mom helped Gil place the bird inside. He fed the bird with worms that he dug up in the flower beds and supplemented its food with Gran's birdseed. They succeeded in saving the robin. It was a joyful day when they released the bird from the cage.

Gilbert with baby Robin, whom he nursed back to health. *Courtesy of the Author's Collection.*

This house holds other, less pleasant, memories. Leo's abuse of me finally came to a startling end here. He was in the habit of molesting me while I was sleeping, and this day was no different. Mom had sent me to bed for a nap in my room while she and Gran cooked a meal in the kitchen. The next thing I remember is Leo lifting me in his arms and carrying me to his bedroom. I was half awake by this time. He didn't speak a word to me but laid me on the bed, removed my panties, and started molesting me. At some point, Mom checked my room and discovered me missing. That's when I saw her walking into Leo's bedroom with a look of rage on her face. She let out a blood-curdling scream and started pummeling Leo with her fists. Her screams terrified me. She was shaking when she put my panties back on. Then she scooped me into her arms, ran to my room, and put me back in my bed with stern instructions to stay put as she abruptly walked out. Scared and thinking I had done something wrong, I heard Mom's raised voice in the kitchen, telling Gran what had happened. Once she had calmed down, Mom returned to my room to say that what Granddad had done was very wrong and wasn't my fault. Shortly after that she had me examined by a doctor to see if I was still intact, which was equally embarrassing for me. The doctor pulled mom aside and whispered I was okay, but I could hear him anyway, although I didn't understand what he meant. Looking back, I have since wondered why the doctor did not report the molestation to police. Nor do I understand why Gran stayed with her husband after hearing the news. The odd thing about Leo was that he never spoke a word to me during his molestations. Fortunately, this silent predator was never violent with me. In the years since, I don't like being in the same room with him, but too often Mom makes us visit them anyway, and as we leave their home Mom always says, "Give Granddad a kiss goodbye." Gil does, but I disobey. Mom and her parents follow each other from city to city and state to state, like we're doing now, so there have been times when Gil and I are never far from Leo's reach. To this day, I have not forgiven him and avoid him if possible.

After Mom's divorce from Dad was final, we finally moved out of our grandparent's house because Mom had met and married Jack Laughrey, a railroad engineer. Although we were living in the same city as our grandparents, we were no longer within easy reach of Leo. However, we continued to celebrate holidays together.

Jack and Mom moved us into a two-story, white clapboard house on Miller Street near a quay. The house was large and comfortable. A wooded area surrounded the neighborhood and Gil and I occasionally wandered into the woods to pick blackberries. We made our tummies ache from eating so many of them, staining our faces and fingers purple. Across the street from us was a nice house with a white picket fence along the front. The yard was filled with beautiful tree roses. Within that house lived a bratty girl my age named Sharon. She was always bragging about her possessions and also had a habit of calling me names. I think she picked up on my sensitive nature. One day I reached peak anger and decided to defend myself. I'm not particularly proud of what I did, but as she was walking home from school and taunting me, I beat her up. In the melee, I broke her glasses. Immediately I felt guilty and suddenly feared the consequences. I knew my stepfather had a volatile temper. What would he do to me? I was shaking and crying when I got home and told Mom what I had done. As it turned out, Jack did nothing. I couldn't believe my good luck.

Gil and I witnessed many arguments between Mom and Jack. Some of these occurred after Jack accidentally burned down the Purthas' home. We had all celebrated Christmas at their house. Immediately afterward, Leo and May went out of town; Mom and Jack agreed to look after the house and feed Gran's canary. The house was heated by a coal furnace in the basement, which needed periodic stoking. Jack had never stoked a furnace before, so he guessed how much coal the furnace would need. He guessed wrong. After he had the coal into furnace, Mom and Jack debated whether to leave us home while they went to the grocery store, a few blocks away. Fortunately, they took us with them. While we were shopping, a massive fireball exploded through the floor and out the roof. Witnesses claimed the fire ball went about one hundred feet into the air. Everything in the house was lost, including Gran's canary and our Christmas presents. The house was not insured. At least Gil and I are alive to tell the story.

On another occasion Mom was cooking a pot of chili when Jack came home from work. I don't know why they started arguing, but Jack suddenly picked up the pot and threw it at Mom. Both she and the wall were covered with dripping hot chili. He stormed out of the house, leaving Mom burned and in tears.

In the early days of their marriage before things blew up, Mom, Gil, and I attended the Church of Christ, located at the end of our block. Jack did not attend with us because he was a Baptist. As the number of arguments increased, Mom stopped taking us to church. However, at the age of nine I decided to go to church one day by myself. Like previous Sundays, our soft-spoken, white-haired minister asked if anyone in the congregation wanted to be baptized. As if I were being pulled up and forward by invisible threads, something lifted me out of my seat and propelled me until I stood before the minister. He instructed me to change into a cotton gown and meet him at the baptismal well, which was up a flight of stairs and overlooked the congregation below through an open window. He was already standing in the water and invited me to join him. The minister prayed over me, put a cloth over my nose, and then gently bent me backward into the water. When I arrived home, my hair was dripping, and in my hands, I held a commemorative Bible. Mom, who was so stressed out by now that she had noticeably lost weight, was so focused on her troubled marriage that she barely acknowledged my independent decision. Very soon after, she had a nervous breakdown. Years later Mom told me Jack had become involved with another woman.

Once again, the Purthas stepped in to help their daughter by taking us under their wings. When mom had her breakdown, we no longer had family living in Michigan City, because our grandparents had previously moved to Downers Grove, Illinois, a suburb of Chicago. So, the Purthas caught a train and returned to town to collect the three of us. We lived with them in Downers Grove until Mom recovered her health.

Downers Grove is a city of twenty-five thousand people on the outskirts of Chicago. We had easy access to a major train station. Once Mom's divorce from Jack was final, she found work as a bookkeeper at a television repair shop. She rented a small two-story white house on a corner a few blocks from work. The house had previously been a real estate office. In fact, the sign was still on the side of the building when we moved in. There were a couple neat things about the house that appealed to Gil and me. For example, there was a huge tree near the back door. Gil drove Mom crazy climbing it as high as he could. She would stand at the base of the tree and beg him to come down. Reluctantly, he obeyed. Gil loved the physical challenge, and there was always a chance he could peek into the birds' nests. Part of our backyard butted up against a large plot of land that was totally overgrown with plants that resembled corn stalks and were so tall a grown man wouldn't be visible if he was standing up. Naturally, Gil and I explored that forest. Together we broke down enough of the stalks to create a hideaway. And then one day we discovered someone else had been, or was currently, doing the same thing as us, because within one large circular area, the ground was littered with a sparkling treasure trove of fancy shaped bottles. We thought the bottles were so interesting that we picked up a few and took them to show Mom. She exploded with anger and told us not to play there anymore. She said the pretty bottles used to hold hard liquor. Their presence meant a man was likely hiding in our forest and getting drunk.

A few months later Mom introduced us to a new friend called Jack Smart. He worked as a repairman at Dale's TV. Unlike Jack #1, who was tall, lanky, and blond, Jack #2 was shorter and a full-blooded Cherokee Indian with jet-black hair and eyes. His face was covered with acne scars. Being focused on adjusting to our new schools, Gil and I gave no thought to their friendship.

When the spring semester ended in June 1961, Mom shocked Gil and me by saying she had arranged to send us to Texas to visit our father and our brother David. She had never raised the idea with us. I was eleven by then, and Gil was nine. We were extremely excited, but we were also frightened because Mom said she would not travel with us on the train but had arranged for a lady minder to keep an eye on us during the journey. Talk about mixed feelings! When we boarded that train, our knees were trembling. The scenery flew past the train window, not unlike our drive to Arizona now. The landscape began with green rolling hills and lots of trees and then eventually transitioned into drier land and unfamiliar plants. The soil changed from black to red. Dad, his sister Betty, and young David greeted us as we stepped down from the train. The minder told Dad that I had a stomachache most of the journey, probably due to stress, and Gil was constantly asking how much longer the trip would take. Neither of us had seen or heard from our father since we left Texas as preschoolers. We were virtual strangers. There was some discomfort on all sides as we tried to get reacquainted. During our years apart, I had written to Dad a few times, begging him to reply, but he never answered my letters. I thought, "Why does he want to see us now?"

Dad and Betty drove us to their brother Waylon's house for lunch. Another new face. All I can remember from that visit were the dark brown dishes on the table and that we were a little too stressed to eat much while among strangers. After lunch, Dad and David said goodbye to us and set off back to Plainview. We were surprised and disappointed. "Why did we come all this way if he's leaving us already?" He then said we would see him and David again later in the summer. We were deflated.

After Dad drove away, Betty first drove us to Paducah to see our grandparents, Ira and Deedy Johnson. Ira was somewhat frail, but Deedy was fit as a fiddle. They were so happy to see us they were shedding tears. It seemed odd to have adults swooning over us because that never happened at home. Afterward Betty drove us to Chalk, a tiny village about fifteen miles outside of Paducah. There she introduced us to our aunt Mildred, her husband Clayton, and their three children. Randall was the same age as me, Hal was the same age as Gil, and Linda was two years older than me. We didn't know we had Texas cousins. Our uncle Neil had two children by 1961, but they lived in Indiana. We never met them. Prior to this, except for school, Gil and I had always been surrounded by adults. Now, the Ryan family had generously agreed to let us live with them for the summer. Even though the Ryans were quite poor, they made room for us in their tiny shotgun-style house, with its outer walls covered in native rocks. Later in the summer, Dad brought his blended family to see us in Paducah. We met his wife Flora, her two children Darrell and Nancy from a previous marriage, and Danny, a child they conceived together. David, of course, was also there. Once we all got to know each other, Gil and I were overwhelmed with joy, although Darrell and Nancy didn't seem very pleased to meet us. Despite their standoffish behavior, the rest of the family welcomed us as if we had always been a part of their family.

Clayton, Mildred, Nancy, Hal, and Randall Ryan, Chalk, Texas, 1961. *Courtesy of the Author's Collection.*

Back row, left to right: Darrell, Nancy, Daniel, Flora, and Marlin. *Front row, left to right*: Gilbert and David, 1961. *Courtesy of the Author's Collection.*

The contrast between life at home with Mom and the Ryans' home in Chalk couldn't have been starker. First and foremost, we noticed the way the Ryan family lived, worked, played, and prayed together. There were a lot of practical activities going on, and there was a lot of love and respect in their household. There might have been disagreements in the Ryan home, but Gil and I never witnessed a cross word among them.

The Ryans farmed cotton for as far as our eyes could see. The fields were not far from their back door. They also had a herd of cattle. I don't know how many cows they owned, but some of them were never far from the farmhouse. On one side of the house a barbed wire fence corralled the cows away from the house. With their own hands the Ryans had created a pond in the area, which was fed by a windmill; the cows shuffled around its banks to drink. The boys built a raft and floated it on the pond, using a big branch to control its drift. Gil enthusiastically joined the fun. On the opposite side of the house, about a stone's throw away, stood a wooden building dedicated to storage and laundry. Mildred used an old-fashioned agitating machine and a metal tub, which were close to a hand pump. Keeping her family clean was hard work, especially when they all came home after plowing, covered in dust and dirt. She did not have a dryer, so everything had to be hung on clotheslines. Mildred put metal stretching frames into the legs of the men's wet jeans and then hung them to dry in the blistering sun; they looked funny blowing in the wind. At least the jeans never needed ironing like all their shirts, and the jeans always had nice creases down the front. Those creases made the cowboys look tidy and handsome, which was always the case when we went to church. Girls notice these things.

On one occasion Gil and I rode in the back of an old pickup when Clayton and Ira went out to inoculate the cattle. The needles were huge! Swarms of grasshoppers jumped over our heads like popcorn on the stove, scaring the daylights out of me, but Gil couldn't have been happier as he grabbed them and inspected their bodies. Less enthusiastic about bugs than Gil, I got into the cab when the men got out. There were so many new experiences and much to learn. Gil was in his element, but I had trouble with all the bugs. There were plenty in and around the house as well. One time Linda found a tarantula in her bed, which we shared that summer; another time I nearly stepped on one in the shower. I hate spiders! We also had freedom to roam the pastures and to ride Prince, their pony. After one of those rides, I ran to Mildred in terror because I found blood when I went to the toilet. Mildred immediately calmed me down with a gentle smile and set me straight. In simple country terms she told me this was normal and necessary if I hoped to have children of my own when I grew up. After that she took care of my needs, and we didn't speak of it again. Mom had never prepared me for this transition in life.

Other than keeping windows open, there was no way to cool the house, so some nights we kids slept outside. We'd lay blankets on a patch of grass and watch zillions of stars in the sky. They seemed so close you could touch them. We competed to see who could count the most shooting stars. Some nights we heard coyotes howling, which gave us chills. In the dark, Hal and Randall played what they called a snipe hunting game with us. They told us the snipe was a small, strangely formed animal that could be caught using paper bags. They walked us into the nearby pasture, told us where to sit on the ground, and instructed us to make funny noises to attract the snipe. If one approached, we were to quickly shut it in the bag. Then suddenly Randall and Hal disappeared into the night. They left us alone. In the darkness we heard strange noises. We were scared, until a few minutes later the boys reappeared, laughing at us. They confessed that snipe hunting is a practical joke. Afterwards we had a good laugh at ourselves. Randall, Hal, and Gil spent hours rabbit hunting and gathering quail eggs, while Linda took a shine to me and tried to teach her pubescent cousin how to look pretty, according to her standards of beauty. She plucked my eyebrows and put Vaseline on my eyelashes and lips.

One particularly hot sunny day, Hal and Randall noticed buzzards circling over the pasture in the distance. They told us this meant an animal had died and asked if Gil and I wanted to help them find it. Of course, we did! The walk through the pasture was rough; there were lots of cacti to step around, rocks to trip over, and scrubby brush that scraped our skin. I don't know how far we walked, but we eventually found the carcass of a cow. It was mostly intact, except for its rear end, where several vultures were sticking their ugly naked heads into the beast to eat the organs. The scene was gross. That done, we walked toward a nearby deep gully. Just as we approached the edge, the most magnificent bird I have ever seen suddenly appeared from below the edge and then swooped over our heads. It was a great horned owl. The wingspan looked to be as wide as Clayton is tall. It had a nest just below the gulley's edge, and we apparently disturbed it. Gil and I watched it soar into the air, our mouths hanging open. When we returned to the house, the first thing we all did was run to the hand pump. Even though the water is hard in Texas, it was the sweetest thing we had ever tasted. We splashed the water all over our sweating bodies.

I marveled as I watched Mildred cook a huge breakfast every morning for Clayton and the boys and another feast when they all returned from ploughing the cotton fields. Whenever possible, Gil was allowed to ride along on the tractors. All the guys came home late in the day covered in sweat and dust. Mildred was also a brilliant seamstress; she made shirts and beautiful cotton dresses for Linda. Her ironing board was always nearby. I don't have any memories of Mildred resting, except after dinner and at church. We attended the Church of Christ in Paducah twice on Sundays and once on Wednesdays. But it was not all work and religion: despite the heat and the swarms of bugs circling lighted lampposts, nighttime baseball games in Paducah were a blast for everyone. On some hot evenings, the whole family sat on the rear stoop and ate mouth-watering watermelon. Those were the happiest days of mine and Gil's lives.

Near the end of our summer holiday, mom wrote us with important news. She and Jack #2 had gotten married. Then she told us they would pick us up in Paducah rather than returning us home by train. When they arrived mid-August, seeing them together felt a little strange. This man, whom we barely knew, was now our "daddy," and we were asked to "please" call him that. I went along for a while. After Gil and I said tearful goodbyes to everyone, we climbed into our parent's big Pontiac and drove the long trip back to Illinois. I suppose it gave us an opportunity to, sort of, get to know Jack better. Still, before we pulled away, Mom asked if it would be possible for Gil and me to visit again next summer. The Ryans agreed. Of course, Gil could not leave the farm without a memento. He had a mason jar with a lid that was pierced with holes. Inside was his pet tarantula. I was creeped out the whole trip. The next day Mom suddenly panicked, screaming that the spider had escaped. You could have peeled me off the ceiling of the car. Then she confessed she was teasing me. Not funny! Without realizing it, we also brought home Texas accents. Once we were back in school, the kids made fun of us.

When we arrived at our home in Downers Grove, Mom had another surprise up her sleeve. I think she must have felt guilty when she married Jack without telling us, because she had redecorated our bedrooms in our absence. This did make us smile.

Not long after we were back in Downers Grove, Mom and Jack moved to a large Victorian home and enrolled us in another new school district. During the fall we had grand fun jumping into deep piles of raked leaves. We only had one winter in that house, which included another near-death experience, or so it seemed. Gil, I, and a few neighborhood kids built an Eskimo igloo of snow against the trunk of a huge oak tree. We created one small entrance to crawl through but failed to put a vent in the top. Proud of ourselves, we all crawled in, one after the other. I even brought a candle and a match because I knew it would be dark inside. Once we lit it, it only took seconds for us to realize we couldn't breathe. All the oxygen was gone. We frantically climbed over each other's bodies to get out of the igloo. We all gasped in relief when the chilled air entered our lungs.

While we lived in this house, Mom indulged Gil's desire to raise birds as pets. She bought him a flock of six, pure-white pigeons, which he kept caged in the detached garage. They were quite beautiful. It was also here that I came across a shocking discovery. I had turned twelve in November. One idle day I decided to explore the nooks and crannies of the big old house, starting with the attic and ending in the basement, which was cluttered with junk and old furniture, none of which I recognized. Along one wall was a chest of drawers. Nosey me, I opened all the drawers to see what was inside. Nothing worth touching in the top few, but the bottom was stuffed with a bunch of paperback books. I picked one up, flipped through the pages, and blushed. They were not the Nancy Drew mystery books that I enjoyed reading. Oh, my goodness! I couldn't believe what I was reading. Today I know those kinds of books are called pornography. The book, while shocking, was also an epiphany for me. I suddenly understood what motivated Leo. I also counted my blessings that Mom had intervened when she did. Otherwise, my fate could have been worse if he had continued molesting me as I grew older. Even though I had attained puberty in the summer, Mom had never discussed sex with me. I didn't even know the word. I was clueless about the nature of men and women and how babies were made. Trembling, I put the book back into the drawer, ran to my room, and never said a word to my parents. I don't know if the books were left there by a previous tenant, or belonged to my parents, but I wasn't going to ask them to find out. For some reason, we did not live long in that house, because we moved again to a plain one-story home with a detached garage on Woodward Ave. Although we were still in Downers Grove, we changed schools again.

Wherever we lived, Mom did her best to make her homes look presentable. This house was no exception. In fact, it was at this time when she told me of her favorite mottos: "We may be poor, but we don't have to be dirty," and "Cleanliness is next to godliness."

Shockingly, Leo's ungodly treatment of Gil was revealed to our mother at this Woodward house. She kept the details from me for a long time, but when she did finally tell me, she explained that she had walked into the detached garage, where she found Leo sexually molesting Gil. At the time he was about twelve or thirteen. I had no difficulty imagining Mom's violent reaction and Gil's humiliation. Prior to this, Mom had already told me that her father had also molested her between the ages of three and thirteen, but she did not give me any other details.

Throughout Gil's life, he has always been susceptible to illnesses and injuries, so Mom often fretted over him for one reason or another. He had tonsilitis, acute appendicitis, respiratory infections, a monkey bite, and lots of smashed fingers. It didn't help that Gil was also a skinny kid, making him the target of bullies, especially as he was so often the new kid in school. Mom was very protective of him. In fact, both Jack Laughrey and Jack Smart were irritated by the amount of attention she gave to Gil. They were jealous. Our stepfathers also didn't have the patience or enough interest to father us in a conventional sense. They never said they loved us. They went through the motions of raising us for a time but never made us feel as loved as we felt in Chalk, Texas.

After the incident with Gil and Leo, we moved out of the rental and into a house on Pershing Ave purchased by Mom and Jack. It was only blocks away from the house on Woodward, so this time we didn't have to change schools. This house was a trilevel design, with an exterior of brick on the lower half and light green asbestos tiles on the upper half. There was a half-circle driveway along one side but no garage. Like so many new homes, there were no trees or shrubs in either the front or the back yards. We slowly started fixing up the house. The living room and kitchen were on the central level, and three bedrooms and one bathroom were on the top floor. I was allowed to paint my bedroom, and I helped Jack lay linoleum tiles on the lowest level to create a recreation room. Jack paneled the entire room and added a wall to hide the washer and dryer area. He also built a bar and a built-in cabinet for the record player. We had a modest period of normalcy in our household, except perhaps for the number and nature of pets we adopted. Mom always had a soft spot for animals of all kinds and allowed us to indulge our whims in that regard. On Pershing, we had two dogs, one cat, and a spider monkey (for a short period of time!). At the previous house we also had an alligator stored in a fish tank, but it mysteriously died. When I turned fourteen, Jack tried to teach me to drive. Unfortunately, that huge Pontiac Bonneville was more than I could handle. Nevertheless, when he thought I was ready, Jack took me to the DMV to be tested. I was terrified, so I failed.

As I turned into a moody teenager, Mom and I butted heads a lot. She regularly criticized me for one thing or another, and yet she always wanted me to style her hair before she and Jack went out on the town and was very pleased whenever someone told her that she and I looked like sisters. She was only seventeen years older than me, so I suppose I shouldn't be surprised. Around this time, I was developing an interest in boys, so I wasn't paying a lot of attention to Gil's activities. However, I was aware that Gil always seemed to be in Mom's good favor. Despite my frustrations with her, I admired Mom's singing voice, and I thought she was beautiful. One day I asked Mom if I could take voice lessons. Without explanation, she just laughed at me. She burst my bubble and confidence. I never asked again.

Gil and I thought life was moving along smoothly, until the day Jack bought a blue BSA motorcycle made in the UK. He was very excited with his new toy and wanted to show it off to his friends, most of them so new we had never met them. He and the guys rode around town doing whatever men do on two wheels. Whenever they roared into our driveway together, the noise was deafening. On one occasion, Jack took Gil and me to the school playing field where he gave each of us a ride on the grass. Then he said to me, "Would you like to drive it?" As it turned out, the bike was too heavy for me to hold upright, so driving it was impossible. Gil begged to be allowed to drive it, but he was smaller than me, so Jack said no. Over many weeks, Jack spent a fair amount of time with his motorcycle buddies. They must have visited a lot of bars because he frequently came home drunk. Sometimes he was so drunk, he couldn't wake up in the mornings to go to work. Both Mom and Jack liked to party with friends, but this was too much for her to deal with, so the arguments started. There may have been other problems between them, but all I know is that their fights were becoming a nightly event. Neither Gil nor I wanted to be in the house when they were fighting like cats and dogs.

My awkward teen years converged with Mom and Jack's nightly fireworks, which resulted in a big mistake on my part. I was frequently grounded for arguing with Mom, while Gil was allowed privileges. I was jealous. I also have a strong independent streak, which seemed to threaten Mom. One Saturday, after Mom and Jack left the house, I thought of a way to get Mom's attention, never anticipating the negative consequences. I wanted to make her miss me. So, in my fourteenth year, but nearing fifteen, I rummaged the house looking for loose change. I found some in pockets and purses and even some coins in the sofa cushions. All I could gather was four dollars, but it was enough to buy a train ticket and have a couple dollars left over. So, I wrote a note saying, "Long time no see, I hope!" and ran to the train station.

The train traveled about twenty miles when I finally decided to get off. After exiting, I wandered Main Street for hours, passing the time by looking in windows and occasionally sitting down on a bench. I didn't eat anything. By late afternoon, I began to wonder where I could sleep for the night. I first thought of gas station bathrooms, and then I had a brainstorm. I headed to the theater where they were showing a film called *It's a Mad, Mad, Mad, Mad World*. The movie was a 1963 comedy, but after watching it about three times, I wasn't laughing. The film was chaotic. I didn't need any more chaos. About 9:30 p.m., I went to the lobby to use the payphone. I put a dime in the slot and called a boy I knew fairly well. He and I chatted for about thirty minutes, and then I noticed two policemen walking through the theater doors and in my direction. The boy's parents had alerted Mom, who called the police. They had already sent out an APB about my disappearance, but I made it easy for them to catch me. I left quietly with the police, glad my quest for attention was over; also, I was hungry. At the police station, I received a severe reprimand about my behavior and was told that had they caught me after midnight, I would be going to a home for juvenile delinquents rather than to my house. They also told me about another girl who had run away whose body was found in the nearby woods.

My stunt shattered Mom. After the police dropped me at the house, she became hysterical; she was both crying and screaming. She assumed that I had run away with a boy, which was a ridiculous idea, and said she would never forgive me. I have often thought that if Mom had told me earlier about Gil's experience with Leo, I think I would have better understood why she was so protective of him and gave him special privileges. I don't think I would have run away. In fact, I'm certain I would have done all in my power to protect Gil from Leo. Regardless, I had made a bad situation at home very much worse. As I went to my room, I wondered how my stunt was going to affect our family in the coming days. Meanwhile, Gil looked puzzled by my antics and did his best to disappear into the woodwork so he wouldn't get involved.

The next morning, I tried to explain my reason for running away, but my words fell on deaf ears. Nevertheless, we tried to get back to a normal routine by not speaking of the matter again. Mom and I walked a tightrope for weeks. Jack's unchanging drinking habits added fuel to the tension. Their fights became virtually continuous. I got so sick of listening to them that one morning I made an absolute promise to myself that I would *never* marry an abusive man and live a life like Mom's. Unfortunately, we were about to experience another life-changing disaster and I was right in the middle of it, but this time not by choice.

One morning before Mom left for work, she said Jack was sleeping off a hangover, that he would not be going to work, and that I was not to wake him. I needed some clothes out of the dryer. As I headed from my bedroom to the recreation level, the phone rang. That put me in a panic, so I ran toward the phone in the rec room. Before I reached it, I slipped in a puddle of dog pee and hit the floor face down. I had a ring on a chain that landed between my chin and the floor, which cut open my chin. I was knocked unconscious. When I came out of my stupor, I staggered toward the stairs, collapsed part way up, stood again, and managed to round the corner to the next flight of stairs, only to faint once more. Finally, I got to the top, bumping against the wall as I made my way to Jack's bedside to get help. I felt nauseous and fainted next to his bed. This time Jack woke up. I tried to tell him what had happened, but I was slurring my words. Then Jack scooped me up from the floor and carried me to my bed. Even though my chin was bleeding and he had not tended the wound, Jack lay next to me for a little while. Then his hands started to roam over my body. When I realized what he was doing, I screamed Mom's name several times even though I knew she wasn't there. It scared him, so he stopped. Once his head cleared a little from his hangover, he drove me to the emergency room. He watched for a minute while the doctor stitched my chin, then ran from the room and vomited in the hallway. Jack's cocktail of a hangover, mixed with blood and remorse, was more than he could handle.

When Mom came home from work, Jack told her about my trip to the hospital. He also apparently confessed to his semidrunken behavior because Mom later asked in an accusatory tone if anything inappropriate had happened. I, of course, never wanted to think about the incident again. I just wanted the memory to disappear from my mind, so because of the tone in her voice, my reflexive answer was a lie. I said, "No!" If she had asked me in a gentle, concerned way, I may have told her the truth. In hindsight, I would like to believe that in his semidrunken state, Jack mistook me for Mom, because I was wearing her hand-me-down, baby doll pajamas, but I'll never know.

We all tried once again to act as if everything was okay, but we couldn't keep it going for long. I turned fifteen in November. Mom decorated the house in preparation for Christmas and even shopped for gifts and put the presents under the tree. As the holiday neared, I made the naive mistake of inviting a girlfriend to spend the night with me. She was the first girl who had ever been invited to our home. For me this was an opportunity to forget our troubles. Wow! That idea turned out to be a big mistake and a huge embarrassment, because about 1:00 a.m. Mom and Jack got into a severe argument. My friend and I peeked out the bedroom door and saw Jack throwing punches at Mom, and then he deliberately knocked over the Christmas tree. The ornaments and presents scattered everywhere. We scurried back inside my bedroom, but Mom had caught sight of us, so she came to my room and told my friend to immediately call her parents to collect her. My friend was happy to leave.

Like a familiar refrain from an old tune, when Jack was out of the house the next day, Mom, Gil, and I ran away from him forever. We rapidly packed up some belongings and Mom's poodle and piled everything into the Pontiac. Our other dog, Christy, had died earlier when a neighbor poisoned her.

The cat, meanwhile, had gone to another home after it killed a rabbit in our mother's bedroom to feed its kittens. Throughout all these ordeals, Gil kept quiet as a mouse. He did his best to stay out of sight when home, or out of the house altogether when he could escape. As we hit the road, I realized that I had only finished my first semester at Downers Grove South High School. It was a brand-new school with about two thousand students, and I had been looking forward to attending there until graduation. Now that dream was gone in a flash.

As always, Mom decided to run to her parents for support. They had inexplicably moved again. This time they were living in Eureka, Illinois, a lovely small dormitory town with a population of less than three thousand people, known as the "pumpkin capital of the world." Mom's disabled brother Jack also lived in Eureka, although his home with Anna was on the outskirts of town. Our 120-mile journey south to Eureka was treacherous, as a winter blizzard followed us virtually the entire way. Mom's knuckles were white from squeezing the steering wheel to keep us from sliding off the snowy roads. Visibility was low.

By some miracle we arrived at Uncle Jack's doorstep, but by then the snow drifts were touching the roofline. I don't know how she found the house. Inside the house the wallpaper was loosening at the seams. We spent our Christmas there, such as it was. When the snow cleared, we went to the Purthas' house in town and stayed with them for several months. I didn't like being this close to Leo again. Mom enrolled us in school for the spring semester and found a bookkeeping job. Surprisingly, Gil and I managed to complete three full semesters of school in Eureka. The schools were small, but the teachers and the overall environment were very pleasant and welcoming. Life in Eureka was much more laid back than in urban Downers Grove.

Despite its small population, Eureka was something of a wealthy college town. To be honest, the thought of attending college had never entered my mind. I didn't know anyone who had ever gone to university, so it was a foreign concept, especially since completing K-12 was proving hard enough for Gil and me. The college was a private liberal arts institution associated with the Disciples of Christ, enrolling fewer than five hundred students. It was also the alma mater of Ronald Reagan. The town's other wealth was probably earned by locals who worked in Bloomington, Illinois, only thirty-three miles to the southeast. In any case, I thought the red brick buildings with bright white pillars and window trim were very pleasant to the eye. There was something special about the place. After I earned my driver's license, I enjoyed cruising past the campus, as well as exploring the surrounding country roads.

I made a few casual friends, but we didn't socialize outside of school. Gil and I had learned not to trust anyone. I did enroll in an art class for the first time and really enjoyed it. Twice a month in the summer there were barn dances with a live band. I always went there on my own and left on my own. I dated one boy for a time, but we fell out. Neither Gil nor I attended or participated in any school sports activities. Such things had simply never played a part in our ever-shifting lives. During the summer I worked part-time as a waitress in a small cafe. The job helped pay my gas bill. Fortunately, gas only cost thirty cents a gallon. I could have shucked corn as an alternative job, which a lot of the kids did, but it didn't have any appeal for me. Gil wasn't old enough to work, so he spent a lot of time at home with the Purthas. One memorable day, Mom asked me to appear as a witness in her divorce petition against Jack #2. The judge asked me a lot of questions, and I told him all that I remembered. She did not ask Gil to corroborate my testimony. Mom was granted her divorce.

During this Eureka idyll a new man entered our lives. As these memories are running through my mind, that very man is sitting in front of me now, driving our car to Arizona. Bill Schulz appeared in Eureka seemingly out of nowhere. When Mom introduced him to us, she said he had previously worked as a repairman for Dale's TV in Downers Grove. Gil and I were speechless because we had never met him. He certainly wasn't one of Jack's motorcycle buddies. Standing about five feet, ten inches and weighing 180 pounds, Bill had intimidating muscular arms, pale skin, and sharp blue eyes that contrasted with his strawberry-blonde crewcut. He looked very German, like his name. Mom proudly told us that Bill had fought as a Golden Gloves boxer. We learned that he was six years younger than her and that they were dating. What could we do but go to school and try not to think about what might happen next? We were teenagers and frankly not very interested. However, their relationship changed very quickly. One day, they told us they were going on a trip, so Gil and I were left alone with our grandparents. When they got back, we learned they had gotten married; again, Mom did this without telling us in advance.

Immediately upon their return to Eureka, Mom and Bill found a nice single-story brick home to rent, and it is just as well, because our grandparents and Uncle Jack were making plans to move to Arizona for Uncle Jack's health. Both events made it possible to get out of the Purthas' house. While we lived in this home, Gil revealed to me that he was interested in falconry. He had read some books on the subject in the school library. I was a bit shocked, though, when I saw what he was doing in in the back yard. He already knew how to raise pigeons, so he had managed to trap a wild one. Just as I walked out the back door, I saw Gil grab the pigeon's head in a lock hold, and then he broke its neck right in front of me. "What are you doing?" I screamed at him. He said he needed to make a lure from the pigeon's wings, which he planned to use to trap a falcon. The next day he showed me a pair of wings tied together with leather; the bloodied wings were hanging from a long leather cord. He demonstrated how he planned to use it by swinging the lure in circles above his head. He said this was how falconers drew the birds to land on the falconer's arm. I didn't fully appreciate what he was doing, but I was glad he had new hobby, even if I couldn't understand why anyone would want to do this. He added to his falconry paraphernalia by constructing a falcon's hood and tethers using leather. Mom or our grandparents must have paid for his materials. Unfortunately, his hobby was put on hold, because we only lived in that house until the semester ended.

I don't know if Bill found any job in the area because they never talked to us about money, but Mom said they hoped to set up their own TV repair business. Apparently, they couldn't afford to follow their dream in wealthy Eureka, so on sudden notice Mom said we were moving to the village of Roanoke, about nine miles to the northeast as the crow flies. They rented a grungy old building to set up the business. Access to the village was primarily along dirt roads. The worst part was that they yanked us out of the Eureka school district and enrolled us in Roanoke schools. The population in this old coal mining village was even smaller than Eureka, and the residents were not wealthy. This area was not a safe place for children to wander off as Gil and I did in Chalk: the terrain included abandoned mine shafts that were four hundred feet deep.

Mom and Bill rented a fusty, two-story farmhouse situated in the middle of vast corn fields. Three memorable features included the out-of-tune upright piano, which Gil and I played duets on, a party-line phone, where locals could hear each other's conversations, and a big red barn replete with the bones of dead livestock. It was very creepy. I'll always remember one severe thunderstorm in Roanoke. I was driving home from Eureka when it started. The dirt roads were slimy. By the time I reached the house, the rain was pouring down in buckets. The corn fields had been totally flattened by straight winds. Thunder pounded overhead. Blasts of lightning provided the only illumination I had as I ran from the car to the dark house. The door wasn't locked. The electricity was off. Nobody was home. I was covered in goosebumps. I felt like I was role playing in a horror movie. All I could do was sit out the rest of the storm alone in the house and listen to the boards of the house creak. About an hour later, Mom, Bill, and Gil walked in the door. This whole evening felt like an omen.

Just as this memory popped into my mind, Mom looked over the backseat and spoke to me and Gil again. She told us a little more about why we were running away. Bill had been arrested for writing bad checks on two separate occasions. Each time, he was put in jail. Today, she bailed him out again. She also claimed that while Bill was in his cell, he heard a conversation between two prisoners in an adjoining cell, plotting a surprise visit to a farmhouse in Roanoke where some new folks with a teenage daughter lived. These men had plans for her. If those men said anything else within Bill's hearing, Mom didn't tell me. However, she said Bill knew the men were discussing our house, and me, so that was another reason to leave town. Mom wasn't in the habit of telling tales like this one, so I shuddered and was glad we had left. As for the bad check charges, my gut tells me there is probably more to the story than we are being told. Bill just tightened his jaw and kept on driving. And now I wonder if Bill wasn't only looking out for cop cars. What if Bill knew these men, and there was bad blood between them?

Land of Disenchantment

Between 1961 and 1962 our dad had moved from Plainview, Texas, to Albuquerque, New Mexico, so during the first half of our summer 1962 trip we stayed with the Ryans in Texas; the second half of that summer we stayed with Dad in New Mexico, so Gil and I had seen this terrain before. Over the next few days, we headed southwest to Wichita, Kansas, then south to Oklahoma City, and eventually merged onto Route 66. The passing scenery was becoming increasingly familiar after we left Oklahoma City. Mom and Bill gave a roadmap to Gil and me so we would have something to do in the backseat, telling us we were their navigators. We directed them through the Texas Panhandle as we headed toward Albuquerque. Once again, we saw cotton fields, pump jacks, and scrub mesquite.

While staying with Dad in 1962, Nancy and I did not get along too well, nor did Darrell and Gil. Where Darrell was a bully, I'm sure Nancy felt jealous of my presence in *her* home. She told me, "You aren't allowed to touch anything!" Dad worked during the day. Flora kept watch over the kids. At some point, she sat me down at her sewing machine and taught me how to make a summer crop top. I was thrilled to learn a new skill, and I've been sewing my own clothes ever since. She also nursed me through a very severe sunburn that ran the full length of my backside, which I acquired after I fell asleep while sunbathing in the backyard. Flora healed my blisters by repeatedly applying cold, wet compresses using cloths soaked in baking soda. Despite this apparent warmth, we haven't exchanged letters since that summer.

Bill made the transition off the Caprock and onto the arid eastern plains of New Mexico. We passed through the towns of Tucumcari, then Santa Rosa, without seeing anything notable. This started to change though, as from Clines Corner, we could see a mountain range rising in our path. The mountains got bigger and bigger as we got closer to them. Our loaded car struggled some as it climbed from Edgewood into Tijeras Canyon, which was crowded on both sides by a forest of pine trees. Roadside curio shops were selling Indian fry bread and Navajo rugs. Finally, a large green road sign indicated ALBUQUERQUE NEXT 9 EXITS.

My thoughts are drifting again. Ten years have passed since Mom and our father divorced. So much has changed in those years, but even still I feel my relationship with Dad is tenuous. As Route 66 merges with the busy, traffic-lined Central Avenue inside Albuquerque's city limits, Gil and I are watching people in cars and on the sidewalks. Could any of them be our father and brother? Silly thought! Under the circumstances, there is no way Bill and Mom are going to stop for a visit with Dad and David. She would be too embarrassed. As Central Avenue leads us across the Rio Grande, up to Nine Mile Hill, and back onto Route 66, Albuquerque is only visible in the rearview mirror. I'm thinking, "There's another chapter gone from my life."

Prescott

Our escape from Illinois finally ended in Prescott, Arizona, at least temporarily for me. Uncle Jack and Anna had bought a nice home situated halfway up a pine-wooded lane. They were expecting us. Mom asked Gil and me if we wanted to stay with Jack for the remainder of the semester while she and Bill went to Mesa to find a place to live and work. Gil chose to go with them; he never wanted to be far away from Mom. I was so upset by recent events that I agreed to stay with Jack. At least I could be away from my parents for a while, and I could finish the school semester in peace. As soon as I was enrolled in Prescott High School, Mom, Bill, and Gil headed to Mesa. Mom's reason for choosing Mesa as a place to begin a new life was twofold. It was a large city with job opportunities, and Leo and May Purtha lived there.

Prescott High School was brand new, and the unusual architecture was quite different from what I was accustomed to. It was very nice. Once again, I was the new girl in school and found it awkward to fit in with my classmates since I was starting midsemester. My first day at school didn't begin well. First, they assigned me to home economics—the third such time I had been placed in this course at various schools. I was irritated. As I entered the classroom for the first time, I learned that the teacher was taking her students on a field trip, but for some reason I was to stay behind. To pass the time while they were away, I was instructed to clean the oven. I had seen Mom clean ovens, and it was a dirty, smelly job. I could have spit fire, but instead, after she left, I burst into tears and didn't even attempt to do what I was told. When the teacher returned, I learned that it was a self-cleaning oven. I had never heard of such a thing. I then thought, "If it's self-cleaning, why did I have to do anything to it?" On another day I was told to buy fabric for a sewing project. I was totally embarrassed because I had no money whatsoever. Once again, I burst into tears, but this time in front of my teacher. In the end the principal authorized giving me charity funds.

On the weekends I attended some youth club dances or walked down the hill to the gas station to chat with the workers. At home, Uncle Jack had a horse. He said I could ride it anytime, but I would have to put the saddle on by myself. He showed me how to do it only once. I later took him up on the suggestion, saddled up the horse, and trotted off into the pine trees. After a while the horse decided he was going home—in a hurry! He suddenly turned and started running like the wind. I clung on for my life, ducking under countless tree branches. That was the last time I rode the beast.

Mesa

At the end of the spring semester, Mom and Bill drove back to Prescott to pick me up and took me to Mesa. We pulled up in front of a duplex apartment that wasn't very appealing on the outside. When I walked in the door, though, I was shocked when I saw the kitchen. Somebody had painted the tiny room a shade of royal blue. The kitchen resembled a cave. The rest of the rooms had not suffered a similar fate. In fact, they were utterly boring. When the semester started, I enrolled in Mesa High School. Gil had already completed a semester there, so he had made a few friends. I have no idea how Bill earned money, if he did at all, and I can't remember where Mom worked, but any job she ever had was clerical. One day a stray kitten wandered into our postage-stamp yard, so I brought it inside to care for it. Mom said I could keep the kitten, but it had to stay outdoors at night because Gil was allergic to cats. That was news to me. The next morning, I found her dead at the curb. We only stayed in this duplex a short time.

Our next apartment was much nicer and fully furnished. We were still in the same school district. Palm trees towered overhead. A few blocks away stood a Mormon temple, surrounded by orange groves. On a hot summer night, the perfume from the blossoms drifted through the air. It smelled heavenly. Across the street from the apartment was a Taco Bell, which became my favorite place to eat, and on another corner was Apache Lanes, a bowling alley. When school started, I found myself enrolled in home economics—yet again. Another bummer. On weekends during the semester, I worked at the bowling alley as a waitress. Fortunately, the school offered a cooperative office education program that allowed senior students to be trained in clerical skills such as typing, shorthand, filing, etc. I took to those lessons like a duck to water, earning high marks in every skill I learned. The best part was that learning these skills gave me confidence and meant I would be able to earn a living wage. I had no college plans. Part of the training included working in the afternoon at local businesses for school credit, as well as a paycheck. I was put to work in customer service at Valley National Bank.

The Final Blow

Since Gil and I spent our days in the classroom, and I worked two part-time jobs, he and I did not spend much time together. He wasn't interested in my activities, and I wasn't interested in his; it was a boy/girl thing. I was also dating and wrapped up in my infatuations. Gil was doing his own thing, but he rarely talked about his activities. However, I was aware that he was pole vaulting at school and enrolled in Distributive Education. Like all teenagers our age, especially of different genders, our lives were diverging in different directions.

We never had family dinners together, so for a while Gil and I were unaware of how Mom and Bill were getting along. However, as the weeks wore on, and because we were home at night no matter where our activities took us, we eventually realized there was serious trouble brewing in their marriage. Déjà vu. History was repeating itself. Bill was coming home drunk every night. They argued about his behavior and about money. One memorable evening Gil and I went to bed in our rooms, and Mom and Bill in theirs. As usual Bill had come home drunk. In the middle of the night, he got up for the toilet, but in his drunken state stumbled into my bedroom instead of theirs. He was half naked. As he started to climb onto my bed, I flew off it and started screaming for Mom. She angrily dragged him back to where he belonged.

It wasn't long afterward that the situation in our home got dangerously violent. Mom, Gil, and I were home on a Saturday afternoon when Bill charged drunkenly through the front door and immediately started arguing with Mom. His face was livid with anger, and he was shaking his fists at her. As they screamed horrible words at each other, Bill grabbed a heavy piece of furniture and tossed it across the room. I was standing behind him when that happened, so I ran to the door, opened it, wanting to run out, but I was worried about Mom and Gil. I paused, with my heart wildly beating. In the next moment, Bill charged toward Mom, but skinny fifteen-year-old Gil wedged himself between them to protect her. Then Bill turned his rage on Gil. I knew he had been a Golden Gloves boxer and was terrified that he was going to seriously hurt my brother. In the next moment, I saw Bill grab Gil by the throat with his left hand and push him hard against the wall, clench his right fist, pull his arm back, and finally thrust his fist toward Gil's face. Miraculously Gil managed to duck at the last second. Bill's fist went straight through the wall. At that moment I ran as fast as I could to my boyfriend's apartment and asked his father if I could use his phone to call the police. Of course, they and all the neighbors in the apartment complex knew what was going on, so he handed me the phone.

Somehow in the interim Gil and Mom had managed to escape from our apartment. They ran to the apartment of another friend. I joined them. Very quickly sirens approached. While the police negotiated with Bill, our neighbor arranged to take us to a safe house; to leave without Bill seeing us from his vantage point, we had to crawl out a bedroom window at the rear and climb into a waiting car. We were told it took the police about two hours to entice Bill out of the apartment. Fortunately, he didn't have a weapon, but his fist alone could have killed. He was arrested and taken to jail. The police charged him with disturbing the peace, not physical abuse or attempted murder. After a few days at the safe house, Mom quickly found us a small house to rent.

Following this attack Gil made a decision that would stick with him for the rest of his life. He was sick of being bullied at school and at home. He realized he wasn't strong enough to defend himself, much less Mom, so on his own accord he started training at a karate studio in Mesa. Mom paid the fees. He put his heart, body, and soul into learning the art. Little could Gil imagine how much he would achieve in this arena or that one day he would personally edit the memoirs of Bruce Lee, the world's most renowned kung fu expert.

Divorce followed very quickly. We were also visited once by the FBI about Bill. After they left, Mom told us Bill was in a Florida prison charged with murder. She also told me that at some point during their marriage, Bill confessed to her that he had killed a man by pushing him down an elevator shaft. Since those awful days I have seen Bill's arrest records in the State of Illinois. He spent five years in jail for armed robbery and car theft; there were multiple DUI charges, assault, and battery, and much more. He used several aliases, including William Harr, William Gustav Schulz, and after their divorce, William G. Johnson: he stole my maiden name. Bill began his crime spree at eighteen, immediately after being released from an orphanage where his mother had dumped him when he was twelve because her new husband didn't want anything to do with him. So, there is more than one way to traumatize a child in ways that have consequences later in life.

Months later Mom started dating a new man, Joe Mansi. He was Italian, was a couple inches shorter than her, and had a large family in Connecticut. Joe seemed a likeable guy, and that remained true for several years. While we were still living in this small house, Mom and Joe flew to Las Vegas to get married, again without telling us. Afterwards they moved the four of us into a nice apartment complex. Fortunately, I was engaged by then and married after graduation in August, so I got out of their house rather quickly. During the early summer Gil decided that he had had enough uproar in his life; he didn't need another stepfather. He also didn't seem pleased that I was getting married. He wouldn't look me in the eye and just shook his head, but I was nineteen going on twenty and ready to spread my own wings. So, at the age of seventeen, Gil packed his bags, said his goodbyes, and rode his motorcycle twelve hundred miles to Stafford, Texas, near Houston, to live with our father and brothers, all of whom he barely knew. I was surprised Dad had agreed to this arrangement.

In my mind, Marlin had abandoned us as children and gave no financial or moral support as we were growing up, so I was puzzled. Why would

Dad now welcome Gil into his home? Ronald will tell that story. For the remainder of Gil's thirty-eight years, he and I corresponded occasionally and talked on the phone, but rarely were we able to see each other until his final days. He filled his life with foreign adventures and an encompassing desire to become an author. He dreamed of writing a semifictional book based on his life. Now Ronald and I are having to write that book for him.

Years Later

During the first year of my marriage, I finally talked to Mom about her father. I had been told years earlier that Leo started molesting Mom when she was only three years old, but that was all I knew. This time, Mom provided a few more details. She said he continued molesting her until she was thirteen, at which time he attempted intercourse. She stopped him by threatening to tell her mother if he persisted. Now I wonder whether Mom blackmailed Leo. She was only thirteen when she auditioned with the radio station and was hired. Leo was the only person in the family who could drive her to the station. Did he agree to let her do this in exchange for her silence? It was during this conversation that she gave me more details about Gil's molestation. I asked her why, to this day, she still seemed comfortable in Leo's presence and why she didn't keep us away from him, to which she answered, "I forgave him." She never forgave me for running away.

CHAPTER 4

NEW BEGINNING

(As told by Ronald)
Stafford, Texas

That night Gil found himself sitting on the ground before a small campfire at a rest stop outside Las Cruces, New Mexico. He had ridden his motorcycle four hundred miles, and yet time had flown by so quickly that his first day's journey seemed over before it had begun. He leaned against his backpack, and with the aid of a campfire light, unfolded the roadmaps he had picked up at a gas station. As he marked his route for the next day, Gil recalled a few years earlier when he, Jeanne, his mom, and her previous husband had made a last-minute escape from the police in Illinois. On that grim day they were headed to Arizona. His mom tossed state roadmaps into the backseat and informed the teenagers they were to navigate the journey. For the most part, the adults followed the escape route that Gil and Jeanne chose for them. With little else to do in the cramped backseat, this had kept their minds busy. The first map he squinted at in the flickering light was of New Mexico, the second was Texas. Tomorrow he would traverse, first, southern New Mexico, then most of Texas before reaching his destination in Houston.

Gil was going to East Texas to finish high school. Remaining in Mesa, Arizona, was impossible. Jeanne had just graduated from Mesa High School and was engaged to be married soon. This meant Gil would be left to cope with sharing a cramped apartment with his mother, Elsye, and his new stepfather, Joe. Fortunately, Elsye was sympathetic to Gil's dilemma and placed a call to Marlin, Gil's biological father, in Texas. Marlin quickly agreed that Gil could come to Texas to live with the family and complete his senior year of high school. Impatient to depart, Gil insisted on riding his BSA motorcycle the twelve hundred miles from Mesa to Houston. Marlin felt concern about Gil's choice of transport because of his youth, but as he was an avid motorcyclist himself and was aware that Gil had been riding a bike for some time, he set aside his worries because he was keen to reunite with his son. They had not been under the same roof since Gil was about two and a half years old, when Marlin and Elsye separated in Plainview. Father and son both relished the idea of being together again. So, with the past behind him and optimistic about the future, Gil wrapped his denim jacket about his upper body and dozed off to a chorus of chirping crickets.

He rose early the next day, as the temperature was quickly rising along with the eastern sun. Today was to be a long day in the saddle, seven hundred miles long. If he did not arrive at Dad's doorstep by evening, he knew Marlin would be worried. Gil gathered his bedroll, munched one of the sandwiches his Mom had put in his pack, and set off. From Las Cruces, I-10 went south to El Paso and followed the Rio Grande for a way, then curved east and south toward the heart of Texas. Hour after hour after hour, sand dunes dotted with yucca cacti and scrub mesquite trees flew past his sight. Eventually the scenery gave way to green grazing pastures and then an abundance of rolling hills that sprouted groves of post oak trees. By the time Gil entered Austin, his body was dog-tired, but pride pushed him to keep going. He still had three hundred miles to go, and the sun was setting on his back. He powered on into the evening until the Houston skyline rose from the ground in front of his handlebars.

It was late when Gil neared our neighborhood in Stafford. He exited the interstate, slowed his machine, and navigated his way through the suburban streets. The weariness of two long days and twelve hundred miles was finally behind him. After gripping handlebars and facing the wind for such a long distance, every inch of his body ached. As he made his way into the new housing development, his sun-weary eyes surveyed row after row of new brick homes until he found 13102 Suzanne Street. Relief, mixed with uneasiness, welled up in his chest as he parked in the driveway. He set the kickstand, dismounted, and stretched his sore limbs. After a few moments to gather his thoughts and his emotions, he slowly walked to the front door. Before he could knock, the door flung open, and Gil was immediately embraced by our Dad. An embrace that was long overdue.

The home Gilbert stepped into included familiar faces from two summer visits in the early sixties and one unfamiliar face—mine. Shortly after our father divorced Elsye, he remarried. His new wife was Flora Moore, a native of Plainview and a single mother of two children, Darrell and Nancy. When seventeen-year-old Gil arrived in Stafford, Darrell was two years older than him and had recently enlisted in the marines to serve in the Vietnam War. Nancy was the same age as Gil. David was fifteen. Daniel was eleven. I was just six years old, so Gil had never met me. Now that Gil was living with us, seven children bore the Johnson name. However, among the lot of us, the Marlin Johnson household collectively had two different mothers and three different fathers. Gil, on the other hand, had lived with his sister Jeanne and a string of stepfathers, so a strong family unit was a welcome change. As a young adult, I had difficulty responding to friends' inquiries about how many siblings I had.

In no time, Gilbert ingratiated himself with his sister and all his brothers, whether related fully or partially by blood. Nancy had been complaining for some time about there were too many boys in the house, yet Gil's charm managed to win her over during the time he lived with us. Darrell's absence due to his enlistment relieved some of the ever-present sibling tension. David responded to his reunion with Gil as a celebration, and the two got along wonderfully. Daniel and I were fine with having another older brother. The four boys shared a single bedroom. Each night was like living in a summer camp dormitory. The conversations and pranks were lively, to say the least. Our parents were already well-versed at doling out love and discipline in equal portions, so one more child was not an issue. And Gil's perpetual playful demeanor, as well as his helpful attitude toward chores, left us all asking ourselves why he had not moved in sooner.

Dad quickly recognized Gil possessed a greater sense of independence than his other children were permitted. Regardless, Dad expected Gil to fall in line with all the family rules, which included curfews, haircuts, wardrobe modifications, and mandatory church attendance. In our house, there were some absolute must-dos, and weekly Bible class was one of them. We all went to church twice on Sundays and once on Wednesday nights. Somehow, we all fit into the Volkswagen station wagon and made our way to the

Stafford Church of Christ. By all indications, Gil had no problem complying with this rule. Whether or not he agreed with everything he heard from the pulpit or discussed in Bible class, everything he experienced in the church setting was consistent with what was expected of everyone in our home. Gil seemed to bask in the stability and the normalcy of it all, a rare experience for him since church attendance was an irregular event in his previous life.

At some point during the year that Gil lived with us, Dad gave him a pocket-sized, red leather New Testament and Psalms, which Dad had lovingly used for many years. At the back of the Bible, Dad had written some notes in his distinctive draftsman-block lettering. Gil also added some notes of his own at the back, specifically two short annotations. On line one he wrote *faith, hope, charity I Cor. 13:13*, referring to the thirteenth verse of the thirteenth chapter of I Corinthians, commonly known as the love chapter: *And now abideth faith, hope, charity, these three; but the greatest of these is charity.* On line two Gil noted *charity Col. 3:14*, which is from the third chapter of Colossians: *And above all these things put to charity, which is the bond of perfectness.* These verses had some meaning for Gil. Contemporary Scripture translations sometimes substitute the word "kindness" for "charity," and if Gil was known for anything, it was his kind nature. In his heart and in his actions, Gil personified what he had gleaned from the Bible.

Gil enrolled at John Foster Dulles High School for the 1968–69 year. He quickly set out to make a good impression on his fellow students. Assimilating to a new school had become second nature to him by this time, as he had bounced from one school to the next countless times since grade school. While in Mesa, Gil had enrolled in Distributive Education Clubs of America (DECA), so he joined the club again in his new school. David was also a member. Gil's worldly experiences probably made him seem more mature than his classmates, which may be the reason he was elected club president, and he had a fun nature. DECA was a popular offering in high schools for students interested in pursuing a career in business or finance. Gil's and David's DECA affiliation helped both obtain paying jobs even though they were still attending high school. Two major retail chains in the Sharpstown Mall hired them. Air-conditioned malls, while common now, were a new development in the 1960s. This mall contained forty-three stores on one level. It was so popular that celebrities shopped there on a regular basis, including Dan Rowan, a famous comedian who cohosted a primetime show called *Laugh-In*.

Gil worked at Foley's department store, David at Bostonian Shoes. Several times a week, the Johnson brothers would don their perma-pressed slacks, white oxford button-down shirts, and a razor-thin, dark-colored tie. Their work uniform was completed by a navy blue sports blazer emblazoned with the logo of their respective employers stitched to the pocket. A sharp pair of penny loafers completed their ensembles. Off to the mall they went to find their place in the world of commerce.

While employed at Foley's, Gil befriended a young, female coworker. One day this young lady confided to Gil that she was having difficulty breaking up with her abusive boyfriend. She was afraid of him and worried about walking alone to her car at night. Brothers in arms, both Gil and David gladly offered to escort the young lady to her car at the end of her workday. Right on cue, the brute showed up in the dark parking lot. Gil, without hesitation, went into protection mode, a posture he knew all too well. His body tensed; his left shoulder nervously ticked upward while his head tilted slightly to the right, a tic the family had seen before. All his senses were on red alert. Less than two years earlier, he had placed himself between his mother and sister to ward off a drunken, belligerent, and dangerous stepfather. (After that incident, he was motivated to learn the art of karate.) That said, this time Gil had an unfortunate disability; his left arm was in a sling because of a recent motorcycle accident. Gil had been over-confident on his bike and taken risks. As he did two years earlier, Gil first tried diplomacy. David chimed in as well. This time the Johnson boys' tactics successfully de-escalated the situation without using force. The young lady was permitted to get into her car and drive away without incident. How fortunate for both boys, because this boyfriend was a hulking mass of flesh and muscle, and he was very angry.

After being reminded of the parking lot incident, David fondly recalled an earlier childhood memory in which eleven-year-old Gil had taken action to save his life. In the summer of 1962, David was allowed to travel from Albuquerque to Arizona for a short trip with Gil, Jeanne, Elsye, and her husband. They were together only a few days. On one of the days, they stayed at a motel; the kids got into the pool to cool down. Elsye and husband were in their room a few yards away from the pool. Gil knew how to swim; Jeanne did not. David was still learning. After some horsing about, David found himself in over his head and struggling to reach the pool's edge. Gil saw what was happening and swam to David's rescue. Gil always had a soft spot for animals and people who were in danger, so his nurturing nature responded instinctively to save his little brother.

One girl in high school took a shine to Gil. He and Mary hung out together on occasion, but she became too clingy, so Gil began to avoid her until their friendship eventually ended.

Up to this point, we all believed we knew Gil, so our religious household was unprepared for a revelation that came to light. In fact, this event may have precipitated Dad giving Gil the Bible. Somehow, our dad had come across pornographic materials in Gil's personal possessions. Worse still in Dad's mind, the materials were gay pornography. His shock was palpable. I was too young at the time to be involved, but as David recalled, Dad immediately sat down with Gil to discuss his and God's views on homosexuality. Because the two boys were so close in age and spent so much time together, Dad drew David into the lengthy conversation. Our dad, while possessing his own authoritarian views of right and wrong based on his upbringing and church teachings, fortunately did not inherit his own father's temper. Grandpa Ira would have beaten Gil with a switch until his backside bled. Instead, Dad took a more sympathetic, diplomatic approach by discussing homosexuality from various vantage points. At the conclusion, our father challenged Gil to seriously consider his interests in light of God's teachings. Other than the fact Gil had dated Mary for a short while, this was the first time anyone had so much as a hint of Gil's sexual interests and thus the first time anyone in authority had challenged his sexual behavior. Gil seemed to take our father's advice seriously and agreed to do his best to meet Dad's expectations. If nothing else, Gil feared losing our father's affection after being deprived of him for thirteen years. Dad's fatal assumption was that Gil's interest in the gay lifestyle was only a matter of choice and thus could be changed by willpower and faith alone. Dad also was unaware that Gil had been sexually traumatized by his maternal grandfather, and Gil wasn't going to be the one to tell him about the sexual lessons Leo had taught him from about the age of two and a half until his early teens.

The balance of Gil's senior year was uneventful. After final exams, Gil collected his diploma but did not attend the graduation ceremony. Instead, he enlisted in the US Marines Corps at a local recruitment center. In a letter to his much-loved Aunt Mildred in Texas, Gil told her he joined the marines because he enjoyed hard physical exercise, and marine trainings are the hardest. He also intended to make use of the GI Bill to pay for his college education following discharge. Then he boarded a plane and flew to Phoenix to prepare for the next phase of his life.

Private Gilbert Lee Johnson, USMC

Gil was sworn into the United States Marine Corps at the Phoenix Junior College auditorium on June 17, 1969, along with a gaggle of other young recruits. His mom and her husband Joe looked on in disbelief. The Vietnam War was in its ninth year, and the US troop deaths continued to rise. Hopes for a cease-fire seemed nonexistent. In addition, protests against the war were occurring across the nation. Elsye, and hundreds of thousands of other parents, were anxious for their sons' lives.

Gil believed he was fully aware of the potential dangers ahead, yet he brashly plunged forward anyway. He was used to living life dangerously, almost as if he didn't care what happened to him. As a budding writer, and sensing that upcoming events may be important, he decided to keep a private record for posterity.

Private Gilbert Lee Johnson, 1969.
Courtesy of the Author's Collection.

For the duration of boot camp and basic training, he kept a pocket-sized diary with him and made notes whenever he could fit in a few moments for introspection. On the title page, Gil dedicated the diary "To Dad." Inside, each entry read like a letter to our father. After the embarrassing discovery of gay pornography, Gil desperately wanted to regain Dad's approval, and now that he was following in the footsteps of his stepbrother Darrell, maybe Dad would love him for his efforts despite the issues that had upset the family.

An early entry in the diary said, "I'm on board a jet leaving Phoenix. There are two interesting civilian girls sitting next to me but I'm too tired to hardly talk. Oh well." Several days later Gil faced the reality of bootcamp. He described it thus: "I'm writing this 3 days later (after the event). It was one of the roughest things I've ever been through. We were called everything from bitches to slime and pigs. I felt like jumping out a window." A few weeks later Gil got a letter from Dad which lifted his spirits, and he resolved not to quit: "Got a nice letter from Dad. Hope I can live up to what he's expecting." Gil resolved to carry on, writing, "I have just about made up my mind to go all the way in training. It will only last a few weeks & what I do will mean so much later, to my family – and myself. GERONIMO!" Gil was not going to let himself or our father down. Another entry conveyed Gil's worries about going to war. During a class on marine history, the recruits were shown raw combat footage from World War II of the Battle of Iwo Jima. Gil wrote, "I hope I'll never have to see anything like that. It wasn't just unpleasant – it's something terrifying. There's no way I could explain the clammy felling I got watching it."

While at Camp Pendleton, Gil made his most heartfelt, and at the same time, self-critical entry in his diary. He was standing in the chow line one evening when he heard a member of his platoon yell a derogatory slur at a private in another platoon. The slandered private was a slightly built man from Guam; these soldiers were called Chamorros. They were allowed to enlist in the US military because Guam is a US protectorate. In the eyes of some soldiers at Camp Pendleton, Chamorros were considered ignorant and illiterate. The offended private responded with a kick, and then calls for a fight echoed around the room, while others stood silent, including Gil. Before things got out of hand, Gil's drill instructor, Staff Sergeant Feyerchak, stepped in and brought the fight to a halt. Later that night, the sergeant sat his entire platoon down and admonished the privates for failing to come to the aid of the undersized kid from Guam, even though he was from another platoon. "It was the right thing to do," said the sergeant to his platoon. Gil was upset with himself that he had done nothing to help. It wasn't as if he hadn't helped others in need before. Why didn't he do so this time? That night Gil decided to pick up where he left off in Mesa and continue his studies in karate.

When he finished basic training, Gil took a short furlough before his specialty training began. While on furlough, Gil visited us at the end of October. During that stay, Gil saved the day for our brother Daniel, who had been trick-or-treating and came home with a long face. A neighborhood bully had snatched Daniel's entire bag of candy and run off with it. The budding thief had no idea what was about to happen next. Gil asked Daniel if he knew the thief and where he lived. Daniel said, "Yes." Without a moment to lose, Gil flew off the couch, escorted Daniel out the door, and down the street to the bully's house. Gil rang the doorbell. Fortuitously, the thief opened the front door. He looked up at the tall, stern young man sporting a marine's crewcut; next to him stood Daniel, grinning like a Cheshire cat. Gil was blunt and to the point. He told the boy his behavior was totally unacceptable and dishonorable, and that he must return the bag of candy. He did as he was instructed without arguing. Daniel was thrilled as he and Gil turned away from the door. Gil had become his hero for the day.

Upon returning to duty, Gil reported to the Defense Information School (DIS) at Fort Benjamin Harrison, in northeastern Indianapolis, Indiana. Unknown to Gil, a century and a half earlier our paternal great-great-grandfather had migrated to Indiana in search of better opportunities. In Gil's case, Indiana only brought back traumatic memories. When Elsye and Marlin separated, she moved Gil and Jeanne to her parents' house in Michigan City. Leo took his grandchildren under his wings, and just as he had done with his own daughter, he molested both children. While Jeanne's trauma ended comparatively soon, Gil's trauma was repeated over and over as time passed in their household. With those memories lingering in the recess of his mind, Gil mentally disassociated himself from those events. He had no intention of ever telling our Dad about his history. It was at this time when

Gil wrote a letter to Aunt Mildred in Texas, remembering happier days: "I used to wish that your family could just stay the way they were when I was little. You don't know the relief it was to me to be out there where all of you were so nice and, well,—together."

The DIS school was staffed with personnel from all branches of the military. Students learned how to become journalists working in print, radio, television, or photography. They also received advanced supervisory training in editing, public affairs, media, and community relations. Gil was a whiz at typing, which was made easier with the light-to-the-touch, electric IBM Selectric typewriters. He also excelled at administrative supervision. These skills aided him throughout his professional life.

Upon completing DIS, and due to Gil's work in journalism, he was granted the privilege of choosing where he would like to be stationed. His options were California, North Carolina, Arizona, Okinawa, or Hawaii. He chose Hawaii.

Lance Corporal Gilbert Johnson

The island of Oahu is an enviable destination of any mainlander looking for a tropical escape with its quintessential sprawling, pure white sand beaches and vast tropical mountain peaks. It is also the site of the US Navy's Pearl Harbor base, home of the Pacific Fleet. Camp H. M. Smith is not far inland from Pearl Harbor and in 1969 was home to the US Marines' Fleet Marine Force Pacific. The base housed thousands of soldiers and sailors and their respective families. Gil was assigned to the position of press information man at headquarters where he served as a member of the newspaper staff. Much to Gil's relief, his weapon would be an IBM Selectric typewriter rather than an automatic weapon and K-Bar. His writing career began in earnest.

The base newspaper, the *Leeward View*, had a staff of several dozen enlisted personnel and a small officer staff. The newspaper was published once a week with a respectable circulation of about a thousand. Each edition consisted of four to five pages of general base-related business, intermural sporting events, and domestic affairs associated with family life on the base. Lead stories included national events, major stories affecting the Marine Corps, and snippets from the Southeast Asia theater. Recurring columns included Chaplain's

Desk, Community Calendar, and the Military Marketplace. Its format and function were very similar to the *Paducah Post*, the small-town newspaper Gil's paternal grandfather faithfully read decades earlier. Rather than serving a farming community, the military base paper serviced the marines and their family members with base events and news of the world at large.

The articles Gil wrote for the *Leeward View* covered a broad scope, but without doubt, his most cherished topic was personal fitness. He did not have to convince his editor of its importance; historically, the marines were fanatical about the issue. One article written by Gil from early 1971 was a short piece titled "Rank Disintegrates at Noontime." It led with, "They're in the Marine Corps, and although one may be a general and the other a private, they find themselves working side by side with little regard to each other's rank." The gist of the article was that rank mattered little during physical fitness training. Gil included a photograph of himself with a caption saying, "Brown belt from Camp Smith's karate club, Corporal Gil L. Johnson uses one of the weight room's mirrors to perfect his kicking form."

Black Belt in Karate

By the late 1960s, karate was graduating from being a mere national fad into a legitimate national health and fitness movement. Hollywood got wind of this emerging trend and began releasing motion pictures with martial arts woven into the plots. A 1967 sleeper titled *Born Losers* introduced a character named Billy Jack, a half-Navajo, Green Beret Vietnam War veteran and hapkido master. In the plot, Billy Jack is associated with a countercultural school for children. He is eventually forced to use his martial arts skills to protect the school's director and a group of students from small-town thugs. A simple plot, perhaps, but the surprising success of the movie lead to three more films in the franchise, of which the best known was *Billy Jack*. The unforgettable scene from this film found barefooted Billy Jack standing nose to nose with the story's antagonist. Billy Jack stares at his foe with a penetrating gaze and states, "I'm gonna take my right foot and whop you on that side of your face," pointing to the man's right temple. "And you want to know something, there's not a damn thing you can do about it." In a microsecond Billy Jack executes a flawless arching kick, leaving the bad guy stunned and prone on the ground. Thousands of young boys and men left the theater, looked up the nearest karate dojo in the Yellow Pages, and signed up for the next available class. Billy Jack films lit the fire of public curiosity about the martial arts. But perhaps the most famous of all karate films was released in 1973. *Enter the Dragon* ignited a bonfire of interest in the martial arts. The film's star, Lee Ju-fan, professionally known as Bruce Lee, was a Hong Kong–born Gung Fu phenomenon.

The collective family of martial arts originated in Asian countries. Karate and judo pioneers arrived either from Japan or Okinawa and gung fu (or kung fu) adherents from China. Sailors and marines stationed in the Pacific theater after the end of WWII, especially in Okinawa, witnessed these men practicing their unfamiliar forms of fighting and wanted to learn these self-defense skills. Eventually the Okinawans trained Americans in the use of karate. In return, the Americans taught the Okinawans how to box. The exchange of techniques fostered international relations and turned on a spigot of interest that flooded across the States. One such serviceman who returned to the United States after the war with a burning desire to promote this new self-defense craft was Robert Trias. He settled in the Phoenix, Arizona, area and opened its first martial arts school using the Shuri Ryu karate system. Two decades later, a teenager named Gil Johnson walked into one of these schools and signed up for lessons. He developed his skills to a level that allowed him to participate in a competition. He invited Jeanne to watch. She thought he performed amazingly well and was proud of him. Even though he came away from the match with a bloody nose and bloody knuckles, he grinned from ear to ear with excitement and vowed to continue learning the craft.

Tatsuo Shimabuku was one of the most revered Okinawan karate masters. Even though he barely stood one inch over five feet tall, and never weighed more than 120 pounds, his skills were so masterful that no one ventured to challenge him. During World War II, Tatsuo trained the Royal Japanese Army in self-defense techniques. At war's end he returned to his home village and continued to teach the local villagers in his backyard under the palm trees. When the US military set up a permanent base on the island of Okinawa, scores of marines showed up at Shimubuku's front door, all wanting to learn his fighting techniques. By 1954 Shimabuku broke from his own sensei's karate system and developed his unique system, which he called Isshin-Ryu, or "The One Heart Way." A select few of Isshin-Ryu followers, with their sensei's approval, returned stateside and opened their own dojos (schools) teaching the techniques they learned from Shimabuku. Thus, the American Okinawan Karate Association was formed in 1969. Gil joined the association in October 1970, just after he arrived at Camp Smith. His certificate of membership was signed in neat Japanese characters by Master Tatsuo Shimabuku himself.

For the next year, Gil's weekly routine consisted of working in the office five days a week and training at the gym during lunchtime. Several times a week, Gil packed his gym bag and made his way to the dojo in the evening. True to the Japanese philosophy of respect and discipline, the training sessions were performed in a regimented pattern. Students bowed when entering the dojo, removed their shoes, then changed into their *gi* (uniforms). They were also expected to bow before their instructors. Prior to starting formal class, everyone stretched and warmed up, strengthening their hands by striking a *makiwara* (wooden board) or heavy bags. At the scheduled time, the senior instructor (*dai sempai*) called students to line up facing him according to their grade, senior persons to the right of each row. The *dai sempai* had the students face the Buddhist altar, where a picture of the isshin-ryu *megami* (goddess) was hanging, as well as pictures of the sensei (master), and the sensei's karate teachers. Everyone simultaneously bowed, then faced the trainer, and bowed again. Next followed a prescribed series of upper body exercises, including punching, striking, as well as lower body exercises like blocking, and kicking, kneeing, and limbering.

The most distinctive features of a karate education in the early 1970s were *kumite* (sparring) and a series of *kata* (individual prechoreographed movements). Isshin-Ryu placed a stronger emphasis on *kumite* than *kata*. The master believed the aesthetics of correctly performing a *kata* meant little if it could not be translated into actual combat. Students wore *kendo* armor during these hard contact sessions. The *kendo* gloves and padded skirt also included a groin cup. Though stressed less during training, *kata* executions were still important. *Katas* developed an individual's mind, body, and spirit in preparation for fighting. To accomplish this, Isshin-Ryu training featured special breathing methods. The first *kata* taught was *sanchin*; it was performed using ten breaths and completed in 106 seconds. Next was the *seisan kata*. *Seisan* means thirteen, so students were taught to perform the *kata* in thirteen breaths. The subsequent *katas* progressed in complexity and the number of movements.

Finally, in September 1971, Gilbert L. Johnson, stood proudly in his *gi*, and with all attendees lining the perimeter of the dojo, held his hands as his side and bowed his upper body in respect before the panel of senior instructors. He awaited the sensei's decree. The supporting document of this age-old ritual reads:

> *Mr. Gilbert L. Johnson has satisfactorily completed the course in Karate Training and competed in matches held in the American and Okinawan Karate Association, conducted by Isshinryu Karate Instructors, therefore is given the rank of SHO-DAN (1st-DAN).*
>
> *In Testimony whereof and by virtue of vested authority I do confer upon him this Certificate of Proficiency.*
>
> *Signed by Tatsuo Shimabuku*

In lay terms, Gil was conferred with the prestigious black belt, first degree. His certificate was indexed as no. 1708. His goal realized, one can imagine the pride and satisfaction that Gil felt at the achievement of this longtime dream. No longer would he be incapable of answering the call for help from any of his

Gilbert Lee Johnson, First Degree Black Belt, self-portrait, 1971. *Courtesy of the Author's Collection.*

loved ones, or any others who needed him in times of duress. This conferment shaped many events during the balance of his life.

Two weeks before Gil was discharged from the marines, he wrote one last letter to Aunt Mildred to express the depth of his appreciation for the time he had spent with her and her family. No matter where he was, or what he was doing, those memories kept him going.

Dear Mildred and Clayton,

About sunset, I walked across the athletic field on my way to the bowling alley to get something to eat. It had rained for the first time since I got here in February and there was a red, sunset rainbow in the clouds. But even before I saw it, I could smell the rain and as I always do when I smell summer rain, I thought of you. I thought of all those evenings when the air went cool, and you could smell a storm coming on from miles away. And I remember how we would play in the dark and sleep outside with the coyotes. And I remember how both of you would sit in the house and read while the bugs flew against the screen and how you would sometimes call us in for iced tea.

If either of you had any idea of how much that time meant to me and how much more it means to me now, I think you'd be very proud. I can close my eyes sometimes and be back there with all of you. If I ever become the writer I hope to be, you'll be known by every reader who knows me, and everything you taught me will be taught to them. That's a promise.

. . . I realize that my memories of the summers on your farm are just like your memories of the little boy from Illinois. That's to say that they're gone and can never be captured again, but it's something we share, and I like that. Take care and please give my love to Hal and Randall and Linda when you see or write them again. And say hi to Grandma for me.

Gil

Back row: Nancy Ryan and Jeanne Johnson. *Front row*: Gilbert Johnson, Hal, and Randall Ryan, 1961. *Courtesy of the Author's Collection.*

Interlude in Albuquerque

After leaving the military, Gil was welcomed into the Johnson home once again, but this time, our family lived in Albuquerque, where we had moved because Dad had found a new job. Gil said he wanted to study journalism at the University of New Mexico, which was not far from where we lived. He completed the fall 1972 and spring 1973 semesters studying expository writing, Shakespeare's tragedies, general psychology, the study of literature, magazine article writing, and photography, among others. Gil treated his photography assignments as examples of journalistic reporting, with an artistic touch. He didn't choose easy subjects. Instead, he literally moved into a seedy hotel in the most dangerous part of Albuquerque so that residents living within could get to know him, trust him, and allow themselves to be photographed. His black-and-white images portrayed disheveled and drunk

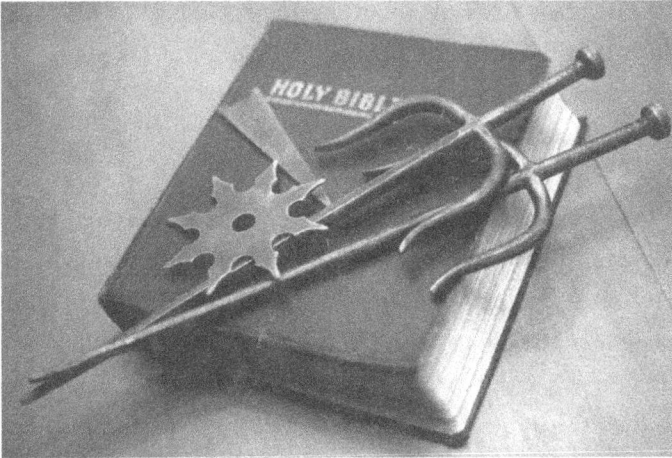

Photograph by Gilbert Johnson. *Courtesy of the Author's Collection.*

men and women, mostly elderly, as well as night scenes of rundown buildings. One photo stands out from the rest because its symbolism is personal: the Holy Bible rests upon a table, and lying across it at a diagonal are three martial arts weapons: a throwing star, a dart, and a pair of *Sai*. *Sai* weapons were one of the first Okinawan weapons that emerged in the martial arts, with a purpose both offensive and defensive.

During this interlude Gil met a beautiful young woman named Dana at church. They became close friends, and the family loved her. Gil clearly cared very much for her, as indicated in letters he wrote to her and family. In Dana's mind, their relationship was becoming serious. When his last semester ended, rather than finding the courage to tell Dana

Dana Fisher. *Courtesy of David Johnson.*

that he wasn't ready to think about marriage, Gil packed his bags and left for California without giving her any indication of his plans. She didn't learn of his departure until he was gone from her life.

Milian France

Gil was mesmerized. He didn't hear a word she was saying, but he knew her name was Milian France. She had an open smile, sandy blonde hair, and a vivacious personality. Her brown eyes sparkled with pure energy, and her laughter was contagious. On this fortuitous day, Milian was giving a presentation as part of an assignment and showed the class a 16mm art film and then began a discussion about its artistic meaning. Gil sat in the front row, unnervingly staring at her throughout the hour. Milian recalled asking herself, "Who IS this guy, and why is he staring at me?" After class ended, as was typical, the instructor invited the students to meet at a local dive for dinner. Gil and Milian both eagerly jumped at the invitation. As the evening wore on, Gil and Milian focused their eyes and conversations on each other, as if no one else was in the room. The chemistry between them was immediate and mutual. During their conversation they each revealed their backgrounds and future plans. Both were surprised to discover that the other had attended the University of New Mexico. Whereas Gil studied there for two semesters before moving to California, Milian had studied there for four years and earned a BA degree in art and education. Gil also learned that Milian was seven years older than him, but her girlish manner made her seem younger. She also let him know that she had a toddler son and was still hurting from a recent divorce. She needed something to jolt her from postdivorce doldrums, which is the reason she enrolled in creative writing at Santa Rosa Junior College. Milian sensed that Gil was so enamored with her that she told him she was reluctant to start another relationship so soon. Not to be deterred, Gil confidently said, "You and I are going to know each other for a very long time!"

Gil's statement was prophetic. What began as a friendship soon resulted in them becoming project collaborators and finally lovers. However, their relationship was, from the beginning, unusual. Milian explained, "There were complicated rules to our romance, and I always had to second guess

Gilbert Johnson and Milian France. *Courtesy of the Author's Collection.*

them. Things that normal couples did, we didn't." One rule was when and where they could meet. Gil did not want Milian dropping by his apartment unannounced. His said he did not want to inconvenience his roommates. There were also certain restaurants and taverns that were off limits for them to frequent together.

Less than a year into their budding romance, Milian discovered the reason for Gil's rules. While at lunch with a girlfriend who also knew Gil, the friend expressed surprise when she learned that Milian and Gil were in a relationship. Milian sensed an ominous twist coming. A mutual friend of theirs named Bart, whom all knew to be gay, had mentioned seeing Gil hanging out in gay bars in San Francisco on weekends. Milian was surprised but not shattered. This revelation gave some clarity to their relationship.

Not long after this conversation, Milian confronted Gil. She asked, "Is it true? Are you gay?" At first Gil was angry that someone had spoken about his personal business, but then he collected himself. "It's not that simple," was his response. A long awkward pause ensued. Finally, he got the courage to explain, "The only way I can describe is, it is like having a taste for apple pie. If you're raised on apple pie, you occasionally have a taste for apple pie. That's all it means." Another long pause ensued. Finally, Milian had the courage to ask, "By apple pie, do you mean . . . ?" Gil interrupted, sensing what Milian was about to ask him. "I was brought up a strict Christian and I believe in what the Bible says. I had no problems in the marines. I pray, every day, that it's finally over. But I can't marry you until I'm positive that every single bit of it is out of my system." He went on to explain, "I especially can't bring a son into the world until I'm certain I'm completely cured."

"You want to marry me?" she squealed. The mere mention of marriage and children gave Milian a sliver of hope that their complicated relationship might be heading in the direction she hoped for. At that point, their conversation ended.

What Milian did not ask Gil was, how was he going to get "completely cured"? Years later she learned, from one of Gil's neighbors, some details about his form of self-therapy. After a weekend of sex-binging with nameless male partners in San Francisco, Gil would return to his apartment in Santa Rosa. Apparently feeling tormented with shame and guilt, he was heard talking to himself long into the nights, pacing the apartment floor, praying out loud to, and arguing with, God about why he couldn't break this addiction and why wouldn't God stop his compulsive behavior. In an obtuse way, Gil reached out to our father for help in letters but never disclosed the raw details of what he was struggling with. In one poignant letter, dated September 1974, Gil skirted around the real issue by using vague allusions to his problems. Without mentioning sexuality, he indirectly tried to explain his mental confusion and an utter frustration with his life.

> I've often wondered why so much has happened to me, why I see things differently from so many people, why I've been led so much. I can see from whence I came, and I know, vaguely, where I'm headed. So many times, I've weaved across a particular path, a direction, and incidences always bring me back along one general course. The whole matter is so complicated it defies explaining, but I _see_ every detail

*of it. I've been "allowed" to do things I shouldn't do and have prayed
till the sweat and tears rolled out of me to be taken away from those
things, only to return . . . There are other times when I can pray for
the impossible and it's like asking for a drink of water.*

He then went on to reveal:

*When I dip into the dark places to learn them, and learn them I
must, I feel like I may not find my way back again. So often Gil Johnson [referring to himself in third person] wakes up mentally and finds
himself wandered too far, I feel like a freak, a tourist to every walk of
life and a resident to none of them . . . So much for the mind-boggling
head trip—no, I have not turned spacey, mod, hippie freako (though
I can be that) (I can also be super-straight, Marine tougho, business-
man, and younger than average editor). There's a reason for all that.*

Black Belt Magazine

As if the moral struggle to reconcile his actions with his beliefs was not
enough to deal with, more mundane events around Gil were becoming
problematic as well. His savings were drying up, making it difficult to pay
for classes at SRJC. Wages from odd jobs were insufficient to pay rent each
month. When the financial storm clouds were at their darkest, a slim beam
of light penetrated the night and provided him with hope. A major magazine
offered him a job in Los Angeles. It would mean moving from Santa Rosa,
but the salary and opportunity were too good to pass up. This move would
be a critical test for the durability of Gil and Milian's already complicated
relationship, since she was to remain in northern California.

In the spring of 1974, Gil found a small apartment in West Hollywood
and reported to work at the offices of *Black Belt Magazine*, then located on
Wilshire Boulevard. He was hired as an assistant editor for not only *Black
Belt Magazine* but also *Karate Illustrated* and *Fighters*. All three monthly
publications were owned by Ohara Publications. During these heady times
of growth, the editorial staff had some personnel turnovers, including its
well-known editor, Bob MacLaughlin, the man credited with building martial arts magazines into sought-after publications by the public. Americans

Gilbert Johnson practicing a high karate kick, 1974. *Courtesy of the Author's Collection.*

were hungry for news about the martial arts movement. Aside from Gil, there was another young man who worked as assistant editor. In Gil's opinion, this guy knew little or nothing about karate. So, Gil set out to become the editor in chief but knew he had a long and hard road to travel to prove his worth to management. The work was not that much different than what he had done with *Leeward View* in Camp Smith. This time, though, the subject was vastly more interesting, and the pace was blistering.

By 1974, martial arts programs were establishing roots all over the United States. Dojos were being opened nationwide. The teaching materials, product offerings, upcoming events, and people of interest to cover each month were growing fast, and Gil realized current staff levels were not enough to stay ahead of the growth. He convinced management to hire some photographers and writers from other cities to conduct the necessary legwork of reporting and production. With management's approval, one of the first writers Gil contacted was Milian France. To this point in Milian's life, she had never written a single article or story, other than writing an essay for a college course. Milian was flabbergasted when Gil called her with his offer of employment. Gil lessened her fears of failure and promised to teach her how to write and even how to use a 35mm camera for photographing people and events that she would be covering. Milian finally agreed to take the job, but more importantly, she felt intoxicated that the love of her life had not forgotten her.

A Confession

Their love affair entered a new phase. They would alternate, with either Milian flying to Los Angeles or Gil flying to San Francisco on weekends. Now they had so much more to talk about: collaborating on writing assignments for the magazine, martial arts training, which Milian began to embrace, and creative writing ideas—a passion they both shared. During one of these weekend interludes as they lay in each other's arms, they asked lover's questions of each other. Curiously, Milian asked Gil, "When did you lose your virginity?" But before he replied, she freely told him it had happened to her in high school when she thought she was in love with a boy. There was an awkward pause as Milian awaited Gil's response. He rose from the bed, too perturbed to speak; his nervous tic revealing something was deeply wrong. She asked him again, "How old were you?" "I was six," he whispered. Sirens went off in Milian's head. They were no longer discussing consensual sex between lovers, but something much more disturbing. "Who was it?" she demanded. Gil's head fell forward, and he whispered, "My grandfather. He raped me." Milian screamed out, "The bastard, if I ever run into him, I'll kill him!" Gil cautioned her, "No, he's a good man. I don't bear him any grudge." Surprisingly, there was no malice or anger in Gil's expression. She sensed he was telling the truth. As his last word on the uncomfortable subject, Gil said, "I've never told a living soul. We lived with him. And he never hurt me. And you must realize, that in all those years, it was the only real love I got. The only love . . . "

Many years later, after reflecting endlessly on that conversation with Gil, Milian concluded, "From the age of six, he had been trained to give and receive sexual love from a nice old man right there in the same house. Yet Gil had managed to forgive all that."

Tao of Jeet Kune Do

One day as Gil worked in his office at the magazine, his phone rang. He picked up the receiver and found himself talking with Mitoshi Uyehara, the owner and publisher of Ohara Books. Gil immediately recognized the heavy Japanese accent, since Mitoshi had hired him months earlier. The publisher had an eye for talent and wanted to offer Gil another unusual opportunity. Over the next few minutes, Mitoshi related that he had a long personal and business relationship with kung fu master Bruce Lee, which had lasted until Bruce's untimely death at thirty-three a year earlier. Gil needed no explanation of who Bruce Lee was; the entire world knew. Bruce was the ultimate marquee personality of the martial arts industry. His unfortunate death in Hong Kong occurred due to an adverse reaction to prescribed medications. His tragic loss only increased Bruce's legendary persona. Mitoshi then told Gil that he and Bruce had been discussing a book deal for some time, but other business concerns always got in the way. This hindered the project from progressing. Since Bruce's death, Mitoshi had been communicating with his widow, Linda. She had possession of all her husband's files, notes, and drawings. Finally, the phone conversation ended with the publisher encouraging Gil to contact Linda and introduce himself and his credentials as her husband's potential book editor. However, even though Mitoshi had recommended Gil's name to Linda, the final decision rested solely with her. The twenty-two-year-old assistant editor slowly hung up the phone and sat back in utter disbelief. He was being offered an honorary key to the front door of the martial arts industry. Bruce Lee was the inner sanctum, the who's who of notoriety. All he had to do was gain the approval of a grieving widow.

Once his head cleared, Gil immediately went into action. One of his karate associates was Howard Jackson, a karate and kickboxing celebrity in his own right; he also knew Bruce, Linda, and their children. After Gil spoke to Howard and explained the situation, Howard expressed no qualms about introducing Gil to Linda, so the meeting was arranged. On the appointed day, Howard and Gil drove to Santa Monica, to the house that Linda and her children were moving into. After Bruce's death in Hong Kong, Linda had first moved with her children to Seattle for a while but later decided to settle in the Los Angeles area. When Gil and Howard arrived, moving boxes and furniture were scattered about the yard; friends of the Lee family were lifting and carrying items into the home. The chaos was being directed by an attractive, Caucasian woman with short blonde hair and sad eyes. Gil correctly presumed this was Linda Lee, which Howard confirmed with a nod. Introductions were made, and Linda sweetly introduced Shannon and Brandon, her two young children, to Gil. A dinner date was fixed in the near future to discuss details of the book project.

Not long after the meeting, Linda informed Mitoshi that she was comfortable with Gil leading the project and gave a green light to proceed. The hard work began in earnest. Milian was with Gil when Bruce's boxes of research material were handed over. She recalled years later, "I was with him [Gil] when he got all the notebooks and it was an overwhelming experience, like being handed the tablets of God to go through and rearrange . . . It was all in Bruce Lee's handwriting, with his little drawings and diagrams, much of it cryptic." Gil spent hour upon hour quizzing Linda about various topics or asking questions about interpretations of what he was finding in Lee's papers. The task was daunting but creatively invigorating. Gil and Linda became friends and sometimes drove to the coastline with her kids. They talked about the project while playing on the beach with little Shannon and Brandon. Unknown to Linda, in a letter to our father during this period, Gil suggested that he and Linda were "semi-dating" for a while, but the reality of Linda's age (she was six years older than Gil) and the fact that she was the mother of two young children ensured their friendship remained platonic and businesslike. Milian was relieved.

Bruce Lee became known to the American TV viewers in 1967 when he played the reliable sidekick of the fictional superhero, Green Hornet, on the afternoon program of the same name. After one season *The Green Hornet* was cancelled, and Lee found himself out of work, he opened the Jun Fan Gung Fu Institute in Los Angeles's Chinatown area. Bruce began teaching a new style of kung fu that he had been developing since he was a teenager in his hometown of Hong Kong. He referred to this new style of self-defense as Jeet Kune Do.

Early in the project, everyone knew, including Gil, that it was critical he get into the gym and unlearn some of his karate biases and quickly learn, firsthand, the physical and technical nuances of Jeet Kune Do. There was no question who Gil would have to call upon to mentor him for this transition. Danny Inosanto had been a longtime friend of Bruce who had graduated from being a Bruce Lee student and became an instructor of Jeet Kune Do as well. Danny was now to be Gil's instructor.

> *Danny's class is interesting. Basically, it could be called, "Throwing oneself into the lake to learn how to swim." I really like it. We put on boxing gloves and go at it full-contact with the hands and half-power with the feet—anywhere. My first partner was an over-six-foot policeman with a build like Atlas (only more flexible). Didn't do too badly, but the gloves are sure hard to get used to and my nose is really taking a beating. There are some drills of course, to sharpen combat timing, accuracy, endurance, and power. Notice the word combat. There are very few static drills. The art is based upon Bruce's concept of fighting—"do your own thing, as long as you know the principles of combat motion." He named it "Jeet Kune Do" for convenience and described it as the "style of no style."*

Another student present when Danny introduced Gil to his class was Chris Kent. Chris was a teenager at the time but had already been studying Jeet Kune Do with Danny for over a year. Chris, like Inosanto, went on and dedicated his entire professional career to promoting, teaching, and authoring books and videos on Jeet Kune Do. Gil and Chris began their friendship as sparring partners in class, then workout partners on off days. Chris helped Gil understand a student's perspective of Jeet Kune Do, and Gil helped Chris understand the martial arts scene at large. Chris recalled driving from his parents' home in Santa Monica to the Black Belt offices and hanging out as Gil worked on the book project: "He [Gil] had Bruce's papers spread out all over the floor of his office. Sometimes Gil would ask me questions about where I thought certain passages should be located within the book. Some of Bruce's notes were from western fencing, other notes from boxing. Since I fenced in high school, I was able to put into context some of Bruce's notes."

Gil spent the better part of a year mimeographing Lee's notes, transcribing critical passages, and indexing material by themes. One element of the finished book Linda was adamant about was that no photographs of any person demonstrating a particular movement or punch would be included. Bruce had voiced this same point before he died, saying his book would not be a "How-To" manual. This was an unusual decision, since established practice in the industry required the use of formulaic images to demonstrate a particular movement. In the end, Gil and Linda agreed that the only images to appear in the book would be Bruce's loose, energetic line drawings and renderings of stick figures.

In the introduction, Gil wrote, "With the help of his wife, Linda, I collected and scanned and thoroughly indexed all the material. Then I tried to draw the scattered ideas together into cohesive blocks. Most of the copy was left unchanged and the drawings and sketches are his own. The book's organization, however, could not have been justly done were it not for the patient attention of Danny Inosanto, his assistant instructors, and class of senior students. It was they who took my eight years of martial arts training, threw it out on the floor and turned the theories into action with *their* knowledge. They have my gratitude both as the editor of this book and, separately, as a martial artist."

By mid-1975 the manuscript was completed and titled *Tao of Jeet Kune Do*. Ohara Publications released the two-hundred-page hardback book to the public the same year. The finished product, however, looked somewhat underwhelming at first glance. There are no eye-popping images of Bruce Lee's shirtless, fabulously athletic body anywhere within its pages. The only image of Bruce Lee is on the cover, and even that one is subdued. The book opens with Bruce's philosophical quotes about Zen, the art of the soul, Jeet Kune Do, and organized despair. The chapter titled "Preliminaries" addresses simple fitness training techniques, accompanied by minimalist pen sketches illustrating correct posture and positions. These are followed by Bruce's analyses of parts of the body—head, arms and hands, trunk, legs, and so on. The chapter on "Qualities" addresses his philosophy on coordination, precision, power, endurance, balance, body feel, good form, economy of motion, vision awareness, timing, cadence, and attitude. "Tools" focuses largely on a stunning variety of kicks, punches, and grappling techniques, all philosophically explained according to Bruce's thinking. The "Preparations" chapter explains feints, parries, and manipulations. "Mobility" begins with a quote: "Attain stillness while moving, like thy moon beneath the waves that ever go on rolling and rocking." In this chapter Bruce philosophizes about distance, footwork, and evasiveness. The "Attack" chapter is very direct: "There is

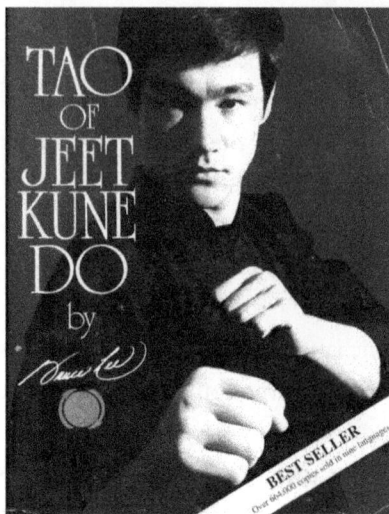

1998 cover of *Tao of Jeet Kune Do* by Bruce Lee. The book, edited by Gilbert Johnson for Ohara Publications in 1975, has been published in numerous editions and printings over the decades and has sold millions of copies worldwide. *Courtesy of the Author's Collection.*

nothing much in this art. Take things as they are. Punch when you have to punch; kick when you have to kick." In this section Bruce outlines the psychophysical process of attacking, describes how to prepare oneself, and discusses the various modes of attack. All the chapters are illustrated with Bruce's line drawings, which express a vibrant energy despite their simplicity.

Even though Bruce was lost to his wife, family, the martial arts world, and fans, Gil's personal knowledge of the art, along with his organizational and writing talents, helped to breathe life again into Bruce's philosophical teachings. It's as if Bruce were whispering into Gil's ear, telling him the order in which his methods should be explained. Bruce's vision, coupled with Gil's editorial skills, created what many believe to be the Genesis text for the modern amalgamation of all martial arts studies, commonly called mixed martial arts. The book sold over 750,000 copies in nine languages.

After the publication of *Tao of Jeet Kune Do*, other writing opportunities came Gil's way. Danny Inosanto, fully aware of Gil's talents, engaged his new friend in an endeavor to coauthor another martial arts manuscript. Together they published *Filipino Martial Arts As Taught by Dan Inosanto*, released in 1980. Their writing partnership became a friendship that lasted years.

Bruce Lee's book was the crème de la crème of opportunities in Gil's career up to this point. While he found the experience a labor of love, immensely satisfying, and worthwhile, he still had not lost sight of his ultimate dream to become a novelist. He wanted to write something that would live longer than him and be original to him. However, once again he temporarily shelved that idea when another adventure presented itself. He was going to Iran.

CHAPTER 5
THE IRANIAN REVOLUTION

"Dark dawns remember evening's browning tones. I sit alone and preen my wings to spread them in a brightening sky. My time will come."

Gil Johnson, *undated poem*

Bazdari

The taxi left the pavement traveling faster than it should have until it came to a skidding stop on the dirt shoulder of Route 51. Sand and rocks boiled up from the old Paykan's bald tires, filling the air inside the compartment with dust. The two passengers in the back seat coughed and held on for dear life. Gil was accustomed to this style of driving but frequently thought Iranian taxis drivers were even more reckless than their Los Angeles counterparts, if that was possible. The other passenger, Gil's peregrine falcon, Damien, perched upon his trainer's gloved left hand, voiced his dissatisfaction by emitting a high pitch screech, which only made Ahmad, the taxi driver, smile with glee.

As the two exited the back seat, Gil spoke in Persian to ask the driver to return in two hours for a fare back into the city and promised to sweeten the transaction with a few extra rials. The driver quickly agreed. They exchanged amities, "May Allah protect you," as the Paykan sped off in the direction from which they had come, back to Isfahan. After a moment, Gil looked around to get his bearings. He had come this way along Route 51 countless times while on business trips but never actually stopped at this location. Looking east, the terrain was void of anything noteworthy, showing only arid plains and craggy outcrops. Off to the west of the highway were patches of grain crops, mixed with barren hills, that met a thin line of trees following the meandering Zayandarud. Together Gil and Damien set off down the embankment towards the tree line in search of quarry.

Isfahan, Iran. Photograph by Gilbert Johnson, 1979. *Courtesy of the Author's Collection.*

The locals were never surprised to see a man carrying a hunting bird, since falconry had been a part of Iranian culture since prehistoric times. The birds helped trainers capture prey to feed their families. However, the Iranians were pleasantly bewildered when they saw an American in possession of a *baz*. Each time Gil ventured into the bazaars near his apartment carrying Damien, the scene generated lighthearted conversation with the shopkeepers, which gave Gil opportunities to converse with his neighbors in his new language. Gil had loved birds since he was very young. When he was a teenager in Illinois, he read a book on falconry in the school library. His heart raced with excitement and he began immediately creating the kit necessary for raising falcons, even though he did not have a bird. One day he would. Many years later Gil became aware that Arab kings and princes were avid falconers, reveling in the sport of hawking—capturing wild game using hawks and eagles—or that the Kirghiz of Central Asia had developed falconry into a science. No matter how poor a nomad might be, he possessed a falcon or a hawk that he would never sell. The Persian language referred to this sport as *bazdari*—falcon keeping. Gil dreamed of someday raising his own *baz* and hunting wild game as did the ancients. Jeanne fondly remembered (although appalled at the time) the day her teenage brother ripped the wings from a captured pigeon in the family backyard. Attaching the bloodied wings together with a strip of leather, he affixed the lure to a length of leather cord and practiced swinging the lure in the air, as he would do years later to train a falcon to hunt. While still in Marine Corps basic training along the Southern California coastline, Gil made an entry in his journal describing the grassy hills as beautiful falconry country. Some letters home from Gil while he was in Iran, and later Saudi Arabia, had dark splotches on the pages. He circled and captioned them: "Bird Shit."

Today was a big day for Damien; Gil had high hopes. He had purchased Damien when the bird was juvenile; to date, it had not captured a pigeon or partridge on its own, even though the instinct is innate. Gil incrementally trained Damien to fly further and further away from him over time, giving the falcon a reward when he flew back to Gil's gloved hand. Occasionally Damien flew circles overhead, diving at terrified critters, but never swooping for the kill. Instead, he returned to his perch to beg for morsels. But the time had come: Gil felt Damien was now ready to graduate to capturing prey on his own volition.

As trainer and hunter approached the tree line, Gil slowly removed the hood from Damien's head. Immediately, Damien turned his head toward the forest and stared intently at prey in the far distance, which only he could see. His claws tightened on Gil's gauntlet in anticipation of flight. Slowly, Gil released the jesses, or leather straps, from Damien's legs. He stretched his arm toward the trees and emitted a sharp whistle. Damien immediately shot into the air like a missile leaving its launch pad, his jesses dangling in the air and the sound of his ankle bells disappearing on the wind. In seconds, Gil lost sight of the falcon. He was concerned but also proud of Damien's hunting instinct. Meanwhile, all Gil could do was walk, listen, and scan the sky. He walked for what seemed to him like hours, but in fact it was only minutes later, as he came around the base of a small hill, that he heard Damien's rapid kack-kack-kack-kack sound. Gil approached the kacking on tiptoe, left ear turned toward the sound to hear better. What he saw next almost brought him to his knees. A few feet away, magnificent Damien hovered, wings spread, over the prostrate body of a grey partridge, killed from deep lacerations. Damien made eye contact with Gil, blood dripping from his beak, and gave a triumphant squawk, as if saying, "Look what I did!" Gil was beside himself with joy; tears welled up in his eyes. All his pent-up emotions about possibly losing his falcon had proven misplaced. Trainers keep their falcons well fed so that the bird will not be hungry enough to eat the prey, so Gil bagged the partridge to use later as food or treats, although he tore off a small piece to reward Damien for a successful hunt.

With Damien tethered and his hood in place, Gil sat on the ground, took a cigarette from his chest pocket, and lit it. After a long celebratory exhale, Gil's thoughts traced back to December 1976, about one and half years ago, when he spotted an exotic classified advertisement in the Los Angeles Times. Northrop Corporation was seeking experienced office personnel to support their supply chain operations in the Middle East. After working several grueling years at *Black Belt Magazine*, he had spent time working freelance, without any financial success. Earlier in 1976, he journaled, "I have $10 to my name. I'm lonely, and this little bed seems, again, like a cot in a cell. Times like this I pray—without words, without requests." Gil hadn't forgotten his dream.

> *I just want to write and sell about three scripts in the next couple of years. With that done, I want to accomplish two things. (1) Buy an A-frame in Northern California, and (2) Secure an agent to sell what I write and keep me informed, and periodically commute to Los Angeles.*

He went to work for Northrop in January 1977 and was making more money than he would have in the States, so he had every hope he was on a pathway to his ultimate goal.

Gil's reverie turned back in time, again. He had another, much more personal reason for leaving Los Angeles.

He relived their conversation in his mind. Out of the blue one evening, he rang Milian and asked her to go on a late-night drive. As was typical for him, he didn't bother giving her an explanation about where they were going. Their romance had been cooling off for a while. They were getting together less and less. Deeply in love with Gil, Milian was worried. The silence between them on the drive was deafening. Eventually Gil's rusted MG turned off Los Feliz Boulevard and began to climb up Fern Dell Drive.

"Are we going to Griffith Park?" Milian asked.

"Yes, we are," he responded.

Milian looked out her window at a large sign on a grassy knoll, which said GRIFFITH PARK. This was the most popular tourist destination in the entire Los Angeles County area. The four-thousand-acre city park hugged the eastern slope of the Santa Monica Mountains and featured many popular attractions.

Gil pulled into a parking area. Without speaking, they got out of the car. As they walked hand in hand, Gil led Milian toward a walking trail among the trees. Near them someone was playing a saxophone; its deep, brassy woodwind sounds echoed through the eerie darkness. Suddenly, a man popped out from behind a bush and rushed in the opposite direction. Milian gasped, but Gil kept on walking until they climbed the gentle slope and stopped by a large rock. He lifted himself up, sat on the rock, and gazed at a wedge of warm city lights visible between two hills. Milian anxiously looked at him. "I was already steeled for the worst, the big break-up. And I had made up my mind not to care. I could be very bull-headed when I had to," she thought.

The saxophone squeaked, then started a new round of deep, smoky blue notes.

To Gil, Milian said, "If we were writing this scene, we'd have to leave out the saxophone. It's way too corny for a movie."

"A lot of musicians play out here at night," Gil said.

"Are they all that sad?"

"Most of 'em."

Milian leaned back against the rock, gazed at the glimmering view, and waited for a reaction from Gil. Before he could speak, they were startled by a second man sneaking through the bushes near them.

"Who are these people?" asked Milian.

"Gay men come here to meet and have sex because the police have a hard time busting them."

Milian looked down at the ground in silence. Gil twiddled a stick in his fingers.

"Remember when I told you about . . . apple pie?" he asked.

"Yes."

"Somethings been happening to me lately. I . . . I think I'm a little more bisexual than I thought," he said.

"What does that mean?" she responded.

"I've had a relapse now and then. But now, I don't seem to be able to control it as well as I used to."

"Maybe you shouldn't."

"NO! I believe in the Bible! I will not give in to evil, do you hear? It's an abomination! I am an abomination!"

"You are not! You were an innocent child."

"No! I know what I am when I'm with guys. I rise up out of my body and watch what it does. You don't know what men do with men. You could not imagine."

Tears filled Milian's eyes. She leaned against the rock in dismay. Gil jumped down and stood rigidly beside her. Neither looked at the other.

"So, I guess this means we're going to break up . . . "

Gil whirled. He grasped Milian around the waist, fell to his knees, and burst out crying.

"Oh, no. No! Please, Milian, you can't leave me! You're all I have left in the world. I need you. You can't leave me, not now. Please!"

Tearful, confused, and astonished, Milian knelt in front of him, and wrapped her arms around his body.

Years later, Milian recalled her thoughts at the time: "It was like having the brake and the accelerator on at the same time. I felt I would internally hemorrhage. But oddly, the thought of Gil with other men wasn't as bad to me as the thought of other women."

After this unnerving evening in the park, days turned into weeks. Neither Milian nor Gil tried to call or speak to the other. It was Milian who eventually initiated contact.

One day, Gil returned home from the office and found a large manila envelope in his mailbox. It was from Milian. He ripped open the envelope. Inside was a typed copy of *Lurking Shadows*, a screenplay the two of them had been working on together. Milian had slashed a heavy, violent X across the first page. On another sheet of paper, Gil found a new, hastily drafted contract. Milian laid out terms for them to continue this project. Like King

Solomon, Milian had split the screenplay in half. Each would be responsible for their half if it was to be continued at all. Years later Milian said, "I had to divorce Gil. That meant dividing up the script we wrote together. I bore him no rancor. The contract I drew up was fair."

Even though Gil and Milian had not spoken in all that time, in the interim Gil was still thinking about her and turned to his journal with these thoughts about their awkward discussion:

> *I am caught between two worlds and can be totally accepted by neither one. Strange that I, so often thought to be beyond my age, would be called immature. And somehow it's true.*
>
> *Still, until I can embrace one of the two worlds entirely to the exclusion of the other, I must learn again to live alone, to study, and work, and grow on my own, using the rest of the world as a study, a training and proving ground. As I am alone, I must develop the strength and skills, the power and background, to defend what I am as a* man.

Damien jolted Gil's thoughts back to the present by impatiently flapping his wings to gain his keeper's attention. Gil checked his watch and hoped the taxi driver would honor his promise to return to pick them up and take them back to Isfahan. Proudly, Gil gathered up Damien, who by this time was mellow, and made his way back to the highway. Ahmad was waiting.

In the early days in Isfahan, he still had Milian on his mind:

> *"Working with Dr. Jack Ward, Thomson discovered that a person's force field detects the frequencies of the force fields of other people at a distance and is affected by them." – I HAVE BEEN (as I've noticed) FOR YEARS! "People's force fields immediately sense fear, aggression, panic or friendliness in another person." MILIAN! I'm validated! By doctors and scientists around the world! I saw you at the airport (while sitting at my desk) meeting me, and tears started streaming down my face for joy (at the desk). They burst out of my eyes before I knew what happened, and the feeling disappeared and left a glow. Thanks for your letter.*

Gil journaled with regularity, but it took him six months to write his first letter home to Dad (by this point he had been transferred to Tehran):

When the Iranians heard about your telex, that I'd not written for six months, they were appalled. They wanted to put me in a sack and stone me, neglecting my parents. My responsibility, they said, for staying in touch with the people who raised me, for showing loyalty to my family. My family understands, I said. I live in the present, and in dreams of tomorrow. A quirk in my character. My family knows. No good, I should have written a note, a postcard, something. Iranians are family oriented and, of course, they're right in this case. When I got Jeanne's telex, I wrote two pages in a dream-swept mood that embarrassed me afterwards.

A quick rundown of work activities. I began as a parts chaser (no one here knew what that was either), unloaded a few trucks, and was "promoted" to material control specialist, keeping track of all the supplies and materials coming in. I was moved into a hotel room with this older fellow who had been in Iran for eight or ten years before joining this company, and who was being lined up for some kind of management position. He asked me a lot of questions about administration, and I wrote a few procedures for him. He became a director, and I became the acting manager of Administrative Services in Isfahan. I'm in charge of telex, postal, translation pool, typing pool, graphics, repro, and distribution, and I wrote a lot of procedures for different departments. I made the Vice President's secretary cry, supposedly, and on the basis of that it was decided that I was too undiplomatic to be a good manager. I was sent to the Tehran Headquarters Office, uniquely corresponding with my boss's move to Tehran, and enshrined in the office next door. I advise, write procedures and directives, and I keep my nose behind my desk. I am still on parts chaser pay, socking away a little less because of the expenses in big city living, and every other day I get a fresh promise for a raise, possibly a new manager's position since I'm controlling most of the same functions here. I was hurt, depressed, angered by the transfer, ready to quit, slightly obnoxious, and I still frequently give everybody flak about my pay, but it seems I'm liked in this office, a real popularity winner. My opinion is respected, unofficially. The managers, directors, and secretaries all steal by to ask me questions. Central Files is my biggest problem, how to get all the correspondence tucked away neatly for review a couple of years from now, how to get everyone to follow the procedures I know will work.

Then at 4:30 or so, I leave it all, hop in a car that takes me home or shopping. The driver bribes me with oranges and candy for extra hours on his timecard. I take the bribes, and he runs errands for me, and drives me around till late at night—restaurants, nightclubs, cinemas, homes of friends.

A guy who works for me has become a good friend. His wife is seven months pregnant but makes these huge meals for me when I come to visit, not for me, she says, but Goodarz's brother and their lifelong friend are living at the house most of the time, and she likes to feed them all well. We sit around and get drunk or high while she cooks dinner. I'm teaching them to stick fight, Filipino style, and they're teaching me how to build carburetors. They all speak Farsi half the time, and I'm learning to intrude on the private comments that take place in front of me.

I met some ballerinas and some ballet dancers. A fairly dull group of people. How can awesome dancers perform Camina, and then play pinochle afterwards? They live in such a little world among themselves. Still, they tear my heart out when they dance. I should have been a dancer.

There's a karate studio near the office. I've been invited to participate without paying.

But most of all, I like the people on the streets south of Tahkte Jamshid, the Old Bazaar, the laborers who line the streets in the early morning, leaning on their shovels, waiting for strangers to give them work for ten dollars a day digging ditches or carrying rubbish. They're all villagers, and they stand there holding hands, watching all the cars go by. Some are old and pock faced, bent nearly double from years of hard labor, and some are young with generous smiles. I think they're all beautiful, more beautiful, and real than the ballerinas.

I think of home in Illinois, the grain bins, and silent, snowed-in streets at night. I think of crisp cold days, and muddy roads, and think how right at home these villagers would be in Roanoke Benson, Illinois.

This weekend an Iranian friend took me to a walled pasture where his parents kept some fruit trees outside the city. We passed some farmers hoeing a field. I stood there in coat and tie, with my driver waiting in the car, and tried to tell Mehdy, in my limited Farsi, why I felt so at home with workers. I think he understood. His family are farmers.

Mulberries, melons, grapes, and oranges. This country has got everything that grows. Pistachios are their national nut, and you can buy caviar by the kilo.

The mountains are still in snow, an hour away, but the city is hot and gaseous. I went skiing for the first time in my life. Not a beginner's mountain. Nearly broke my leg but had a great time; got lots of compliments.

I adopted an eagle, a golden eagle, who lives on the terrace outside my apartment. The terrace is at the top of a house of stone, overlooking a garden with flowered trees and a swimming pool. The apartment is an L-shaped single with separate bathroom and kitchen. It's a small place, but the entrance hall that joins the kitchen and the living room has one glass wall to my private terrace with a view of the mountains. I have a glass table, and a set of garden chairs on the terrace, and a waterpipe with Isfahani tobacco that makes you swoon. I smoke it only occasionally when the night is just right. It takes a lot of preparation, a ceremony of sorts. I let my eagle free (his wings were clipped before I got him) while I'm firing up the coals, and he follows me around, snatching at odds and ends, toppling over the pipe, climbing into copper bowls. Occasionally he gets in the house, shreds the paper in the waste basket, empties out all my pens and pencils from the pencil box, attacks the pillows, and carries the telephone receiver around. I try to keep him outside. He pecks at the burning coals, and flies (a little) from chair to chair, or lands on my *shoulder and goes through my hair. Though he's small for an eagle, a 4 to 5-foot wingspan, he lets you know he's there. One day, when he was especially hungry, he flew down from the terrace to the yard of a neighbor several doors away. He stole a bone from their terrier. The neighbors were delighted. I was relieved. He could have eaten the terrier without a lot of fuss. He's been kidnapped twice after flying off the roof. The last time it took several Iranian friends and some detective work to find him. A young Iranian kid had stuffed him into his car trunk. Baked eagle at 90 degrees. He was pretty sad and angry looking when I got him out. I try to keep him tied. It's better for him, but he is pretty clever at getting loose.*

I'm beginning to wonder if I'll ever grow out of this wanderlust, if I'll ever grow up and settle down to a nice quiet, normal lifestyle. I want adventure still, but I don't know how to get it without the humdrum of industry work. These countries are still going through their industrial revolution. Speaking of revolution, have you heard the machineguns that go pop in the night here? The religious leaders don't like the Shah because he moves too swiftly into the future. The students don't like the Shah because he doesn't move fast enough. They've heard of democracy, but don't really know how to go about it without dragging the monarch off his throne. The monarch is very fair; he shoots them both when they step out of line.

Civil Unrest

Since the early 1970s the Iranian government had spent more than $15 billion on military equipment, ranging from aircraft to army tanks. Concern grew within the regime about the ability of the nation's armed forces to absorb so much new and sophisticated weaponry. To meet the concern, they allocated another $200 million to US contractors to train their military and manage the massive supply chain for parts that were needed to maintain the new equipment. Northrop Corporation was one of the primary companies awarded a service contract. When Gil arrived in Isfahan, at least ten thousand American families were already working and living throughout Iran. But now, in the late summer of 1978, civil unrest was boiling across the country.

On August 19, 1978, a horrific terrorist attack occurred at Cinema Rex in Abadan. Arsonists set fire to the theater using jet fuel. The theater burned to the ground, killing 477 innocent Iranians. Religious fundamentalist leaders had been proselytizing that movie theaters were controversial because they symbolized modern, Western influences. The Islamists blamed SAVAK, the Shah's secret police. However, after the revolution, an Islamist confessed to the crime and was prosecuted. Be that as it may, this brutal act set the Islamic revolution on fire across the country. The government and the people all blamed each other. Attempting to quell the masses, the Shah implemented martial law on September 8, and the very next day his military fired into a group of protestors, killing at least one hundred Iranians, on a day that became known as "Black Friday." Early in October, the Shah ordered the Ayatollah Khomeini to be deported. He ended up in France, where he had unfettered access to the media, which gave him a greater ability to influence his followers in Iran. The pressure to get rid of the Shah became so intense that it became impossible to broker a national unity government. The Shah broadcast a promise to never repeat the mistakes of the past, but no one believed him.

Foreigners were increasingly being pressed by the Islamists to leave the country. Some left, some stayed. Gil was fearless. He wasn't leaving. He quit Northrop about the time of the Abadan massacre and moved back to Isfahan, where he rented a small house, and despite the brewing troubles, bought himself the falcon he called Damien, named after his most recent lover. Before leaving Tehran, he passed his eagle on to another falconer.

Isfahan is a large city located two hundred miles south of the capital city of Tehran. During the period 1963 to 1973, Isfahan emerged as a major industrial center with a large steel mill, cement and sugar factories, an oil refinery, and petrochemical industries. Modern bridges spanned the Zayandarud River, and its branches and canals were retrofitted for modern needs. The city was outfitted with recreational clubs, theaters, and sports stadiums. For years before the Islamic revolution, Isfahan was a popular tourist destination.

While living in Isfahan, surviving off his savings, Gil sought freelance journalist credentials from major world news outlets. The unrest in Tehran and other cities told him he was living in a time and place that was going to change political history. He wanted to witness it firsthand and report back to the Western world. He also thought this would be the break he needed to kick start his writing career.

Gil's journalistic principles required he show no bias, an ethic rarely seen in journalism today. He intended to integrate with the people, experience what they were experiencing, and report these events to the world in an unbiased way. To that end he said:

> I tried to keep my position and my home as neutral as possible to keep a wide range of information coming in. In my entry parlor on a table stood a picture of the Shah, a picture of Khomeini, the book of the Koran, and an English Bible. I had SAVAK men for guests (emissaries of the Shah's secret service), as well as soldiers, Khomeini supporters, avowed Communists, Christians, and atheists. I made regular calls on all the main religious leaders in the city and kept a journal of daily events. What kept me friends with everyone was the neutral position I tried to maintain.

Secular and religious outrage intensified through the fall of 1979. Khomeini condemned the military government and called for continued protests. His supporters organized a series of escalating demonstrations during the holy Islamic month of Muharram, to culminate with massive protests on the days of Tasu'a and Ashura, December 10 and 11, respectively. These holy days honor the prophet Hussein, grandson of Mohamed, who was slaughtered by opponents of the Islamic religion. He, with his child in his arms, seventy-two of his followers, and all their families died on the battlefield in the name of Islam.

With those two holy days arriving soon, millions of Iranians from surrounding cities descended on Isfahan and Tehran. This is Gil's report from Isfahan:

> By 1979 the Muslims of Iran were again in the midst of battle. They were fighting for a government based upon the laws of their religion, defined in their bible, the Koran, which was written by Mohamed. This time, their enemies were the king, Mohamed Reza Shah, and all his supporters, because they were too liberal and westernized. Their

leader was Ayatollah Ruhollah Khomeini, exiled from the country in 1964 after serving terms in prison for defying the Shah on religious grounds. Five years before, Khomeini had redefined opposition to the Shah. This redefinition included a people's revolution—a slow, planned struggle to dethrone the Shah, and, if necessary, the sacrifice of thousands of his followers at the hands of the Shah's forces.

The military forces were waiting. Cities around the country were under martial law during evening hours, and even small demonstrations held during the day, had been met with crushing violence from the military. After a long siege of battles that set Tehran ablaze, that destroyed Islamic stumbling blocks such as cinemas and bars, after most of the banks and government operated buildings had been burned to the ground by the people, and thousands of bullets had been spent by the army, the country was silent. Waiting.

There was talk of a 24-hour curfew that would give the army license to kill anyone who so much as peered out of his home. The army took up positions throughout all the cities, and the people set their faces to the East to pray. Some prepared burial clothes for themselves and their families, and a few stopped by my house in Isfahan to say goodbye. Most Americans living in Isfahan took their families to Shahin Shahr and Kanet, the housing compounds outside the city for Bell Helicopter and Northrop Worldwide employees, both companies supporting military contracts. At the compounds, the red DANGER flag was flying, warning Americans not to leave the guarded tracts. The few Americans remaining in Isfahan closed their doors, locked their windows, and moved to the rear of their houses, turning off their lights in the evenings, whispering in the dark.

The day before Tasu'a the people would gather at Mosalla, the largest outdoor mosque in Iran, in the south of Isfahan. There they would hear instructions for the march called by Khomeini.

That morning I walked the couple of miles from my house along silent, vacant streets to Sassan, the local taxi office. The people there had known me for a year, when I was still working for Northrop, traveling through the city and to and from Shahin Shahr and

Khatami Air Force Base in Chevrolets paid for by the company. After leaving the company and joining the news services, I had switched to the little Paykans more common in Iran, and my business continued with Sassan at cheaper rates.

When I reached the taxi office, the room was packed with drivers. No one was traveling anywhere in the city. When I laid a movie camera on the counter and told them I wanted a man to take me to Mosjed Mosalla, they laughed.

"Did you know they caught an American near the mosjed this morning? They poured oil over him, held a torch to his face, and told him to go and tell his friends to leave Iran."

"You're saying I pay double the regular fare?"

"I'm saying no one will take you. They'll kill you if they catch you near the mosjed. They'll tear you into little pieces."

No one made a move. Just then Ahmad walked in. Ahmad and I had gone out together several times with Damien, and chasing down machinegun fire, trying to get close enough to take decent pictures with no telephoto lens. More often the surrounding streets were blocked by truckloads of soldiers waving people away with machine-guns, firing into the air sometimes, adding to the racket.

Off we went in Ahmad's little yellow Paykan, one bullet hole in the trunk from an earlier adventure. Ahmad was grinning in his demented way. I was wearing blue jeans and a Levi jacket, going through in my mind the dialogue I would use if we were caught—the clothes would pass, but my bright, bright blue eyes would not.

We crept down the street that Ts to the left and right in front of the mosjed gates, passing the mud and glass homes of old south Isfahan, with their high mud courtyard walls and heavy iron doors. Shortly, we were swimming through the crowd, headed to the mosque. The packed crowd of people had opened several blocks away, then closed behind us, engulfing the car completely. I took my jacket off, laid it over the camera body, and started filming through the windshield, and I chanted to the driver in a whisper, "keep going, don't stop, slower, faster, keep moving." My window was open, and I forgot that

I was speaking English. A turbaned religious leader stuck his head in
the car, and scowled at us, but was left behind in the press of people.
"Did he see you?" Ahmad asked.
"I don't know, keep moving."

Ahmad drove near the looming gates of the mosque, navigating his way through the streets and crushing crowds of people, many of them peering into the car. Gil kept his eyes covered by the visor and bobbed his jacket-covered camera up and down over the dashboard to take pictures. They eventually got free of the crowd, but then Gil told Ahmad to turn around. They drove two or three times up and down the street, dodging people as they went, in search of a parking spot, which they found near the corner of the mosque. Gil exited; the driver stayed in his car. Gil climbed up a low, mud storage house built into the wall and sat on the grassy roof to get a better view of the crowds, while hoping not to be conspicuous. From that vantage, he said:

I swept the covered camera slowly from my lap in the general direction
of the crowd, a giant swarm of black-clothed people, flowing in a
current to and from two separate gates, and swirling in the yellow
dust. Thousands of eyes, thousands of lives, etching their forms on a
tiny strip of film. The power of such a crowd! I took the camera from
its hiding place in my lap, and pressed my face to the viewer, breathed
in slow, deep breaths while the film ticked away, sucking up the masses
that poured through the lens. Some people started my way. Someone
shouted from below in front and from in back of me, from the street.
From the street, Ahmad was motioning me to hurry. One last, slow
sweep of the acres of humanity and, down in the car, we sped away.

On the morning of Tasu'a, I had made plans to meet with Crystal,
an American teacher in Isfahan.

Crystal, whose last name Gil never mentioned, worked for the American School of Isfahan. At that time, the school had over six hundred students, whose parents worked for various US corporations. She and Gil were only friends.

Massive crowd of women wearing chadors, Isfahan, Iran, 1979. Photograph by Gilbert Johnson. *Courtesy of the Author's Collection.*

Crystal was one of the few Americans in the city who spoke fluent Persian, much better than I, and who had a fierce predilection for the Iranian people and their concept of an Islamic Republic. She had seen the crushing tactics of the military, and feared SAVAK, the government's secret service organization, the way only an Iranian might. She was for the revolution. More than that, she was perhaps a part of the revolution. At this point, however, she wasn't sure if the Iranians would agree with her. For my own part, though still neutral on the basic political questions, I was sure two Americans wouldn't be welcomed. Most Americans were working on military contracts, supporting the armed forces. The Americans had been given full and fair warning. None had yet been seriously harmed, though Iranians themselves were being shot nearly every day by people with whom the Americans worked. In turn, the Iranians regularly asked the Americans to stop supporting the military. When they didn't stop, they were threatened and asked to leave. When threats didn't work, the Iranians wrote signs on their walls and burned their cars. When that didn't work, they went into their homes, asked them politely to stand outside, while they ransacked and destroyed their belongings. And sometimes they bombed them, not with the intent to kill, but with the intent to frighten. There were some exceptions. They killed an

American officer who, supposedly, was helping engineer the martial law tactics. Already, guns were plentiful in the city but, in Isfahan at least, they used them selectively. They sought out and shot a few SAVAK agents who were widely known for their torture tactics. They could easily have shot many of the Americans who still wandered on the streets wearing bright yellow baseball caps, and bright blue and traffic-orange parkas, Bell Helicopter issues, or the blue caps and blue nylon, fur-collared jackets of Northrop people. They carefully placed a bomb under the bed of a Savak man who had chased down and shot a pre-teen boy for shouting, "Death to the Shah." They could have done the same to Americans, but they didn't.

As far as I could tell, the way Americans stood out in Isfahan, other than their distinctive dress, was through their lack of knowledge in the country's simplest points of etiquette, and by their loud talk. Most of the Americans in Isfahan had been recruited from small towns in Oklahoma and Texas. Perhaps they didn't understand. A few, drawing on their experiences from the Vietnam war, said they were waiting "for things to get rough" so they could collect their combat pay. For these sorts, it became a joke. A few Bell Helicopter employees started wearing t-shirts with the slogan "Stay and Die for BHI," all of which to the Iranians, whose families were really being

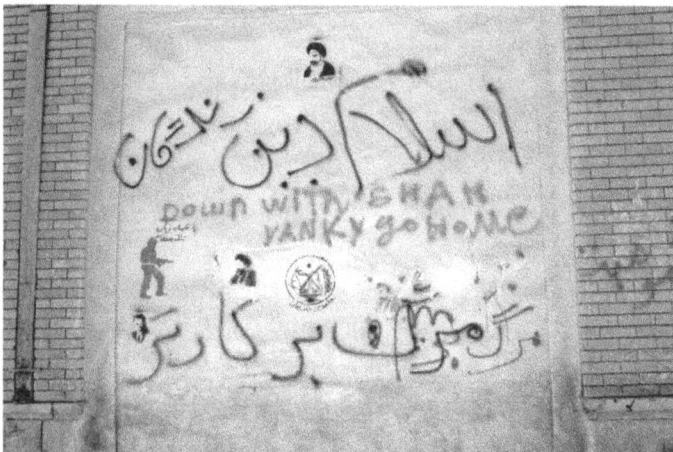

Sign in Isfahan, Iran, 1979, telling Americans to go home. Photograph by Gilbert Johnson.
Courtesy of the Author's Collection.

killed, seemed a very bad joke. Still, the Iranians persisted, and didn't harm the offending foreigners, but warned them and asked them to leave instead, sometimes eloquently and kindly.

One example of this included a letter placed under the Americans' doors, outlining who had to leave the country and the reasons why. Foreigners were becoming obstacles to building an Islamic Republic. The letter then explained that this group of foreigners would be given one month to leave, after which they would be eliminated one by one as though they were the enemy. Because the French had given Khomeini refuge, the letter said, "The French will be excluded for the time being and also all foreign journalists will be excepted." Neither Gil nor Crystal fit any of the categories of unwanted foreigners, so Gil wrote:

We prepared to see Tasu'a and Ashura and to film, if possible, Iran's climactic moment without drawing heavy attention. Crystal would wear a chador, the modest full-length shroud of Muslim women. And I, what could I do? I'd left the tattered worker's coat in Shahin Shahr that I bought for the occasion. I wanted to find a place we could film the marches without being seen, a high building somewhere maybe, with a window overlooking one of the streets the crowd would take.

They were stymied when friends, shopkeepers, and private homeowners refused to let them on their property to film. They were all worried they would be caught harboring the enemy, and their homes or shops would be burned. However, one of Crystal's friends, named Parvis, finally agreed to assist them the following day.

On the morning of Tasu'a, Crystal and I waited until noon, and finally assumed Parvis had changed his mind. The crowd would pass Crystal's house in just minutes, so I took the camera and went outside alone. Parvis had just arrived, excited about the approaching marches. He went with me to an intersection where people were waiting, and helped me climb with the cameras onto a low roof where I could take pictures. He then ran back to Crystal's, and brought her, dressed in her chador, and she faded quickly, quietly into the crowd.

Parvis stood beside a tree, and talked quickly to the people who noticed the foreigner on the roof, taking pictures. Some children came and tried to talk to me, partly curious and partly taunting.

"Hello. What are you doing?"

I held the camera up.

"Take a picture of us."

I took a picture of them.

"Take another one. Are you a foreigner?"

Parvis stopped them, and sent them away, but not before they attracted attention from people scattered in the waiting crowd. The people could see Parvis was with me, and off and on they walked up to him, asking questions. His answers seemed to satisfy. Except for occasional looks to see if I was still there, they concentrated their attention on the march.

From between the leafless trees I could see the swell of people down the street, moving toward us like a giant crawling animal, rumbling as it neared. An 8-foot painting of Khomeini, lofted high in front, led a procession that swept and blurred the features of the street for as far as I could see. The beginning of the street had been completely swallowed by the crowd. In the front, a line of men leaned like living lumber against the face of the procession, slowing, and turning it around the corner below me. Civilian guards with pinned-on tags moved the spectators off the street and curbs. The guards pressed their bodies and splayed arms against the mass as it shuffled past. They turned the crowd South where it would crawl along to Mosjed Mosalla.

We shot back to Crystal's house, and loaded up Parvis's little Geyon, a rattletrap half-jeep with a tiny front window. Film, lenses, cameras, paper, and pens.

Arriving at Mosalla, what I'd seen the day before paled. The congestion of people blocked all the streets several miles around the mosjed. Parvis threaded the car down a maze of alleyways, and brought us around to the back of the mosque. We left the car, and folded into the crowd where we were jostled and bumped to the back gate of the giant enclosure. There we stopped to sip some kind of sweet gruel that was handed out at one house by mothers and daughters. We reached the corner wall, and Parvis lifted me up to take pictures from the top. I was met by some young boys sitting on the wall, who held my camera for me, and who tried to help by pulling me up by my clothing. They sat there and grinned and chattered while leaning out from the wall to get into the picture. Crystal couldn't get onto the wall with her chador flapping and tying her up, so she was sent through a hole in the bottom. I could only identify where she was by the tight collection of black-shrouded women who pressed around her, gabbling with her in Persian, laughing, and squealing with pleasure. We were accepted.

When she came out again, Parvis said he would run and get the car to take us out. Already the throng around us was pressing in to talk, to tell us why they were demonstrating, to beg us to listen, to write it all down. It got difficult to move, to even take a couple of steps through the crowd. We pushed our way through with the help of the nearest people around us, and found a window ledge down the street where we could sit and watch the crowd file by while Parvis went for the car.

While he was gone, a group of women spotted us as foreigners, and started jabbering among themselves, throwing us shy, secret looks. A little boy who belonged to one of them crept close by us, and looked mournfully at some dried figs we were eating from a bag. We held one out to him.

"How are you? Do you like the demonstration?" we asked in Persian.

He nodded his head and smiled, then snatched the fig. His mother came to drag him away saying, "Don't bother them. We're sorry. Are you foreigners?"

"Yes."

"And you're not afraid?"

"No, we love Iranians. Why should we be afraid?"

"God bless you."

The mother took her son by the hand and led him away, but she let him creep back, and he ate a few more figs with us. Meanwhile, people passing on the street also identified us as foreigners, people on their way to the mosjed. They grinned and waved and nodded their heads.

"Foreigners."

The word was both a label and a friendly acceptance.

Parvis arrived and took us home. He had duty the next day, and wouldn't be available for the big event of Ashura. But he would call us if he heard anything about where troops might be deployed to stop the demonstration.

That night Crystal and I stared at each other in silence. <u>Foreigners.</u> But not so hated after all.

The night wasn't entirely finished. Evening was the time that had been set aside for the lashing processions. For Ashura, the Iranians go through this same ritual of mourning every year for the death of Hussein and his people. They pile dirt or mud on their heads, and they dance in processions to the beat of a drum, lashing themselves with chains and leather scourges in mock flagellation. It's a bloodless ritual for most city people that, as in Spain among Catholics, can become bloody when performed by religious zealots, especially in the villages.

Though this year Tasu'a and Ashura were used as a political forum, some small groups had planned to perform these rituals on the streets near Crystal's house. Just after dark, Crystal called some American friends who lived in an apartment overlooking the street where the procession would pass. She waited a long time for her friends to answer the phone.

"Hi, this is Crystal."

"Shhhh, I've got to whisper. Where are you?"

"At home. Has the procession started?"

"We don't know. We've turned out the lights, locked the doors and windows, and the family's in the back broom. Can't talk long. What do you need?"

"We just came from the demonstration at Mosalla. Everything's fine. They were really good to us. They were ecstatic that we were interested enough to ask questions and listen to them talk. It's alright, they're not trying to hurt Americans."

"You're crazy. We're staying inside and out of sight, and you better do the same."

"We've got a little movie camera with us. It doesn't make any noise. What we'd like to do is come over and film the procession from behind your curtains. Really, they don't care; we just don't want to interrupt them."

"Are you kidding? They might see you. You'd get us all killed!"

"No, we've been there. We've talked to them."

"No! We're keeping our heads down. No sense in taking chances. You're crazy. So, you speak some Persian, they don't care, they're fanatics . . ."

"Just let us . . ."

"No! We're not jeopardizing our lives for a few pictures. If you're smart, you'll stay out of it. Let the army take care of them."

When Crystal hung up, she was . . . to put it kindly, she was angry.

"That man's got the best camera equipment in the city!"

"Big deal! No wonder Iranians hate them. They don't care, they're not even interested enough to <u>try</u> to learn the language. They sit at home with their American friends and pretend to know all about it, they're . . ."

"Afraid. Leave them alone. I'm going out; give me a couple of film cartridges."

"Not without me, you're not."

The drums from the nearby mosque were already loud. They were [in] the streets. Crystal in her chador, packed the extra camera and lenses beneath it. I carried the Nikon inside my Levi jacket, filled with high-speed film.

The procession was nearly six blocks away, and it took some running to catch it.

Young children, old men, adolescent boys, filed down the middle of the street, all in step, twisting to the rhythm of the drum, laying the chains and scourges across their backs. We filmed from the outskirts of the demonstration, from the shadows of the alleys, trying to avoid attention. We were noticed. A couple of the boys in the demonstration saw the cameras when they turned. They smiled. Before the procession got another two blocks, we were in it, filming close up. They smiled and continued their dedications, past what would become later the headquarters of martial law administration. For now, still no sign of soldiers.

Next was the big day—Ashura, when the families from villages for a hundred miles around would pour into Isfahan for the big demonstration. No word of martial law, yet a few Iranians came by my house to show me the burial robes they planned to wear, and to say goodbye.

"The soldiers will be there," they said, "but if we die for God's cause, God is with us." These sons and fathers kissed me goodbye, tradition with Iranians. A couple I never saw again.

I left early in the morning, and headed to Crystal's house. No taxis were running, but I caught a lift to the main center of town, Meydan Shah. There, as in most of the larger intersections in the city, stood a statue of the Shah of Iran astride a horse. Bronze, I thought, until later that day.

I was looking for another lift to take me to Crystal's house when a yellow Paykan braked a half block way and reversed to where I was standing. Ali, a young Iranian I had fired from a postal job with Northup a year before. He had recognized me and came back. An explanation here, Ali had been carrying two and three jobs at once, and couldn't possibly keep up with the postal demands of 700-plus Americans. We parted friends. After amities I asked Ali where he was going.

"To the demonstrations."

"Terrific," I said, "so am I. With a girl."

"An American?"

"Yeah."

"Great. Go with us."

We picked Crystal up, then Ali's brother, waved to his sisters and family, who were going by another routed.

At Mosalla, the people were as ecstatic as ever to see two foreigners who were interested to hear what they had to say.

"And the foreigners speak Persian!"

Crystal disappeared through the women's entrance, and Ali and his brother and I were hustled through the crush of bodies in the men's entrance. Inside, meeting up again, we were mobbed. The young men in the crowd and the older women directed our way. They parted the masses, and took us to the center of Mosalla. There, where a small building rose above the sea of people, they called out for a ladder. And a ladder appeared. Crystal went first, and the politeness got crisp when her chador flapped around her. Helping hands drew her to the roof, and I followed after. A small group of camera buffs were on the roof taking pictures of the endless ocean of clothing, the sparkle of faces, isolations, recording the rumble of thousands of voices.

"Allah, Akbar!" God is Great!

The ground shook with their chanting and during prayer, when everyone bowed, the rustle of their clothing hit our ears like the sound of a sudden wind. An advantage of high places is that we get a feeling for the true size of the crowds. From that particular building, the people were packed, shoulder to shoulder, nearly back to front, for the

Gilbert Johnson on roof with locals at the Great Mosalla of Isfahan, Iran, 1979. Photograph by unknown person using Gilbert's camera. *Courtesy of the Author's Collection.*

Gilbert Johnson overlooking a sea of protestors surrounding the Great Mosalla, Isfahan, Iran, 1979. Photograph by an unknown person using Gilbert's camera. *Courtesy of the Author's Collection.*

entire expanse of the mosjed grounds, about two football fields. Out-side the mosjed walls, where the people were still marching, pressing toward the gates, they were packed even tighter, from building front to building front, down every street, and alley as far as the eye could see and on the roofs. Every roof was black with people and every expanse of ground for miles around was covered.

"Allah, Akbar!"

That ground-shaking chant sounded in our dreams long after Ashura. For myself, even outside Iran. The effect of the chant gave the crowd an incredible unity.

An instance. While Crystal and I waited the day before on a window ledge outside Mosalla, a group of Iranian men tried to board a little truck already loaded beyond capacity. The driver burst from his cab, and tried to pry some of the men off the truck. An argument started, and instantly hundreds of voices around the truck changed, "Allah Akbar!" The argument ended. The overload of men got off the truck, the driver got in the cab, drove away, and the men got on another truck. We saw that kind of incident, the united will of the masses stopping aggression, all through the demonstrations, all during the revolution that followed. That paternal passiveness saved me from an altercation later when a Shah supporter, a hotel guard slapped me on the street for coming from a demonstration, and tried to drag me in the closed hotel, obviously to beat me up. I was snatched away by the crowd, who at that moment didn't know who I was, just then recognizing me as a foreigner, and I was carried a block away amid a flurry of apologies. The man who hit me, meanwhile, was lectured and derided by the crowd.

Coming down from the building in the center of the Mosalla, we were escorted past a wall of pictures by an old woman who had just been released from prison. The pictures were bloody documentation of people killed in demonstrations, photographic horrors of young men and old, women and children—machinegunned to death. The woman who led us had a preteen son in prison. He'd been arrested a year ago for saying something against the Shah.

Coming out of the mosjed, people came to me with pens and pencils, saying "Write this. Tell the world we don't hate Americans. We only hate what the American government is doing to our people. They put the Shah in power. They help the Shah's soldiers. The soldiers find our routes, burns shops, says it's us, and then kills us. Tell your country what is happening to us!"

"We'll try," I said.

We left the crowd cheering behind us, found Ali's car again, and headed back to the main hotel in town for some more film.

This hotel was also locked, but the guardsman at the door recognized both Ali and me. Ali was a distant cousin, and I was the crazy American who liked Iranians. That particular hotel, the Kourosh, would later become a kind of home base for me when I was covering the demonstrations for the BBC. The hotel staff would laugh, seeing me peel out of the crowds going by, would take me inside, make me tea, and pump me with questions about what was happening in town, where the next demonstration would be, and why the various news services lied about the size of the crowds. That last was always one of the questions. I developed a standard answer for it.

"How do you tell 500,000 people from a million? How do you prove how many there really were, do you count them?"

That usually stopped them, but I could sympathize with their concern. The amount of people who turned out for each demonstration was their only real way of showing the people's consensus of opinion. If the numbers were cut by the media representatives during a particular issue, the world got a different picture of the scope of their involvement. From the media standpoint, most correspondents took the position that they might be accused of exaggeration or overstatement. Quoting one NBC producer, "If you think there were a hundred thousand, say 'tens of thousands.' If you think there were close to a million, say 'hundreds of thousands,' because someone will always disagree." Conservativeness was the rule when dealing with numbers, especially when reporting deaths.

"The hospitals said, '20 deaths.'"

The hospitals were government owned, and official reports were necessarily low. I saw bodies hit the river, dumped from helicopters, and the washing houses of the dead had reports of corpses that never made it to the hospitals. After one demonstration in which the news services had all agreed, the toll reached nearly 30, I accidentally found a room in one hospital with bodies freshly stacked from the floor, nearly to the ceiling.

We left the Kourosh with plenty of film, and headed for the main bridge in town where one quarter of the crowd would be passing on its march through the city. Crystal stayed in the car with Ahmad, and I climbed to the top of the stone bridge with Ali. Again, some young Iranians helped us up. The procession was coming. From the high vantage point, we could see the swell of people engulfing the tree-lined street in the distance. From the faces of the buildings on either side, across both two-lane streets, and crushing the grass on the boulevard between, from every side street they came chanting, "God is great, Khomeini our leader, death to the Shah!" They filed across the bridge in giant platoons for hours.

During one part of the march, Crystal was counting heads from the roof of the car. She counted 5,000 heads in the women's section by fives and tens before tiring. Still, they came, women cordoned off by men attendants walking forward in the front, walking backward from behind—a courtesy for the women. From the top of the bridge the men shouted, "Praise God for our brave sisters!"

The women were all clothed in chadors. Modesty, so exalted by Iranian Muslims, would become an issue later. Some of the women who had fought beside their "chadori" sisters demanded the right to dress without hiding their bodies. One was attacked in a later demonstration by a young religious man. He punched a girl in the face, and knocked her down. Another girl, a friend of the first, stood up in front of Iranian television cameras and said, "Let him believe what he will, but if the man were truly Islamic, he couldn't <u>touch</u> her in public, let alone hit her." The women won their case. Khomeini, who started the issue, backed down and announced, "What I said was, 'It's <u>better</u> that women are veiled;' I did not say they <u>must</u> be veiled." The women won. Modesty is still revered in Iran, but immodesty is not illegal—a point the media who played the issue up in the States, neglected to publicize as much.

Hours later, when the procession had gone by, we were climbing down, and a man stopped his car on the bridge.

"Who are you?"

"Americans."

"What are you doing here?"

"Taking pictures."

"Why? Who for?"

"For ourselves, to take back to America, to show Americans what you're doing and why."

The man thought for a moment, then nodded.

"God go with you," he said.

We left the bridge and headed across town to where the march was leading.

Turning onto one street, we found it blocked by another section of the march. We got out of the car, and headed with the crowd to Mehan Shishome Bahman, where a statue of the Shah stood.

"They've torn it down!"

As we walked, the crowd clustered around us. An old woman stepped up and kissed Crystal. The old woman was crying.

"Thank you for being here. Are you Moslems?"

"No, we're Christians."

"Do you want to be Moslems?"

"We're learning about it."

"Praise Allah, they've been to Mecca!"

A middle-aged man pushed his way through the press of people.

"Do you know how many people are here?"

"About a million? We didn't know Isfahan had so many people."

"Two million. Isfahan and all the villages for a hundred miles around. They're here today, just for the demonstration. I'm from Malek Shahr. Look . . ."

A young man, carrying photographs on a wooden cross, stopped and turned the cross our way. The crowd closed in, but between the heads I could see more polaroid pictures of dead children.

"Killed by soldiers two weeks ago."

During this, a separate group took Ahmad by the hand, and led him off several paces. Some heated conversation followed. Ahmad returned, took me by the hand and led me into the street with the marchers. It was pressing things a bit to say I was part of the Islamic demonstration, but when they chanted "God is great!" I chanted with them.

Looking for Crystal, who was intermittently consumed by the people, I stumbled. Looking down, I found an arm from the proud statue of the Shah. The Shah's image lay prone in the street, battered by the shoes and sandals of thousands of his people, subjects in a kingdom who no longer wanted a king. We marched into the meydan and found pandemonium. People were yelling, "Get the women back!" A handful of men were still peeling away the marble slabs from the giant pedestal where the statue had stood.

Cars were intermingled in the crowd, caught in the march, and young students directed them through, waving aside the masses with both arms.

A little boy picked up a stone and threw it in the direction of the concrete column, now nearly stripped of refinement. Two men grabbed the boy's hands and said with emotion "Don't throw <u>anything</u>." Though the streets for miles around were hopelessly congested, not a single privately owned shop or home had been touched, only the image of the Shah. Since one appeared on every major intersection, it stood to reason that each one would be taken down.

Smoke in the sky! About a mile away in the direction of Sabze Meydan, a huge pillar of smoke rose like an omen.

Ahmad, Crystal, Ali, and I fought our way to the main street leading in that direction. There we found an old man in a three-wheeled pickup truck, and Ali begged him for a ride.

"Follow the smoke."

"They're burning the statue," he said, and he smiled.

Others began jumping on the truck, threatening to overload it, till Ali told them he was taking the foreigners to take pictures. The men jumped off and ran with us, pushing away all hitchhikers until we gained enough speed to keep going.

Sabze Mehdan was a chaotic boil of people. The government-owned bank, burned previously in another demonstration, was getting a fresh load of wood to be burned again. The Shah's statue, already down and chopped to pieces, was throwing flames from gasoline. The people were ecstatic. Sabze Mehdan, the site where a hundred and some people were machinegunned recently, was exonerated, destroyed—except for the privately-owned shops, still untouched.

"The foreigners! There they are!"

Word had gotten around that we were moving around in the city, asking questions, taking pictures.

"BBC!"

I was not yet working for the BBC, the British radio station that broadcasted in Persian and English every night. But it was a natural assumption, and if it kept everybody happy, I wasn't about to try to explain the difference. The word swept through the crowd, and the entire meydan turned in our direction. They rushed us. We got as far as the entrance to the bazaar before we were overtaken.

They started literally crawling over each other to reach us. A line of men somehow formed, their backs to the crowd, holding them off us. The line got tighter and formed half a circle. I help up hands, gesturing for the people to back away, and those who saw me threw their weight against the mob, dug in their heels, and splayed their arms. Crystal, Ali, Ahmad, and I broke and ran. Fifty yards down the tunnels, the crowd caught us again. From the darkness, we could see silhouettes of hands and clubs, waving beneath the dust filtered skylights. The faces close by were joyous, but the momentum, weight and din of the crowd were a monster. We couldn't control it, and in an instant we were enclosed again, the half circle of defense, against a wall, afraid to talk, because every time we spoke the crowd surged toward us. Crystal fell back against the wall, and slid slowly down it. Her eyes went blank, and our circle stumbled with the weight of the crowd, all leaning to see where she had gone.

"We respect the women, that is why we protect them."

The statement surfaced in my mind like a voice.

"She's afraid!" I shouted and gestured to the crowd to move back. "She's afraid you'll hurt her—there are too many people!"

The circle of friends fought the weight of the crowd with a frenzied kind of energy. The men within reach of my voice joined them, and they sent the word ringing from mouth to mouth.

"She's afraid! They're afraid! Back up, you'll hurt them!"

We gained a couple of seconds, and ran down the vaulted chambers of the bazaar while our friends used their new allies to form lines across the tunnel to hold off the press of people. We turned corners, ran up ramps, dropped down stairwells. We broke free of the bazaar, and stumbled into the street several blocks away. Sabze Mehdan was still pouring into the bazaar. The truck we had left was still waiting, the old man driving, toothless and grinning. Only now, the truck had an awning to hide us. If we could just walk calmly, without attracting attention.

"There they are!"

People were suddenly running for us. I threw Crystal into the truck and dove after. Ali and Ahmad pushed and kicked bodies from the back of the truck before we gained any measure of speed. One boy fell off the back on his back, and I heard his head crack on the asphalt with an audible pop. He got up and staggered. Another young boy was still clinging to the outside of the tailgate, and I had to stop Ali from pushing him off. We were moving too fast. I reached around and grabbed the boy's belt, and held him till we got across town. When we slowed in an alley and Ali staid were stopping, the boy got off. But we didn't stop. We kept going, heading back to the Meydan Shah. In the back of the truck, far from afraid, sat Crystal, eyes were on fire with excitement.

"Nobody's going to believe us! They almost <u>loved</u> us to death!"

The irony in what she said! All the Americans in hiding, and here we were being chased down and mobbed, nearly loved to death, for no other reason than just being foreigners and being present. We all broke out laughing and couldn't stop until we reached Meydan Shah.

"They're pulling the statue down!"

"Wait a minute," I said. "This time we'll be more careful."

We parked and scrambled out of the truck. The boulevard to the statue crossed in front of us a block away. People were running toward the statue.

"If we're seen together," said Crystal, "they'll mob us again."

I was mainly concerned with getting a picture of the statue coming down. Crystal handed me the camera, and Ahmad grabbed my hand and took off in a run, pulling me behind him. Soon we were running with the crowd. Ahead, high on a pedestal in a shaft of afternoon light, the horseback figure of the Shah severed at the waist and crashed to the ground. The rope-tethered horse toppled over, and fell on its side at the top of the column. I shot pictures as I ran, and, finally standing on the grass at the foot of the column, I steadied myself for a shot of the horse coming down.

Someone grabbed my sleeve, and made a lunge for the camera.

"You're a foreigner! Are you SAVAK, are you CIA?"

The young man was taken and pushed back by the crowd. A group of Iranians made a circle around me to keep away the mass, already pressing in.

"He's BBC!"

The surge began.

"Hurry!" said Ahmad.

I clicked off pictures as fast as I could, then the horse was down. Sledgehammers appeared, and the Iranians beat at the horse and figure already engulfed in gasoline flames. The figures broke into shards.

"Tell the world our government kills us!" "Death to the Shah!"

Another man snatched a shard of the statue, and ran across the street with a group of friends. There, buried in a clutch of bodies, stood Crystal, asking and answering questions. The crowd parted slightly, and the man handed her the piece of pot metal, presented it with both hands as if were an offering. She held it up and shouted, "Down with the Shah!" and the meydan cheered with approval. We discussed that later. Statues around the country were still being replaced with far less effort than it took to take them down. Neutrality was still important. This eventually resulted in Crystal and I going to demonstrations separately, this and the fact together we were mobbed beyond our abilities to control the situation. Singularly, we were also mobbed, but somehow could control the crowds around us.

When I finally reached Crystal, she was swamped with well-wishers. We walked down the boulevard in the direction of the truck. We were followed. In fact, the entire meydan turned its attention in our direction. With every step, the crowd that walked with us, that pursued us, got larger, more aggressive. We jogged inside a swarm of people, all jogging with us, until everyone was running with us, away from the statue. When we turned the corner, I grabbed Ali and Ahmad.

"Try to stop them. Try to keep them from following us."

They gathered some friends they had found and fanned out to stop the crowd.

"Don't be afraid." A young religious leader in full-length robe appeared beside us, and in English tried to assure us, then asked who we were.

"Americans," I said.

"Don't be afraid, don't ever be afraid. They won't hurt you."

"We know, thank you, there's just too many of them."

He turned and held out his arms and the Iranians near him braked in their tracks. They were pushed from behind by the surge of people, but they took each other's hands and formed a line. A few ducked beneath their arms, and fanned out likewise, forming a second line.

"God go with you."

The young bearded moola smiled and waved us away. We never saw him again in the city.

"Where are you going?"

Some Iranians further down the street turned to jog with us.

"Away from the crowd."

"We've got a car."

Ahmad appeared.

"Tell Ali to meet us by the Iran Tour Hotel with his car," I said. We ran off with this new group of strangers. We all regrouped at the hotel, but not before hearing the crowd was headed for the SAVAK building to burn it.

The SAVAK headquarters building was just down the street from Meydan Shah. What the religious leaders in town knew, that the average Iranian was left unawares, was that the headquarters activities had been transferred to a building across town. The building the people were about to attack carried routine files and a skeleton crew. Still, it would be enough to bring the army.

"Why?" I asked. "They said everything they needed to say in a peaceful demonstration. The world heard them. Why provoke the army?"

"SAVAK carried away our children, and tortured our families. They're hoods, that's why."

No reasoning would change what was already happening, but our group agreed to watch this one from across the river. There, a separate crowd stood on the bank and watched lone figures scale the wall of the SAVAK building, while the crowd milled down the street. The men climbed down, and a sheet of flame engulfed the wall. The crowd down the street from the building, and the one behind us cheered.

I thought to myself, "What's this . . . symbolism? Flames won't hurt a wall." In fact, that's probably exactly what it was. As the peaceful demonstration had ended, and events had become more and more chaotic, the people's excitement at finally being able to say, to shout in public how they felt, grew into a party atmosphere, then frenzy. The crowds grew wild with excitement, hugging each other and dancing in the streets. It was a day of liberation.

The reply from the army took about thirty seconds. A tank appeared from down the street, and opened up with machinegun fire. The people in the streets fled screaming, and bodies fell. The tank barreled down the street, pumping bullets into the crowd, then turned and chased a group of people who had appeared behind it several blocks away. Up and down the street it went, spraying bullets. It fired the canon several times into the air, then stopped and watched while the people fought each other to get off the street. We got into the car.

"Where to?" asked Ali.

"Across the river."

"Are you crazy"? shouted Ahmad.

I looked at Crystal for her vote and she nodded.

"They've chased the crowd back," I said, "They won't keep wasting shells and bullets."

It was a guess, of course, but the tactics of the military had been fairly consistent.

Across the bridge the street was quiet. People darted quietly between the buildings. The bulk of the crowd was far down the boulevard, still running.

The entrance to the street from Meydan Shah was blocked with rubble, trash cans, and iron girder. Far down the street stood the *tank, cannon at ready, still guarding the bodies sprawled in the street. Smoke drifted in and out, blocking our view. We drove on.*

The remainder of the day was a city gone wild. Cars raced up and down the streets, lights on, horns blaring, windshield wipers pulled forward, rocking back and forth to the beat of the horns, "Marg bar Shah!" Death to the Shah!

That became the password of the day. People no longer said, "Hello," to each other. They raised their fists in defiance and shouted, "Marg bar Shah!"

Our group was famished. We'd gone all day without eating, and all the shops were closed. Someone said the shopkeepers were feeding the masses down in the bazaar on the south side of town. We headed in that direction. All across town it was the same, chaos and shouting, blaring horns, and flashing lights.

Down in the bazaar, food was being prepared in huge cauldrons. It would be another hour.

Ahmad left to contact his uncle. When he returned, he told us to follow him. We entered the bazaar and walked the vaulted caverns for what seemed like miles, turning each corner carefully, half expecting to see soldiers. At one corner a spring well was set into a tiny, lighted room, built into the wall. We stopped there for a drink. Probably because our senses were so alive at the time, that cool well held the sweetest, most delicious water I've ever tasted.

We reached Ahmad's uncle's house, and were welcomed by the family and a group of friends that grew larger by the minute. By the time supper was served, there were nearly twenty people in the house. Oil cloths were laid down in a long line through two room. Crystal and I were the guests of honor. I love water pipes, but after a couple puffs, the pipe was taken by an old toothless lady who hoarded it for the rest of the evening. Crystal was a hit as usual, playing the social politeness games inherent in the language with all the deftness of an Iranian. They loved her!

Conversation stopped, however, when it was time for the BBC broadcast. In all the Iranian homes I'd been in, BBC airing time was an inviolable trust. They listened to it as the only news service that gave a fair picture of the events taking place in their own country. The television and radio in Iran were government-owned and controlled, but the BBC was broadcasted from London. And British reporters didn't need an entry visa from the government to operate in Iran, a political loophole that let them pretty much come and go as they pleased.

What we listened for that evening was word of the day's events and whether martial law had been moved forward from the 10 p.m. curfew. Everyone was satisfied with the reports, but there was no mention of curfew. We turned to the Iranian stations, then turned on the TV set. The Iranian news services said that small demonstrations had occurred and made no mention of martial law.

One man came in and said martial law had already begun. Probably just a rumor, but since it was already about eight o'clock, we decided to leave early, just in case.

The streets were almost dead, a few last cars racing quietly to their homes. We entered one intersection and came across army soldiers.

"Heist!"

We stopped on the command and waited for the soldier as he approached the car, rifle aimed toward us.

Ali asked, "Sir, what time is curfew tonight?"

The soldier didn't answer but slung the door open and ordered us out. When Crystal got out, wrapped in her chador, he told her to get back in the car. Other soldiers appeared and trained their guns on us. One threw Ali against the car, spread his hands on the hood, kicked his legs apart, and ordered us to stand the same way. We complied, but another soldier said something to me that I couldn't understand. Then he kicked me and repeated what he had said. He kicked me again, and I aid in Persian, "What do you want?"

Ahmad interrupted from his position against the car.

"He's a foreigner. He doesn't understand what you're saying."

The soldier stopped, looked at me, then hauled me to the rear of the car and threw me up against it.

Another soldier pointed a machinegun at my head. The first dug through my pockets and found some film. He threw it on the ground and crushed it beneath his heel. Another ripped the tiny black Muslim flag from the car antenna and ground it on the pavement. Another crawled inside the car and took the picture of Khomeini from the back window. He cursed and tore the picture to pieces with one hand and his teeth. Then they started on the car. They broke out the lights with their rifle butts and kicked dents in the doors. They shoved us all back in the car, fired their guns above us, and ordered us to leave. Considering the events of the following day, we were grateful for the gentle treatment.

We didn't head for home, which was clear across town, but instead took refuge in another friend's home near the bazaar, a beautiful 200-year-old mansion with indoor wells and baking ovens made of stone. The boy's parents welcomed us like family, dressed us in pajama bottoms for evening wear, and served us fruit and tea. We talked with the family until the late hours, then separated for sleep, the women to one section of the house, the men to another, all bundled in individual fold-away floor pallets.

Next day on the way home, we found the traffic was all channeled through the main intersections of town. Cinemas were burned that hadn't been burned prior to the curfew, and shop windows were broken. As the cars passed the soldiers, the drivers and passengers were ordered at gunpoint to say, "Long live the Shah."

If articles of religion, particularly pictures, writings or tapes of Khomeini were found in the cars, the cars were demolished on the spot. Anyone who refused to say, "Long live the Shah" was beaten. Anyone who dared to say, "Marg bar Shah" was shot. I watched an old man beaten to the ground with rifle butts for complaining when his car was torn to pieces, and one religious leader, for reasons I couldn't hear, has his beard torn from his face.

Later that day, the boulevard was congested with the cars of Shah supporters, blaring their horns, blinking their lights, and waving their windshield wipers. The rest of the city was silent. Truckloads of villagers traveled through the city, waving clubs, and shouting, "Long live the Shah!" Some of these groups were let out of the trucks, and marched up and down the streets, breaking shop windows, destroying anything with any reference to Khomeini. Ahmad buttonholed one villager from a group marching up the street and asked him why he was demonstrating. The villager replied, "Soldiers came into our village and wanted volunteers. They offered us two hundred rials a day ($3.50) and a kilo of rice to demonstrate for the Shah. Some of us," he said, looking sheepish, "were forced to come."

Personally, I watched buses with the Imperial Iranian Airforce bullseye insignias haul "Shah supporters" into Isfahan throughout the remainder of the day.

That evening I got a call. Soldiers had attacked a small pro-Khomeini village in Najafabad, just outside Isfahan, about the same time the orderly part of the demonstration in Isfahan was breaking up. The people were being carried into the two main hospitals in Isfahan for treatment.

I went to one of the two main hospitals in Isfahan where the villagers were being brought. I was met in the emergency room by a man in a suit who asked my name, wanted to know who I was working for, what I wanted, and where I lived. I gave him everything except my address.

"Don't talk to him," said a man in a white smock after the first had left the room, "He's SAVAK."

The man returned with a doctor who gave me the "official report," but by the time they got there, I'd already seen most of the people. One man with a bloated face had been one of seven. The soldiers came up behind them while they were on their knees praying and slit their throats. A little girl with a bandaged face threw up blood on my shoes. An old woman, past caring, lay rasping in bed with tubes dripping into her veins. She wouldn't talk. And an old man with dusty, baggy villager clothes, pierced with bullets, face completely wrapped, died on a waiting table. Najafabad became a local legend. Seventeen families who took the wounded into their homes from this *small demonstration were slaughtered. Soldiers found out where they were and broke into their homes. They killed the wounded and the families that harbored them, including the children and one baby. A line of people waiting to give blood for the wounded at a small clinic in the city was gunned down by soldiers for not breaking up the line when ordered. Najafabad was virtually destroyed, and the remains of the violence, normally cleaned up by the military during curfew hours, was left untouched as an example.*

"But look at the roads they have, the education. The Shah of Iran is our Middle East stabilizer."

Supporters of the Shah's regime may have boasted of nice roads or good public education, but the reality for most Iranian citizens was now death, misery, destruction, and inhumane brutality. With military roadblocks everywhere, and no protection or help from Northrop since he was no longer an employee, Gil found it extremely difficult to leave the country. While to his credit he had made a lot of friends, he told us later that he had to sell or trade everything he owned to get money he needed to pay bribes to move toward the airport. That included giving up Damien. He entirely depleted his savings to escape. According to Gil, he managed to get on the last flight out of Isfahan that was transporting fleeing foreigners. The big plane only carried about twenty passengers.

Within the span of twenty-four hours Gil had witnessed a broad spectrum of human conduct, some of it loving and thoughtful, some of it an extreme emotional frenzy. The consequences of the clash of religious and secular ideologies were shocking beyond anything he had ever experienced in his life. He was in a war zone, enough to give anyone PTSD. Every Iranian blamed the other for their turmoil. Gil's adrenaline rush must have been intensely stressful. Nevertheless, he loved the Iranian culture and its people, and he was a journalist, so he followed his instincts and lived through the turmoil with them so he could tell the world what was really happening on the ground.

In the middle of the turmoil, in late October 1979 the Shah required medical care for cancer, so he considered traveling to Switzerland although he really wanted to go to the States. Through complicated diplomatic maneuvers, President Carter reluctantly agreed to allow him to get treatment in the United States. Rather than a short visit, the Shah's stay in hospital ended up lasting six weeks, which was very unpopular in both Iran and the United States. The revolutionaries wanted him back immediately to be tried and executed. The Carter administration refused to extradite the Shah, which fueled the emotional fires of hatred in Iran for the States. The Shah did not leave the United States until December 15, 1979, just days after the holy days of Tasu'a and Ashura, and then only to go to Panama, where he was also very unpopular. He did eventually return to Iran, briefly, and then fled the country on January 16, 1979, with his immediate family, never to return.

From abroad, in late December, the Shah appointed Shapour Bakhtiar as the new prime minister, even though he was a vocal critic of the Shah. Coordinating from Paris, Khomeini and Bakhtiar began succession proceedings. However, vying political parties made forming a new government very difficult.

Gil watched all these new developments in confusion. The nationalist revolution he witnessed months before was quickly devolving into another ideological battle pitting East versus West.

Making things worse, on November 4, 1979, the unthinkable happened. An overenergetic group of Islamists, called the Muslim Student Followers of the Imam's Line, shattered centuries-old diplomatic protocol and forcefully occupied the US embassy in Tehran, taking fifty-two Americans hostage. Many Americans can vividly recall the singular image of one male hostage, hands tied, head wrapped in white cloth, being escorted by the revolutionaries in front of the media cameras. The entire country watched the events unfold in complete disbelief.

So mesmerized was the American public that ABC began running a thirty-minute program dedicated to the crisis, which aired after the late evening news slot. *Nightline* was hosted by Ted Koppel and included up-to-the-minute details of the Iranian crisis on a day-by-day basis for over a year. Each segment led with bold letters counting the number of days the hostages were in captivity: Day #126, Day #235, etc.

Without research access to LexisNexis, we were not able to locate any world news service stories reported by Gil Johnson. However, his after-report about the Islamic Revolution says all we need to know. He wrote:

All the arrangements I'd used throughout so much of the revolution paled. From the reports I've read of Iran's activities since my return, I can say the reporters are really trying, but it's hard to completely capture the "why" behind a revolution. America began with a revolution, a few "fanatic religious zealots" who wanted the freedom to worship how they pleased, and to govern themselves. Even most of Iranians agree, the events following the Shah's departure could have, should have worked out better. Again, I find myself trying to reserve opinion. I do pray to God or Allah that things will work out for them. And I know that should I one day return, I, even as an American, will still be welcome—because I care.

Times have changed in the more than four decades that have passed since then. Would he still be so optimistic?

CHAPTER 6

SHATTERED DREAMS

(As told by Ronald)

In 1980, the summer before my senior year of high school, I learned Gil had recently returned to the States after living and working in Iran. I wanted to see him again, and he was keen to see me, so he offered to host me. I boarded a plane from my hometown of Albuquerque, bound for Los Angeles. This was my first time flying and my first time seeing the city of angels. He was twelve years my senior, and up until that summer I only had a faint memory of past interactions with him in Stafford since he had been out of my orbit for many years, an unfortunate byproduct of our blended family. I was excited and nervous.

Gil greeted me at the arrival gate wearing an ear-to-ear grin. He was dressed smartly for the era, in bell-bottomed jeans and a solid-colored buttoned shirt, with the chest splayed open. He had finished his outfit off with his favorite blue denim jacket, which had seen better days. Gil gave me a bear hug and ruffled my hair, as he had done years ago. With his arm around my shoulders, we made our way to the baggage claim area.

LAX resembled a human ant pile, with hordes of hurrying people, completely disinterested in everyone else, yet all behaving the same way. We loaded my stuff into his late model Datsun, found our way onto the 405, and drove north to Gil's apartment in Westwood. I was astonished by the miles of red taillights moving in unison in front of the car and miles of headlights driving the opposite direction. I had only been in LA an hour, and already my senses were overloaded. Albuquerque, by comparison, was quiet as a whistle stop. The stop-and-go traffic gave us time to catch up. Gil had left Iran about six or seven months earlier and settled back in Los Angeles. Unknown to me at the time, he had returned penniless from his Iran tour. All I knew was that he had found work with ABC Television. Additionally, he was taking night classes at the University of Southern California to finish his journalism degree. He asked about Dad and my mom; I told him they were fine. Did I have a girlfriend? No! What was I going to do after high school? Go to college. Each time I responded, he affirmed our dad was proud of me.

Gil's studio apartment was on the third floor of an L-shaped, contemporary complex. His front door looked down on a smallish swimming pool. The interior of the studio wasn't messy, but it wasn't particularly neat either. Articles and photographs he had brought back from Iran dominated the space. His IBM Selectric typewriter held center stage on a wooden desk, surrounded by piles of papers. He had no TV and no bed. We both slept on the floor.

On weekdays while Gil worked, I arose late and lounged around the pool for a few hours, reading my paperback editions of J. R. R. Tolkien's *Lord of the Rings*. The highlight of my afternoons was walking several blocks to the campus of UCLA. Having lived most of my childhood on the arid New Mexico desert plains, I found this college campus a veritable Garden of Eden by comparison. One sight disappointed me, though. Sunny California was not sunny. The cloudless sky was continuously dominated by a brown haze of smog.

Our weekends together were especially memorable. I recall each time before we left the apartment, heading out on our next LA adventure, Gil would jokingly announce, "Dad would not approve of you doing this, but we're going anyway!" I loved it. That first Saturday, we drove up winding roads to get to the exclusive Bel Air neighborhoods overlooking the LA skyline. He wanted to introduce me to an actor friend, John Saxon. John was already an established Hollywood figure when he costarred with Bruce Lee in *Enter the Dragon* in 1973. Wow, I was impressed. Gil knocked on the door, which was answered by a Hispanic maid who knew Gil by name. We were ushered into a small den and offered drinks. We sat and skimmed karate magazines until John came in from his bedroom, shirtless and disheveled. Apparently, he had had a late night and slept in. I was introduced to him, and we shared small talk for a few moments until John excused himself, going outside to sit poolside to read a script of an upcoming project he was auditioning for. I pinched myself, sitting in the den of a celebrity's Bel

Air home as he sat poolside reading a movie script. I was in pop-culture nirvana.

On another day Gil took me to Santa Monica Pier. It was there I first gazed upon the Pacific Ocean, a desert rat's dream. I will never forget the first time I stood on the shore of the ocean. The power of it struck me with awe. I felt so insignificant as saltwater waves lapped around my bare feet. The next day we headed to Griffith Observatory. To get there, we had to drive through Griffith Park, a place where our dad and Gil's mom spent time when they were dating in the late 1940s. Gil took delight in shocking me by pointing out which of the picnickers were straight and which were gay. I didn't ask him how he knew. As I recall, most parties were gay couples. Later we had lunch at the Sunset Grill on Sunset Boulevard. Once again, Gil played the gay/straight identification game, and as before most of the patrons were gay men or gay couples. He completed our adventurous day by taking me to a sex toy shop. I saw objects and devices that were as foreign to my young, naive eyes as color is to a blind person. Throughout the time I was with Gil, we made regular visits to his gay friends' houses. In hindsight, it was embarrassingly obvious that Gil was sending smoke signals saying, "I'M GAY!" As a greenhorn in a gay environment, I simply couldn't read the messages. I believe he was hoping for acceptance, but I failed to give him what he needed. In recent years, I have wondered what might have happened had I understood his message and started a dialogue with him on his lifestyle. We know from Gil's self-reflective journaling and other sources that he was morally conflicted by the direction his sexuality had taken. Could a frank conversation between us have opened avenues to mitigate some of his self-imposed guilt and shame? If only I had the power to turn back time.

My summer tour with Gil had to end, so I returned home before school began again. The LA scene in Gil's company was fun, relaxing, if a bit confusing, and I was delighted to have lived beside my brother, if only for a brief time. We hugged goodbye, and I boarded my return flight to Albuquerque. Although it was to be some years before he died, this was the last time I saw Gil alive. From my perspective at the time, Gil's life looked normal and he appeared happy, or at least content. How wrong I was.

I now know he was living two alternate lives, one for family, coworkers, and friends to see and another that was in opposition to his religious beliefs. Like a Pavlovian dog, he had been conditioned by over a decade of child sexual abuse to respond to these sexual impulses. He dissociated his two personalities to deal with deep-seated pain, which led to mental confusion. In a 2010 letter to Jeanne, Milian wrote:

> Gil told me about his grandfather. He told me that his mother had been molested by her father, which explained her behavior to him, and which he understood. But she knew that would happen when she moved in with him, and brought her kids into that environment, which he found hard to forgive. He was under the impression that his little brother also got affected in some way . . . He also told me it had happened to you but didn't go into details.
>
> In any incest family, there are secrets upon secrets, and the only way to get through it is compassion, complete non-judgement, unconditional love, and forgiveness for everyone concerned. Otherwise, it can eat at the soul, which is what happened to Gil, because it remained such a damning secret until it was too late for him.
>
> . . . Recent secrets have been exposed within my family, too, which is a hard, hard pill to swallow. The only way to be free of it is to go back to the Source, to God, and realize that every participant is beloved of God, an individuation of God, regardless of what happened later. By going back to that truth, and looking at each other through God's eyes, and seeing as well as feeling how much God loves us and them, we gain the perspective to move into compassion and forgiveness. People who can't "go upstairs" and view it through God's eyes have a very difficult time.

From a young age Gil enjoyed writing. Like most children, he had to grow up before he could discover ways to use his talent for a living. Since he did not go to college straight out of high school, his education in journalism could only be achieved by studying part time while working full time. When Gil was an assistant editor at *Black Belt Magazine*, he wrote a letter to Dad, in which he said:

When I started thinking about writing, the last thing I wanted to do then was newspaper work. Couldn't and can't stand the thought of sweating through something at high speed, letting it go out, unrevised and without that awakening of a second look, only to watch it disappear in a day. I thought the solution to that was magazine writing, but somehow that, too, is such a temporary thing that it hardly seems worth the trouble of pouring effort into it. . . . What article written a year ago is reread or even remembered by any number of people? . . . I have only one way to go now to deliver a piece of myself and my observations, to somehow say something to those people who come after me and to those people who don't know me but could have been my friends. If I write books, perhaps those books will eventually develop into something useful. At the same time, screen and teleplays seem to be a natural step. They are long enough to be definitive projects, worth developing fully, and not so long that they can't be used as training elements without wasting too long a time on anyone. Eventually, if I'm allowed to live that long, my career will narrow to books to avoid the fast pace in the other. No, books will not die—not as long as there are people who enjoy the sound of silence.

Books were Gil's long-term dream. Starting when he was still working for *Black Belt Magazine*, Gil and Milian began collaborating in their free time on creative writing projects. Gil said, "We've got to write for movies and television. Scripts are short, much easier to write than novels, and that's where the money is." Milian was intrigued and asked, "How do we do it? Physically, I mean. How many sentences to a car chase? How many paragraphs for suspense?" Gil answered, "We need to look at a real script." They decided to visit the USC Film Library and discovered scripts were in the reference section. "Scripts were top secret and hard to come by in those days," Milian shared later. "Gil and I decided 'Play Misty For Me' was one we wanted to learn from. We couldn't check it out, so I had to copy it in longhand to look as though I were taking notes. Gil stood guard. It took all day, but in the end, we had our first real Hollywood screenplay!" With inspiration in hand, they put their creative impulses together and began writing *Lurking Shadows*, a screenplay with a suspense thriller plot modeled after the one they hand copied. This was the same screenplay Milian eventually angrily returned to Gil to express her hurt feelings.

They also signed up for screenwriting classes: "For six months, we took every class we could sign up for. We found new friends who were writers and met weekly at an attorney named Harold's house." On her own, Milian began writing screenplay ideas to present to their working group. Gil was struggling. One day Milian handed Gil her latest creation, titled *Blue Jade*. He looked perturbed, so she told him he didn't need to read it if he didn't want to. Gil replied, "No, no, I want to. What is this, your fourth script?" She answered, "No, just my third. Where's yours?" "On the desk. Right on top of my novel," he grumbled. "Is it finished?" she asked. Grudgingly Gil said, "I can't seem to pop 'em out like you do," to which she replied, "It's just because you have a job. You work all day. You're the best writer in the world. As soon as I make a sale, I'll stake you." Flattered, Gil said, "I can't let you support me while I . . ." Before he could finish she hugged him and explained, "I wouldn't be supporting you, it would be an investment. I'd own a piece of your novel, your screenplay, and your butt. Guess which I'd collect on first."

A few days after this banter, Milian made the cardinal mistake of showing up unannounced at Gil's house. He was cooking a meal for two people, but she hadn't been invited. "Milian, you can't stay." "I didn't plan to," she defensively replied. Gil tried to soothe her ruffled feathers, promising, "I'll call you. Okay? Look . . . you just caught me off guard." She left shaken. They didn't talk to each other for days. It was shortly after this that Gil took Milian to Griffith Park for the great reveal about his "taste for apple pie."

Nocturnal journaling was Gil's method for dreaming up script ideas. In fact, he drew upon his own dreams—when he could manage to get some sleep. He usually wrote them in the wee hours of the morning. When those dreams were put to paper, his writing focused on metaphysical and philosophical ideas, and self-references were common. The contrast between his ability to beautifully tell a story and his peculiar manner of articulating dream ideas is very stark, as if two minds resided in the same body. And his journal entries were often penned in bizarre ways. It is little wonder Gil couldn't sell his screenplays. He once half-jokingly said to Jeanne, "At least I have a book full of rejection letters."

Dream writing sample from Gilbert Johnson's journal, January 1977. *Courtesy of the Author's Collection.*

19 JAN 77
1530

Besides the book of shadow images, how about
a film of symbols, telling a story in philosophy,
where all the visuals are shadows, colors, translucencies
+ transparencies that suggest the emotions, movements
+ developments of one man's mind.

Begin with birth. The tiny spot of light
that grows in the dark, the rhythm of a heartbeat.
A shadowed frightness, lightening strikes and the
wail of first breath.

Growth, that begins in blurry images, opens
to crystal clarity and slowly, ever slowly is blanketed
and deteriorated by hurry, by environment, abuses.
Somewhere, a woman — images of breasts and flowing
hair softness, flush, excitement, tension, climax.
This too passes to whiteness, the beating of
a heart, stillness + the introduction of abstractions.
Everything is repeated in an instant + there is
stillness, blurry whiteness that opens to crystal
clarity.

Screenplay idea, written at 2:30 a.m., from Gilbert Johnson's journal, January 1977. *Courtesy of the Author's Collection.*

Screenplay idea, written at 3:00 a.m., from Gilbert Johnson's journal, March 1977. *Courtesy of the Author's Collection.*

As he struggled, Gil did what many writers do today. He sought a literary mentor for critical feedback. Norman Corwin resided in LA with his family and was a frequent guest lecturer at USC, which is where Gil met him. Widely known in creative writing circles, Corwin enjoyed an award-winning career that included writing and producing radio programs, writing screenplays for TV and movies, and publishing several collections of essays and books on critical thinking. Noman Corwin embodied what Gil wanted to become, both professionally and personally.

Gil shared drafts of some of his work with Corwin via letters. He was ecstatic when Corwin responded favorably, especially when he affirmed Gil's ability and promise. In one of those correspondences, Gil shared this with his mentor:

> I want to write novels . . . or screenplays . . . or plays. But WHAT is going to make it worth the effort, the sacrifice of being young, the writing as opposed to doing, but what will make it worth the real adventure? I think it is <u>Purpose</u>. Purpose in my way of thinking describes the thread that seems to bind it all together. The whole world moves like smoke . . . you can sometimes see the shape of things, then it's gone. An impression is that, in my situation, people are moving forward toward degeneration. I'd like to say something about what I see to help people make choices without imperiling themselves by actualizing all their dreams and fascinations . . . actualizing demands a price, and the price is more often hidden. I'd like to describe the worst . . . and the "what could've been" alternatives . . . from what I've seen. That's a purpose. To me . . . <u>that would be the What</u>.

Mr. Corwin likely did not grasp the deeper meaning of Gil's cryptic thoughts because he was unaware of Gil's childhood history and the secret compulsions that drove his current behavior. However, as we explored all available documents for this biography, I finally understood what he was saying. He was trying to tell Corwin that he perceived *himself* moving toward degeneration, and possibly the people he consorted with as well. By writing screenplays or books, he wanted to help individuals who were also "imperiling themselves by actualizing all their dreams and fascinations"—in other words, those who were struggling with their identities and dangerous behaviors.

Gil had deep-seated sexual compulsions he could not control. He fought the urges, cursed himself for failing, berated himself, and prayed for help. He often journaled about his loneliness and the need to find his own way. That said, in none of his papers that we found did he mention his grandfather's name or perversions. His right brain didn't want to write explicitly about what had happened to him, so his left brain tried to do that for him in dreams. All of this was a distraction from becoming the professional author he hoped to be.

Even though their relationship was getting rockier as time passed, Milian still prayed that Gil would find himself so that they could be together. After all, by this time she and Gil had been sometimes-lovers and close friends for a decade. They had been through a lot together, and apart. When she got a call from Gil's neighbor Ron, she suspected something was wrong when he asked to meet for coffee. He had never done so in all the time she knew him. Experience had taught her these sorts of meetings usually involved bad news.

Milian walked through the crowded restaurant to a room with a row of small booths and saw Ron sitting at the end booth.

She paused, heart pounding, stepped up to the booth, and Ron looked up. Her place had already been set. A cup of coffee awaited her. With a serious look on his face, Ron said, "I thought you might need this."

Milian slid into the booth. "Thank you."

"I . . . I called because I'm in over my head. I like Gil, but I don't know what to do. The worst part is, he's close to getting himself killed," Ron explained.

"Gil? From what?"

"Do you know about the . . .?" Ron asked, showing her a limp wrist.

"Yes," replied Milian.

"Good. Because Gil is losing it. He keeps coming over to my place to talk about the Bible. He wants me to tell him exactly where it says that it's a sin to be a homosexual. I tell him not to worry about the Bible, just do what he wants. But because he knows I'm a former deacon, he evidently thinks I can absolve him," groaned Ron. "I've seen him through his window shades, pacing back and forth from the living room to the kitchen most of the night with the Bible, turning pages, talking to himself, preaching."

"Oh, my God," Milian gasped in surprise.

"At first, I didn't mind, because he's a nice guy. But then he started coming on to Larry. Larry and I have been together eleven years. We're like a married couple. I couldn't believe Gil would come into my house and do a thing like that," Ron complained.

Milian stared at the coffee cup in shock. She gripped it hard with both hands.

"And then, he started bringing tricks up."

"Tricks?" Milian asked.

"Guys he'd picked up off the street. I'm not spying on him or anything. But I work at home, and my table is right there. I see everything."

"I understand."

"First he started with one or two a week. I was surprised because he never struck me as that kind of guy. Then he brought about one up every day. Now it's up to two or three a day."

"Are these prostitutes?" Milian asked.

"Just guys that he picks up cruising. And let me tell you, he's good. I ran into him by accident once in a bar in Hollywood." Milian closed her eyes in pain but listened. "He was wearing a pair of really short cut-offs with a hole right about . . . there. And he's got all the slick moves down—the looks, the body language, all the subtleties of seduction. He's got quite a reputation in those circles. He's considered the best."

"My Gil?"

"And he always called the shots. Until he met this seventeen-year-old kid. The kid wasn't even interested because he had a Sugar Daddy. But Gil wouldn't let go. Finally, the Sugar Daddy told Gil if he didn't back off, he'd be found in an alley, dead."

"Do you think he means it?" Milian asked.

"Oh yeah. Word has it he's put out contracts before. That's why I called you, Milian."

"This is just . . . Unbelievable," she trembled.

"Gil has just gone too far for me," Ron complained. "And I don't trust him near Larry. Look, I can tell this is hurting you, and I'm sorry."

Milian reassured him, "It's all right. He's always kept it so hidden . . ."

Trying to make Milian feel better, Ron said, "He talks about you a lot. He knows how you feel about him."

She looked up at Ron with tears in her eyes and with resignation said, "Well, he's going back to the Middle East. That's how he solves these problems."

CHAPTER 7

SAUDI ARABIA

The Kingdom of Saudi Arabia lies just across the Persian Gulf from Iran, where nearly three years earlier Gil had personally witnessed the fall of Mohammad Reza Pahlavi, Iran's Persian monarch. The country has been an Islamic theocracy ever since the Shah's ouster. In contrast, Saudi Arabia, the largest country in the Middle East, has been ruled by an absolute monarchy since 1932, when the House of Saud united four regions by conquest, establishing the boundaries of the current kingdom. Aside from its seemingly inexhaustible oil reserves, which enrich its kings and princes beyond imagination, Saudi Arabia is also the home of Islam's holiest cities; the Prophet Muhammad is believed to have received the word of God in the city of Mecca and died in Medina in 632 AD. Thus, even while the political power of religious leaders has diminished in the country in contrast to Iran, Saudi Arabia remains dictatorially governed in accordance with Islamic law, which all foreign visitors are expected to follow or risk arrest.

Once again Northrop hired Gil, for an administrative position based in Dhahran, an administrative center for the oil industry near the city of Al-Khobar, and within Al-Khobar itself, a petroleum export hub on the coast of the Persian Gulf in Saudia Arabia's Eastern Province. While he was in Al-Khobar, Northrop housed Gil along with other contractors in a residential compound. Fortunately, the political situation in Saudi Arabia was not volatile when Gil lived there, unlike like the upheaval he experienced in Iran. (Twenty years later, the situation changed: in 2004, Islamic terrorists carrying machine guns entered that same housing compound, killing twenty-two people and injuring another twenty-five).

As in Iran, Gil used his free time to become acquainted with the people and their cultures and to explore the flora and fauna of the province with newfound friends. He also found time to fly falcons. No longer needing to send news reports to the wire services, Gil typed long letters to family and friends in the States, and rather than having to repeat himself from one family letter to the next, he sent photocopies of these essays and occasionally added personalized touches.

Gil painted a colorful picture for us about Saudi Arabia and wrote enthusiastically about his new experiences.

Salom Malacüm,

From the land of sand and camels. September 1st I saw my first sandstorm.

Some quick local color: The women hide behind black veils or beak-shaped masks and bolts of black cloth, and are not to be touched, spoken to, or even looked at for any length of time. They will say hello on a dark street when no one's around, a rather mysterious game—and a dangerous one in a country where they lop things off for unauthorized behavior. The men wear "thobes," white full-length shifts with button-up collars. The "ghutra" or cloth that many wear on their heads comes in different colors, and is topped with a thick, double-wrapped black cord that can be used for a weapon. Weapons aren't necessary here. The streets are guarded by 18-year-old police carrying loaded machineguns, and everyone treads lightly. The police wear green uniforms with berets. The goats wear bras to keep their tits from dragging in the dirt.

Northrop, the company I work for, I'm told holds the largest private contract with the United States government in existence and is making fighter jets for the Saudi Air Force. They also teach the Saudis how to fly the jets. Politically, I think, the United States is "for" the "other side,"... but ... money ... So much for our country's political stand. I type. I was hired as a "Senior Secretary," but most of the work is just typing out the finals of a pricing proposal. For the end of my 2 [to] 3-month assignment with the pricing group, I've been offered another job as a Contract Analyst for $26,000. If I take it, I'll come home first for a vacation.

The Northrop people seem to be a combination of retired military couples, Mormons, and Down South Folk. They spend a lot of

time playing bingo, watching old movies at the recreation center
(an R-rated movie will pack the theater), and distilling moonshine
(alcohol is illegal in Saudi). They've told me a lot about this country:
The Arabian Gulf is full of snakes, the Arabs are "unenlightened," and
probably diseased, and the military "Religious" police ("the ones who
always wear khaki uniforms") will throw me on the ground, beat me
senseless, bugger me, and cut off my hair. Not all Northrop people
think this way, but the percentage is high.

Meanwhile, I've met some interesting friends. My first night sitting
at the fountain downtown (downtown is a quasi-military/Arab/
American area of two square miles), five Pakistani workers from the
commercial airport/military base where my office is located, walked
up smiling, bought me a Pepsi, and invited me to Pakistan. The second night I met about six Sri Lankan (Ceylon) boys who are working
for a catering company that serves Aramco in another town. One,
who has gone back to Ceylon, is studying to be an engineer. Another
is the son of an English teacher. Another's brother is Secretary to the
Minister of Defense in Ceylon. They've invited me to visit Sri Lanka
in February and insist that I stay with their families.

The smoke shop here in Al Khobar is where many of the locals sit
around to talk, think, and watch television. The smoke shop runs for
three blocks down a potted concrete alley where the moon shines down
on Ramadan like a mottled, glowing egg. Ramadan is a one-month
religious holiday, new moon to new moon, where Muslims don't eat,
drink or smoke till after sundown. During Ramadan the smoke shop
is packed at night with Saudi "gentlemen," Yemen and Pakistani
workers, Africans, Sri Lank[an] boys, and one American. I usually
manage to get a table and chair on my own, but if it's crowded, someone always jumps up to offer his. The "shi sha," a 4-foot-high water
pipe, burns a dizzying mixture of fruit skins. It's got a good, mild taste,
but it leaves you feeling tired. You can wash it all down with a Pepsi
though and feel good as new. Pepsi, I think, is the national drink. That
and a very sweet Lipton tea, served in a pot with tiny glass cups like
miniature root beer mugs. When I'm with my Sri Lanka friends, I can

usually intimidate them into letting me pay the two Riyals (70 cents) for the evening, but when I go to the smoke shop by myself, I can never out talk the Arabs enough to get them to let me buy.

On the way home if I'm tired, I stop by the taxi stand and look for Fartha, the driver I picked out of the lot to avoid haggling. Actually, I prefer to walk. The people I meet in the neighborhoods are generally nice. The entire town of Al Khobar is a construction site. The crumbling pueblos are slowly giving way to newer villas and apartment buildings. Everything has been and will be made of sand in one coarse form or another. At night, men sit around on the sidewalks on mats and rugs, and drink tea or Pepsi, and children play soccer in the streets. The bakers work around their brick ovens while the sun is down, and construction workers, who work the day shift, bed down in front of their half-built buildings. Nearly everyone on the streets says "hi" in one form or another, and when I'm lucky, someone stops for a little broken conversation. They all speak English a little bit, and even the kids say "Hello, how are you?"

A place I haven't been yet is the Petromin University, where most of the learned people in the city hang out. There's also a karate club there. I found out about the place through my newest friend, Dr. John Burchard, a marine biologist working for Aramco, who has lived in this part of the world for six years. He's a thin, bearded, boyish looking 45 American, and has a wife, a child of four, four Arabian falcons (Sakirs), three Arabian hunting dogs that look like small Greyhounds and can run about 60 miles an hour, one kestrel, a raven, a flock of pigeons (for the falcons), and a desert rat. I met the doctor through Prince Mugrin. Prince Mugrin is a member of the Royal family that controls Saudi. There are about 3,000 princes, all with varying degrees of influence, and I don't know where Mugrin is in the hierarchy, but he's a congenial, educated man who conducts official business between Northrop and the Saudi government when he's working, and flies falcons with the Bedouins (nomadic desert people) in his free time. He also flies Air Force jets. I met Mugrin by knocking on his door and introducing myself. Pretty cheeky, I suppose, but I *wanted to meet some falconers. He keeps about a dozen falcons on hand at a time, including two peregrines at the moment. About the end of September, Burchard, Mugrin, and I will be trapping falcons for the hunting season coming up. A month or so after that, we'll be flying them against rabbit and bustards with the Bedouins.*

Prince Muqrin bin Abdulaziz is a well-placed member of the Saud family, being the half brother of King Salman and the youngest surviving son of King Abdulaziz. His distinguished resumé culminated in 2015 when he became the crown prince and first deputy prime minister, a position he held for only three months before being dismissed by the king.

Last night I spent all evening with Bedouins. One of them John has known for some time asked him to come over to look at his two sick hawks. He has seven Sakirs at the moment, and keeps them in circular shacks of wooden slats, about five feet in diameter. The shacks are placed in the family's living compound, a series of courtyards and rooms made from concrete blocks. When we got there, just past sundown, they had begun a fast-breaking meal of fruit, bread, tea, and goat's milk. The dining table is a mat laid out in the courtyard with thin mattresses placed around it, and the dates, pears, bananas, grapes, and pomegranates are laid in bowls and round pans. The goat's milk is served in a large salad bowl with a medium-sized salad bowl floating in it for easy handling. After being introduced to the six or seven men present (the women eat separately and stayed out of sight all evening), we were offered the traditional tiny cup of Arabic coffee. Each time it's offered during the evening, you shouldn't take more than three cups. It tastes like mild kerosene but, oddly enough, I got to like it. After we finished the light meal, John, his friend, and I sat around and talked falconry while the other men, who didn't speak English, talked among themselves, and watched John's Saluki play with another Saluki puppy. They were impressed with John's dog because she comes from a locally famous background, and John has her trained to very low-pitched commands. Talking falconry brought up the subject of the sick birds. One was growing malformed feathers, and John planned to

take that one home to study it for a while. The other had picked up a
virus that caused a growth in her throat. That one was wrapped up in
a wet towel to keep it cool and laid on a piece of canvas with a bowl of
water and some salt. She didn't like being handled like that, and for the
next half hour screamed continuously. The growth had formed beneath
her tongue and, let go, she would starve to death eventually, so they
laid her on her back and held open her mouth, and the Bedouins used
a razor blade to make a small incision beneath her tongue to free the
growth. Then he used my pocketknife and a pair of tweezers to dig out
the dry white tissue, stuff that made a lump the size of a marble. When
the growth was dug out, it left a large hole beneath the falcon's tongue,
and the Bedouins soaked a piece of twisted rag in salted water and
cleaned it with that. There was very little bleeding, but the salty water
left the hawk thirsty, so thirsty that she forgot her pain and begged for a
drink when the Bedouins poured more water on her towel. A moment
ago, she had been screaming, but chortled when he poured the water
from his palm to her lifted mouth. When he freed her from the towel,
she ran along the ground, wet wings outstretched, as far as her leg
jessies and leash would allow. She wouldn't take to the platform perch
the Bedouins offered her, so he lifted her by her jessies and gently tilted
her to a standing position on the perch. Wet, hurt, and proudly defiant,
she calmed after a little bit, and allowed herself to be carried back to
her roost outside of the other falcon's cages. She was a fine, courageous
hunter, the Bedouins told us, his favorite bird. When we go back to pick
up the other sick bird, John will leave his friend some medicine that's
supposed to make fast work of the virus before it can grow again.

After the ordeal with the bird, we talked for a while again and
another meal was prepared. This time we had a tomato sautéed rice
dish with pieces of lamb, almost too hot to handle. Handle is the right
word. You grab a fist full of steaming rice and some meat in your
right hand, and mold it into an egg-shaped ball, then pop it in your
mouth. It's a great way to eat.

We left the place about midnight since we both had to be up at 5:00
or 5:30 in the morning to go to work. John explained on the way home

that his friend isn't technically a Bedouin anymore since he's working for Aramco now and living in one place. "Most of his relatives are still Bedouins though, so he's still considered a desert man." Later, John has promised to introduce me to the chief of one of the largest Bedouins "fighting tribes" in the country. As it turns out, several of the men who watched us work on the falcon were "important figures" among the Bedouins. All night they were coming and going, quietly, unobtrusively joining in some coffee, then disappearing. Since I don't speak Arabic yet, much goes on that I don't understand, but the mystery of old culture flowing beneath the new has me mesmerized at the moment. In the Land Rover, heading for Al Khobar, I watch the towers of flame billowing from oil rig gas pipes that run along the sand, into the desert, burning off billions of dollars' worth of natural gas and turning the night sky smokey and brilliant orange. Then I think of the old, thin, leathery Bedouins with the white, wispy beard, who sat next to me most of the evening and hardly said a word but smiled sometimes. And I wonder what he's thinking. You can tell what I'm thinking—blood, screaming falcons, fighting Bedouins, Land Rovers, rabbit dogs and oil wells. I love it! It's hard to write. I've been spending all my evenings speaking in pidgin English and sign language. I'm picking up about one Arab word a day. If it weren't for people like John and Prince Mugrin, I'd probably disappear into the desert with the Bedouins and forget where I came from. I am trying to keep a record of everything, and in a little while I'll be taking some pictures. Forgive me if I don't write often, the days are short.

May Allah go with you.

P.S. I've seen one, lonely camel trotting across the sand between oil-soaked dunes. She left no milk. As you can see, I'm having a blast!

Gil

P.S. And finally making some money.

In another letter, Gil filled us in about his day job, described his disappointment in learning that Prince Mugrin had left Northrop, apparently when

Gil temporarily transferred elsewhere, and then told us more about Dr. John Burchard, the biologist friend introduced to him by Prince Mugrin. Gil also introduced us to Salukis, a breed of hunting dogs popular in the Middle East. Gil and the Burchards took their dogs into the desert for some play-time. When Gil left Saudi Arabia for good, he brought one of Dr. Burchard's Saluki pups home with him to the States. Her name was Dasmah.

> *My first night in I was assigned to a three-bedroom trailer (TDY—temporary duty quarters) in "downtown" Dhahran. The trailer sits in a walled-in area with a dozen smaller house-like trailers around it and a pool that I pretty much have to myself. TDY couples and families are occasionally assigned to some of the other trailers, and once in a while, I'm told, I'll have some single guy (or guy passing through on single status) staying in one of my bedrooms for a night or two at a time. So far, I've had the trailer (which is really more like a small house) and the containment area for my own use—by circumstance, not by status.*
>
> *I'm working for the program manager at the moment. We plan to give it about 90 days to see if we get along together. If not, I still have a slot in Khamis Mushayt. He's a pretty tough cookie—gruff—but so far he's been nice enough to me. He lives across the street from me in my old friend Sultan Mugrin's house. I'm living right on the spot where Mugrin used to keep his hawks. I spent the first four days and nights trying to find Mugrin. It seems he's left the Northrop Corporation ("If I stay with Northrop," he said, "what do I become, a general? What good is that?") He's now Sultan of the Hail (pronounced Hiyal) Province, just north of Riyadh, and he's invited me up to do some hawking and to see his pet wolves. He gave me another friend's number, Dr. John Burchard. John used to work for Aramco, Saudi's major oil company. He's now the marine research scientist at Saudi's University of Petroleum and Minerals here in Dhahran. His new wife, Oota (a nice Swedish girl), came and picked me up and we waited around for John 'til about midnight. It seems something has been killing the fish, dolphins, and sea snakes off the coast for the last several days, so John went on an expedition to round up some of the dying animals to bring them back for an autopsy. On the way back*

he got a flat tire and was arrested by the local police for spying. He was taken to the local emir, who was already in bed, and ended up having to spend the night at the emir's house under guard. The next day, when the emir's secretary saw John's government papers (he's very well-connected here), John was invited to lunch, dinner, asked to come by for another visit sometime in the near future—all the amenities. Chances are that emir won't be an emir very much longer.

John's house is a veritable zoo of neat creatures—always has been. At the moment he and Oota have three Saluki (hunting dogs that look like greyhounds, only larger and thinner and faster). They're used to hunt desert hare. One of the Saluki had pups. Oota killed five of them (by slamming them on the kitchen floor) and kept three. (She's had a lot of Bedouin training.) Better to raise three pups with a lot of care and attention than try to raise eight and give them to whom, to Americans who don't usually appreciate them or have all the dogs they can handle? She thought about it carefully and decided that killing the extra dogs was best and slamming them on the floor was quicker than drowning, as humane and certain as "putting them to sleep" with injections. Their other animals include two grown parrots and a baby, which they're hand-raising, and "Shit-su" (like a miniature Laso [sic] apso), a white cockatoo with a yellow crest (who likes to eat meat), and a crippled saker falcon that the Bedouins gave John for repairs. The falcon's leg had been broken about a year before John got it, and had mended badly at a slight angle, leaving it not much of a grip in that foot. The Bedouins would have killed it long ago, but even in that state it captured seven caraways (birds a little like road runners). John will try to get some surgery done on it in Riyadh. If that doesn't work, he and I will do the surgery. If that doesn't work, the bird will be killed.

Dinner at the Burchard's—curry soup with rice, boiled lambs' brains on toast, chicken legs and quail on a bed of rice. Date cakes and Turkish coffee for desert. Last weekend, John, Oota, and I took all the dogs for a run in the desert. John's Range Rover climbs over any kind of sand as if it were asphalted pavement. We had to travel about a half an hour in the only direction left to find any real desert

Gilbert Johnson visiting biologist Dr. John Burchard's home in Saudi Arabia. Photographer
unknown. *Courtesy of the Author's Collection.*

*near Dhahran. Most of the desert for miles has been strip-mined, and
the sand and rock are being crushed up into fine white powder, used
for cement. The operation takes place outside in dry conditions, so
Dhahran is surrounded by clouds of white rock dust, a health hazard
if you live on the outskirts of the city. Fortunately, I don't. The patch
of desert that John and his wife return to often is marked by several
individual sand dunes, the size of battleships. The windward side
is sliced into a crescent that tapers into points at each end, and the
leeward side is a gentle giant's rolling back made up of tiny amber
pearls. The flat desert leading up to these dunes has a light green
coat of fine spiked desert grass, from the recent rains. There are small*

Gilbert Johnson with his puppy Dasmah and Dr. Burchard's falcons, Saudi Arabia. Photographer unknown. *Courtesy of the Author's Collection.*

bouquets of purple sprinkled through the grass, some hanging from a tendril root, exposed by the wind. Where the grass has survived several seasons, it grows into bushes about thigh level, and the spikes flower with a kind of desert wheat. The stalks are sweet and full of water-juice, even in the hot, blistering summer. Around the stands of high grass, desert candles come up through the sand like black swords. They look charred until they're ready to bloom, which they're doing now and then they pop and plume out with pink and white and yellow flowers. When they're still beneath the sand they're soft and white. The Bedouins chew them to alleviate constipation. When the sun is high the sand is white, and all the plant colors are muted with a slate grey. But as the sun sets, the sand glows like a golden sky, then turns salmon with purple shadows, and the grasses turn a vivid deep green. Right now, because of the rain and the low elevation, you can dig about a foot beneath the surface of the sand where its damp and cool. Another foot or two and you strike water. It's a pleasant time for the people living on the desert. It's a magic time for the dogs. They race across the flats and rake the low-standing water like thorough-bred horses. Their feet are webbed between the toes (keeps them on top of the sand), so when they get hot they dig a quick hole to the cooler sand below and lie in it. There wasn't any hare where we were

*so one of the dogs ran down a desert lizard and trapped it beneath
his paw until I could get to it. I've got the lizard in a terrarium at
home now, sitting on my back porch. He's pink and yellow and sand
colored with long toenails and squared, yellow eye lashes made of tiny
individual curled scales. (Maybe it's a she.) If it gets too hot or cold
outside, he (she?) sinks into the sand like a vibrating penny.*

*John, Oota, and I wandered the desert, looking at birds and animal
tracks in the sand. We found fox tracks (lots of them), beetle tracks
and tracks of different kinds of lizards, mouse and gerbil tracks, tracks
of caraway and raven, donkey tracks, dog tracks (oops—the dogs really
get around), and the dried balls of camel droppings. At one point, John
and I tracked a snake for about a quarter of a mile. It traveled with
another snake for a while, became a single track (a quick romantic
interlude), separated, and disappeared down a hole in a large clump of
grass. Without a shovel we couldn't dig it out to see what kind of snake
it actually was. Gerbils (or Kangaroo Rats) are a mystery. They'll hop
along, make a long bound, dig themselves a shallow hole and cover it
up. You never know where they're going to pop up from. Sometimes,
if you're hunting them and you know they're in the area, you can
stamp your foot close to one and he'll pop out of the sand, and dribble
through the brush before you get a chance to really get a look at him.
People say the desert is just a lot of sand. I think people who say that
have a hard time seeing in bright sunlight. For myself, I like the desert.*

*Bukarah, enshalla (tomorrow, God willing—or sometime soon),
John and I will drive to Riyadh where I'll buy a saker or a peregrine
falcon. The prices are lowest now because the hunting season has
just ended. Soon, the weather will be too hot to fly, but just having a
falcon on my hand again will be enough for me, for a while.*

*This pretty much says it, I guess. I'm enjoying myself so far. It gets
a little lonely at night, making friends with my pillow. Guess I'll get
past that phase of it. I just count money, instead of sleep.*

> *Keep in touch,*
> *Love,*
> *Gil*

Folks at home received one final "mass-mailed" essay from Saudi Arabia in 1983. In this letter Gil and the Burchards spend the entire day and evening in the desert collecting and studying an amazing variety of flora and fauna. Gil couldn't have been in a happier place, or a happier state of mind. He was in his element.

How about a Sunday drive in the country? Here, it's done on Friday (the Islamic equivalent of the Christian Sunday). April 8, John, Oota, and I left about 7 in the morning with the four dogs, lots of provisions, camera gear, and plans to travel to Henna and Thaj, two ancient villages about a hundred kilometers into the desert (an hour's drive). After two hour's drive down the main highway passing Dammam, what began as a casual Friday morning jaunt lasted until one o'clock in the morning of the following day. Fortunately, we took a lot of water. This kind of trip needs a vehicle that floats on sand. John's Range Rover is probably the best in the country and the smoothest for this kind of travel; the differential locks to get all four wheels turning together. Even then, the sand is sometimes so soft, the Rover wades along at about one mile an hour. It has the best suspension of any vehicle on the road, fortunately, because the roads running East and West are washboards of wind ruts. That's one of the clues used to reckon directions in the desert, even at night, because the wind blows approximately North to South. Consequently, the roads running North and South without bushes breaking up the wind are fairly smooth. The sand piles up on the South (windward side) of the bushes, so North and South are marked by the configurations of the land when there's no sun or stars to navigate by.

We spent the first leg of the trip photographing plants like the 'Aban, a green shrub about a meter high, bursting with furry red, berry-like flowers after the rainy season (which is now). Dancing through these bushes are bright yellow daffodils about the size of quarters. Surrounding the bushes are the low, purple bouquets I mentioned in my last letter, and sprinkles of lavender "petunias." After a while, the Arfaj takes over, and the land becomes a carpet of gray-blue tuffs about two feet high. Egg-shaped, deep-purple flowers swaying on long stems are sweet, wild onions with tiny bulbs. We even passed a field of barley, sown randomly, probably by a Bedouin with a flock of sheep. High above, soaring in the sunlight, a Steppe Eagle dropped closer to get a look at the Range Rover. The Steppe has a large wingspan, marked with large areas of white, but supposedly isn't much good for hunting. It's more of an opportunist and would rather drop on a falcon after the falcon has caught its prey. If the falcon doesn't move, it's liable to take both animals in the same quick swoop. Not long after, a desert Harrier flew past. The Harrier corresponds to the American Marsh Hawk, and its feet are really too small to take very large game (probably lives on a diet of lizards and mice), but it has beautiful broad, soaring wings that bend in slow, majestic beats, just enough to slide from one breeze to another.

From the sky to the sand—in front of the Rover, a brownish-green ball about the size of a racket ball, came rolling toward us and disappeared between the wheels. We stopped the Rover, got out and knelt down in the sand. Beneath the vehicle, a 2-inch, black dung beetle was racing back and forth, confused by the sudden shade. She decided to dig in and started shoveling out a hole, using her head like a bulldozer. By the time John backed the Rover up, she'd popped the ball of camel dung into the hole and had started digging a wider space around and behind it. While the ball sunk slowly into the hole, the patch of gnats clinging to her back began disengaging, one by one, and landing on the ball to lay their eggs in the same place she would lay one of hers. The next generation of dung beetle would have its own, ready-made company of gnats.

There, ahead on the road, were the camels, dropping balls for the beetles. We stopped long enough to get some pictures of the mothers and babies. While I walked around, trying some different angles, the babies kept their mothers between themselves and me. They were pretty docile, except for one, probably the male, who roared at me off and on to let me know he was there.

Farther down the road, Oota yelled "Acktun!" By the time I saw something flash through the brush, John had the Rover stopped and was running on the desert. I ran abreast of him for a bit until he darted to one side and dove into a bush.

He came up holding about 15 inches of a Monitor Lizard with its forked tongue flashing in and out like a snake's. I asked, "Does it bite?" "Yes." "Is it poisonous?" "No, but when it's full grown, about four feet long, it'll hold off a dog." Great. Oota was already digging around in the Rover for a tin to put it in. "What does it eat?" "Meat." Great. Later, Oota would decide that it wasn't so great, since she would have to feed it—along with the cockatoo, the falcon, the parrots, and the four dogs, oh yes, and the oil-soaked, red-eyed grebe paddling around in the bathtub. There's a gecko lizard in a cooking pot, in the kitchen, somewhere . . . Such is the life of a biologist's wife.

On to Henna. This part is really sad. John's been going back there for years. It used to be a patch of stone-walled ruins, an oasis dappled in grass and flowers with sweet-water wells, built stone by stone, reaching deep and clear green into underground caverns. While most of the ruins and wells are still there, square buildings and makeshift quarters of cement and tin have cropped up all through the oasis. There are telephone and electrical lines now, and piles of garbage. A grove of tamarisk trees has been completely cut down for more buildings, though there was plenty of desert space all around the trees. What John figures was the largest and oldest tamarisk in Saudi Arabia has been "trimmed" to a "respectable size"—half the tree is gone. A huge herd of sheep had been allowed to live beneath the tree some time back, and the essence of sheep shit has seeped through the ground, fouling the well beneath the tree. A lot of other wells throughout the oasis have been dug out and "improved" upon with layers of cement poured over the ancient walls of rock. We'd planned to have a picnic in Henna, but John was too depressed about what had been done to it, so we drove out into the desert further. We came across a range of mesas, rising out of the desert. They were filled with small, deep caves that animals had been using as lairs. We found a lot of small animal bones and wolf feces in the larger ones, but piles of rock, and the age of the feces, told us that the Bedouins had probably *blockaded the entrances to starve the wolves living there. (The wolves here are notorious for their raids on sheep and children, so the Bedouins take every opportunity to do them in.) I found the entrance to a rock owl's nest in a crack through the rocks. I knew what it was by the castings (little footballs of bones and hair that they throw up after digesting the rest) and I could hear one of the babies making zipper-like whistling sounds, but we couldn't get to them. Bat shit dripped from some of the cracks in the rocks but, again, they were too deep in the rocks to get at. (Bats make great pets.) John found a rare, fan-footed gecko that obligingly came out of his crack and let him take pictures from about three feet away. Their feet have little pads that splay out to grip the rocks, and this variety is about six inches long and grey with bright gold eyes and vertical, split-shaped pupils. Before we left, I climbed to the top of one of the mesas and found piles of rocks, probably Moslem graves, and rocks laid out into circles. John figures those are probably surveying positions. There were a few ravens circling the cliffs and some rock doves, but other than that, it was pretty desolate on top.*

On to Thaj. Thaj is pretty much a "modern" Saudi village now; a settlement of government-funded houses built to encourage the Bedouins to farm. The ancient ruins of the original Thaj lay within a maze of new cement walls and iron doors.

Back to the desert and in a valley of green desert grass and low brush, we found a flock of about a dozen, maybe two dozen, sand grouse. They're not really grouse; actually, closer relatives to the pigeon, but they're large, about the size of pheasants without the long tails. They're gold and dark-brown mixed with a spoon-shaped patch of bright gold on their throats and a streak of red across their eyes. Their bodies are shaped like bullets, and their sickle-shaped wings make them one of the fastest birds in the Saudi skies.

For a while, we stopped the Rover and just listened. There's about a dozen varieties of lark in Saudi, so the desert literally sings with music.

At a sabkha, a low, shallow stand of rainwater that forms during this season, we watched tiny "sand pipers" and their longer cousins, the stilts, foraging for shrimp-like crustaceans. The stilts are black and white, have long legs (about eight inches), and long, spiked bills half as long as their legs. The smaller birds that wade on the shore come about half-way to their knees—a real Mutt and Jeff combination. The crustaceans lay eggs the same as shrimp that are nearly impervious to drying. When the sabkha dries up, they'll lie dormant till the next rain, then fill the water with lively food again.

Just before the light gave way, we watched a flock of about 20 kestrels (small hawks), playing in the wind, headed in the direction of the cliffs where they would probably roost for the night—a stop-off in a long migration North to Turkey.

Night is when the desert really comes to life with creatures—sand geckos with thin, translucent skin and pale green eyes, camel spiders, mice and gerbils, all sorts of wide-eyed animals, such as foxes. Foxes are one of the reasons it's not a good idea to sleep on the ground in the desert. Oota told me about a group of Bedouins on a hunting party who were sleeping together on the ground in a camp. It seems a fox stole into camp and attacked one of the men in the face while he was sleeping. Fortunately, this one wasn't rabid, but they sometimes are. He lost an eye. In a permanent camp, the Bedouins would be sleeping on wooden beds about a meter high. Rabid foxes, supposedly, lose the ability to jump. Several times on the road back in the headlights of the Rover, I was introduced to another reason for not sleeping on the ground in the desert. Sand vipers. They're not very large, about a foot and a half long. The ones we saw were gray with round, puffy cheeks, and wedge-shaped heads. When they curl up in a defensive posture, their scales make a loud, rasping sound, easily as good and loud a warning as any rattler in the States. The problem is at night it's easy enough to step on one before he gets a chance to make a sound, and there seem to be a lot of them. Even more deadly is a sand viper that's a little smaller than the gray variety. This one has some red and yellow markings. I think the distinguishment between the venom of the two goes something like this: the gray one can be deadly; a bite from the colored one is usually hopeless.

Gilbert Johnson milking a sand viper, Saudi Arabia. Photographer unknown. *Courtesy of the Author's Collection.*

I left the sand vipers where they were, but I caught a sand boa (a small, yellowish constrictor, about a foot long) and tied him up in one of my socks. They're very friendly and gentle.

The stars disappeared in some storm clouds overhead, and the roads wouldn't go in the direction we needed, so after about an hour's night driving, we went through some disorientation called—LOST! (So much for sand configurations.) Actually, we weren't totally lost, just going in the wrong direction. Anyway, what should we come across in the middle of the desert with no civilization for miles? What is the one thing you can never find when you're driving around and really need it? No, not a bathroom—there's plenty of space for that if you can relax enough squatting over vipers. No, we found a gas station. Well, it wasn't much of a gas station, but it had people in it (good thing John speaks Arabic). Since we weren't really lost, we didn't ask them directions, but we did stop and get some gas (at 25 cents per gallon), and some Pepsi, just for grins. The reason for bringing the gas station up is my final reason for not wanting to sleep on the desert at night. We were about to leave, and I looked down at my shoe, and there it was. It was black and armored like a tank, about six inches long, and carrying a weapon. I've never seen such a beautiful and deadly-looking scorpion running around loose in my life. Of course, we dove into the Rover for a couple of paper cups and scooped him up. The sandal-footed gas station attendants thought we were crazy, of course, but what do they know about biology—or pets? For the next couple of hours, we bounced along in silence in the dark, with the scorpion and a gecko in separate paper cups, sitting on the dashboard (two paper cups were fitted one on top of the other for each) with my black sock beside them. The sock kept standing up and waving back and forth across the windshield. In back was the monitor lizard, four dogs, a bunch of rocks, and one human (Oota and I took turns sitting with the dogs). I kept thinking about my friends in L.A.

Riding in the dark I thought, how hard it would be for some of them to sit quietly where I was sitting? The three of us kept drifting off to sleep with the desert floor rolling toward us. Then, Oota screamed. Without thinking about it, she had reached up and put her hand on the dash to steady her ride. Actually, she didn't put it on the dash; she put it on the snake, and of course the snake moved. Oota is not afraid of snakes, but half asleep with a black scorpion riding in a cup right over your lap, I suppose it was a natural reaction. Home again, we're trying to figure out where to put all our souvenirs, our little, lively treasures. If you find a package in the mail from Saudi, open it . . . carefully.

Birds and animals of every sort had fascinated Gil from the time he was a little boy when he saved a robin's life. Elsye indulged Gil's animal and insect fascinations by allowing him to own pets most parents would never permit in their homes. Those indulgences, plus his two blissful summers on our cousins' farm in Chalk, Texas, offered him temporary relief and distractions from his grandfather's opportunistic predations. At the same time those experiences planted seeds of curiosity in Gil's mind that grew with maturity and found rich contentment in the company of Dr. Burchard, Oota, Prince Mugrin, and fellow travelers. His beautifully recorded Saudi Arabian experiences gave recipients of his essays the impression that our brother's spirit was, at least for the few years he was in the country, unshackled by ghosts who had haunted his dreams. The strict Islamic environment, where death was a certainty for homosexuals, probably put a check on the compulsive sexual behaviors that had caused him mental conflict, or at least we assume that was the case. On the other hand, Gil's willingness to take risks may have continued in secret. In contrast, Hollywood's free love environment had previously given Gil unfettered license to do as he pleased without fear of repercussions, even though acting on those impulses caused him confusion and self-hatred.

Milian was correct. Gil went to the Middle East to solve his problems. The people and the desert helped him do that, for a few years. In a place as stark as a desert, the mind wanders. The poet W. H. Auden succinctly summarized its aura, which Gil absorbed: *In the Desert of the heart, Let the healing start; In the prison of his days, Teach the free man to praise.*

All these experiences positively affected Gil's way of thinking, yet at the same time, there were moments when he returned to metaphysical thinking about himself and the universe. In one of his last journal entries, penned while in Saudi Arabia on February 24, 1984, Gil's thoughts wandered into a netherworld. He wrote this as a disembodied letter to himself.

This may be one of those strange letters, I'm sitting in my jeep with my dog, who's asleep, and a falcon, overlooking hills of a municipal dump, smokey—like a battlefield, facing a setting sun. It's a lonely place, but I'm not lonely, not at the moment. I'm trying to trap an eagle and the trap is on a small hill about 500 yards away. Packs of wild dogs are scaring the eagles away and playing by the trap. They are fighting and barking at one another, calling each other from back and forth across the hills. They are . . . home.

Have you ever closed your eyes, or stared at one space on an empty wall and felt the people around you? Not people in the same room, but people, souls, minds, thoughts, living beings within, say, a quarter of a mile. Happens to me all the time.

In a quiet moment, if I listen, feel, I get the impression that I can hear, know everything going on around me—how many people are fighting, praying, having sex, sitting alone, crying, laughing—I suppose that's strange, my imagination—but it feels real, as if . . . I could almost hear their conversations, like the pack of dogs who don't even know I'm here.

How can a man be lonely when he (thinks at least) that he can feel every bit of life around him?—as if it were his own. Loneliness creeps in, I suppose, when one is reminded that the feelings belong to someone, something, else. They're not his own.

That may be why, when I make a friend the feeling is even stronger—as if miles, thousands of miles, make no difference. In a quiet moment I feel like I can feel all their changes. Generalities—like seeing the shape of clouds in the distance as they change.

It hurts when I can't be there to laugh off their pain. And it hurts when I can't lean them, quickly, in a better direction. It hurts to feel them drift away. (Probably why my telephone bills are so high.)

This is a strange, strange life.

There isn't any way a man can be there for everyone he loves or feels something for. But we can try by keeping the lines of communication open. We can try.

In August of 1984, Gil wrote a personal letter to Elsye, addressing her by her given name rather than "Mom," as was usual. In a previous letter to Gil, she had enquired about his love life and his plans. This is part of his revelatory response, beginning with reference to a "friend" named Damien.

Elsye:

I'm sending you the Damien letters for several reasons. Damien was going through some serious depressions . . . reminding me of you a long time ago. Oddly enough, my answers to him sound a lot like your recent letters . . . meaning that we seem to be coming to a lot of the same conclusions at this point in our lives . . . a "cosmic" coincidence that probably shouldn't be ignored. Too, it lets you in on a part of my life that has always been a private thorn . . . reference your guesses. I'm not a homosexual and don't think I'm going now in the direction of being one, but (between you and me) I've been there and back again, gone through every "experience" that would satisfy the lurid imaginations of anyone who spent some time contemplating the subject. Still, when a man lives to the age I am now without taking a wife, people start making their own assumptions. Let me also tell

*you something about what I've learned in the course of a number
of painful years, from both sides of the fence. I've learned that sex
doesn't buy love . . . I've learned to love, from my heart most of all,
anyone . . . in whatever way they can understand . . . I still have a
problem becoming completely involved with one, single person . . .
always backing away for distance, mainly because of what seems like
the hardheartedness I've come across in so many people . . . every time
I've left myself too exposed, they seemed to come back and bite me
in the ass, over the smallest things. Always trying to tame dragons, I
guess . . . a lot like you. I still dream of having a wife and children. I'm
still comfortable . . . and excited . . . with a woman in my bed. Day
to day, routine living, I'm probably more comfortable with another
man . . . So, the human experience for me has been an interesting
and diverse one, not without its pleasures and not without a great
deal of pain. It has always been, all of my life, that when I seriously
asked something from God . . . it was mine, automatically. But the
family bit . . . I've been asking for that since I was a kid. The physical
and emotional affection I've felt toward certain men, I've prayed and
cried and beat my chest to have removed. I contemplated suicide,
disfiguration, castration, shock treatment, therapy, and prayed until I
thought I was sweating blood.*

*The homosexual life is a sad existence . . . the odds of making it
through are phenomenal. Yet, despite that, there are people trapped
in that kind of existence who seem so worth the effort . . . It's hard to
explain. All I know is that there are things that came to me without my
bidding (just the opposite) . . . and I plan to use them in as positive a
way as I can manage. If and when the time comes that the task is over,
I'll be relieved . . . but not sorry for what I've learned about human
beings and whatever flecks of understanding that has given me about
the human condition. In one of my letters, I said to Damien that he
had a better chance of being happy in this lifetime than I. The reason I
said that is because he knows completely what or where he is sexually
(he's more polarized). I, on the other hand, am neither this nor
that, which both includes me in people's lives and removes me from*

"normal" life. So, there I am. I live in two separate worlds, as a visitor, and have a few close friends who accept the position I'm in. Isolation is a good philosophical retreat. Most of the time, I feel like I'm on a mountain (or in a hole), pretending the life of an aesthetic [sic], while spending weekends as a decadent visiting in town.

I've learned to never say never (it surprised me when the 007 movies came out with that title). It almost seems as if everything I ever said "I would never do" . . . I did. Almost like God saying, "Ya think you're so smart . . . " That has prevented me, or rather corrected me, from judging others. Read Romans 1:26–27. That particular verse brought me suicidal thoughts, since I couldn't seem to change the way I felt . . . until I continued reading: Romans 2:1, 2:12, 2:11–24, and 5:1–11, etc. Even John in 2 Cor 12:7–10 etc. I don't condone homosexuality. And I can give more reasons why homosexuality as a lifestyle is not something to encourage than most men who are one or the other . . . because I've seen both the positive and negative of both. Also, because I've seen both, I know that the afflictions that plague human beings occur in both and the attributes that bring human beings to some better state . . . occur in both.

What'd'ya think? Still wanna be friends? Probably, since you made your own guesses long before this. I would still like to take you on your word that this is between you and me. I have my own reasons for that. Probably not what you think, since I'm not ashamed . . . any longer . . . of what I've learned (though I am ashamed of some of the ways I've learned). The reasons have to do with my ability to move from one world to another. If I'm labeled, out of context, as one thing or the other, the things that I might still learn in the future would be excluded from me.

Love you, a lot
Gil

P.S. Keep these letters. We may need them later. Feel free to plagiarize anything I've written or said, anytime.

Gil's contract with Northrop ended on February 17, 1985. He returned to Los Angeles.

Jeanne and I both have wistfully played the "if only" game, asking ourselves and each other how different Gil's life might have been if only our father had played an active role in Gil's life, even after his parents separated, and especially had he not been sexually abused as a child for over a decade. Might he have married and raised children, become a successful novelist, or would he have made a career writing travelogues? With his interest in the natural world, he might also have studied nature. Every one of those potential happy scenarios was cast to the wind when his grandfather interfered with Gil's God-given right to a loving, normal, innocent childhood. In fairness, we also wonder who or what turned Leo Purtha into a pedophile. We sincerely doubt he was born with that predilection. Regardless, the consequence of Leo's influence was about to bear its final rotten fruit.

CHAPTER 8
DOWNWARD SPIRAL

Change is inevitable and constant. Ever since Gil was in journalism school in the marines, he developed an affinity for his IBM Selectric typewriter. Writer and machine were rarely far apart. By the mid-1980s, personal computers interfered with that relationship. After his return from Saudi Arabia in 1985 with a pocket full of cash, he purchased a half dozen Intel 386 personal computers and the same number of Apple Macintoshes. Then he opened a word processing center in the upstairs floor of a house, which he and some friends had rented off West Hollywood Boulevard. Personal computers were novel but expensive, so entrepreneurs like Gil made it possible for the public to learn word processing for a small hourly fee. Similar computer services began to open across the nation. Gil outfitted several converted bedrooms with the new devices, which were then daisy-chained to a printer. The enterprise was not a goldmine, but the revenue was enough to pay monthly bills.

Flush with cash to spend on leisure activities, and no longer living under the strictures of Islamic law, Gil was free to act on his impulses, or compulsions, as he described them. He fully embraced the homosexual lifestyle offered to him on a gilded plate in Hollywood. But what he found was not the love he had been searching for, only meaningless lust. In the last year of his life, Gil said to Jeanne in a phone call, "You have *no idea* how promiscuous the gay lifestyle is—anybody, anywhere, anytime." Since he was so familiar with Griffith Park, he may have once again prowled through there on occasion. He also frequented gay bars and picked up men off the street and brought them home. Still, Gil thought that he most likely acquired AIDS at a gay bathhouse.

About three weeks before Gil died, the *Los Angeles Times* ran an article about these institutions:

The private rooms at Mac's Bathhouse in Silver Lake are a hot ticket on Saturday nights. Well-dressed men with gym bags start arriving at the labyrinth-like club before sunset, and by early evening a "No Vacancy" sign dangles beneath a stern AIDS warning posted on the cashier's window, signaling that the 50 personal cubicles are taken.

Those who come later are forced to accept semi-private accommodations. As they trade their street clothes for towels and settle into bunk beds, steam rooms and each other's arms, a gay pornographic movie plays silently on a television and an empty Jacuzzi burbles near the rounded walkway known as the tunnel of love.

Soft voices echo along the dimly lit gray and black corridors where the private rooms are located, and the faint aroma of marijuana wafts from one area. In other cubicles the doors are left open to reveal nude men, alone, paired off or in groups.

"Try to walk down the middle of the hallways," says Doug Myers, owner of the club that's known as the Cadillac of bathhouses. "Otherwise, someone might grab you."

The fact that some men are still grabbing each other at the baths—despite the gruesome specter of AIDS—is clear to anyone who has visited Mac's or the Compound or the Melrose Baths. Not so clear is what the future holds for these clubs, which have been abandoned by both gay leaders and a large percentage of their former patrons.

The clubs still in business sometimes are busy, but there are fewer of them. Of 25 or more operating in Los Angeles County before the AIDS outbreak, 12 are still licensed.

The article went on to describe measures being taken by local authorities to check the growth of AIDS cases:

The county had sued three bathhouses in an attempt to force them to comply with the regulation requiring owners to eliminate private rooms, closely police their customers and ban high-risk forms of sexual contact. But Superior Court Judge Cole refused to force the bathhouse owners to adhere to those restrictions.

The judge also noted that some of the county Health Department's

own doctors did not agree with the county's definition of "unsafe" sex
practices that were banned under the regulations.

Because so many were dying, including some of his friends, Gil was acutely aware of the dangers of unprotected sex. Yet the conflict between his religious beliefs and his sexual orientation could not be reconciled, so he finally didn't care what happened to him. His lifelong penchant for risky activities reached its pinnacle when he consciously chose total promiscuity. He had already considered committing suicide, but religious beliefs had held his hand at bay. However, by randomly choosing sex partners and not bothering with safe practices, he permitted Fate to put a gun to his head. She answered his weeping cry for help.

Gil's last year included humiliating visits to unprepared hospitals, multiple platelet transfusions, and participation in an experimental research study. Unknown to him in the beginning, he had been placed in the control group, so he received a placebo instead of the experimental drug, AZT. Effective life-extending treatments for the HIV virus were still a decade away. Like a rose wilting on the vine, Gil's once athletic body deteriorated to a state of utter emaciation.

About four months before Gil died, he and Milian sat on opposite sofas. They were in a reflective mood. Gil sighed with relief and said, "This might sound nuts, but AIDS has solved the major problems of my life." "What?" asked Milian. Gil explained: "Well, the biggie was the sexual thing, and that's completely gone now. I no longer have to write my novel because there isn't time." Then Gil divulged the most heartbreaking byproduct of his illness. "And my worst fear—that people would find out what I'm really like—has happened. And yet . . . they still seem to want me." Milian gazed compassionately at him. He shrugged and grinned with irony.

Gil had realized, too late, that his family still loved him, unconditionally, whether or not he was homosexual. Regardless of how he came to this situation, he was still our brother, and a son. We were family, and we would have tried to help him sort out his confusion if only he had not been afraid to ask.

At the time Gil disclosed his diagnosis to us, we all were scattered across the southern and midwestern United States. There never was a family meeting to discuss a collective response to Gil's illness. Honestly, we each processed the situation in our own ways. It was decades later when we collectively shared what we had done or said to Gil. And to a person, our reactions were surprisingly similar. His mom, Elsye, spent a weekend with him in LA before he was bedridden. Our dad invited Gil to come home to Albuquerque and spend his final days there. Gil declined. Early in his diagnosis, Gil traveled to Fort Worth to visit Jeanne, Nowell, and their young family, with graceful and obedient Dasmah in tow. He was looking for a home for her. Our father and David visited Gil, ironically to be approached by a prostitute two blocks from Gil's home. As Gil lay in his hospital bed, David asked him if he had found peace with God. He assured David, "I feel comfortable with the belief that God has forgiven me of my past mistakes." He also confessed that if he had an opportunity to live his life over again, he would have chosen a different path. David hugged him and told him how elated he was about his confessions and how much he loved him. Other visits with family and lengthy phone conversations took place throughout his illness. In each conversation we communicated the same message: we love you, and nothing is going to change that.

And so, in a moment, a lifetime of feeling shame and guilt were eradicated. Decades of living a double life were simplified into living a single life. We hope disclosure and love made Gil's last days more bearable and meaningful.

Many of us feel we failed Gil. If this disclosure, or at least a candid dialogue among us all, had been achieved years earlier, would events have turned out differently? What if he had not lived in Hollywood? What if he had not been abused? Only God knows.

Our brother passed away in the night in the upstairs bedroom of his caretaker's apartment, his beloved Dasmah at his side. He was thirty-eight years young.

Our father and our brothers Darrell, David, and Daniel drove to Los Angeles and collected Gil's cremated remains. Those few personal items in his apartment not already given away to friends were gathered up and loaded in the car and taken back to Albuquerque. Dasmah was given a new, loving home in the arid deserts of central Arizona, a place not unlike where she was born.

Gil's cremated remains were interred at the Antlers City Cemetery in Oklahoma. Elsye is now buried nearby.

Gil's Premonition

Four years prior to passing away, Gil wrote the following in a letter to Elsye:

If I ever happen to die in a crash or whatever, for God's sake don't mourn me. I've had a terrific life. Carry my child, which is this idea that we were born to increase each other, promote life and growth within one another. That's the same child I've tried to implant in all my better friends, even in passing acquaintances. Help that child mature, and I'll live forever.

CHAPTER 9

SEXUAL OFFENDER TYPES AND BEHAVIORS

(A synthesis of FBI Special Agent K. V. Lanning's analyses by Jeanne)

Gilbert's tragic experience is not unique. Children have been preyed upon by child sexual molesters of different types since time began, and they will continue to be victims unless parents and caregivers are trained to become good listeners and instinctive detectives, with the eyes and ears of a falcon allowing them to spot potential offenders. Vigilance is always needed, and most sadly, this includes vigilance over people close to you and/or your child, because most child sexual offenders are people we know, love, and trust.

We have all been trained to worry about stranger danger, but in fact, according to a 2003 National Institute of Justice report, three out of four victims know their offenders very well. The same study also discovered that 86 percent of sexual assaults are not reported to professional investigators. Those few cases that do represent only the tip of the iceberg.

In *What Do I Do Now? A Survival Guide for Mothers of Sexually Abused Children*, author Mel Langston says,

> *Most child sexual abusers are men, although women also sexually abuse children. The National Center for Victims of Crime reports women are perpetrators in about 14% of cases involving boys and 6% involving girls. Most child sexual abuse in families is perpetrated by a husband or partner. Older siblings are also an increasing concern. Known community members commit a significant proportion of sexual abuse. Neighbors, family friends, babysitters, schoolteachers, coaches, grocery store clerks, lawyers, pastors, and other trusted community members abuse children sexually. No group, age, gender,*

race, religion, or ethnicity is exempt. Sexual abusers are young, old, male, female, rich, poor, educated, and uneducated.

The conclusion we can draw from these sources is that sexual abuse is more likely to be perpetrated by someone we know rather than a stranger. With that in mind, the following information will raise your awareness about the types and motivating behaviors of individuals who prey on children.

For the purposes of this chapter, and because men are the most prolific offenders, the information that follows employs male pronouns.

Kenneth V. Lanning, a former special agent for the FBI, authored five editions of *Child Molesters: A Behavioral Analysis for Professionals Investigating Child Sexual Exploitation.* His book is a lengthy tome written for the purpose of identifying, arresting, and convicting child sex offenders. He does not attempt to explain why molesters commit sex crimes; rather, he seeks to analyze how the crimes are perpetrated. Even though the book was written for prosecutorial purposes, some of the information within should be of interest to parents and caregivers, so we provide here a summary of Lanning's key types and patterns of behavior. You are the first line of defense for your child, so file these facts in your mind and be on the lookout for these situations. Because of Lanning's book, I now know which typology group and behavior fits our grandfather Leo Purtha.

Before continuing, parents may be wondering how it is possible that most offenders are known to the victims. Lanning warns us about the "nice-guy offender." This is the person whom everyone seems to love: the good neighbor, best coach, most popular teacher, Big Brother or Big Sister mentor, scout leader, pastor, nun, counselor, to name just a few possibilities. The offender can also be someone who befriends a single mother or becomes her live-in partner or spouse. When these people play a prominent role in your child's life, and especially if he or she spends more time with your child than you do, be very cautious. This is true even if the offender is a prominent member of the community. Many offenders deliberately choose their occupations, and their personal relationships, for the purpose of having access to children whom they can molest. Furthermore, ambitious parents who want their children to excel in school, sports, modeling, and show business sometimes unwittingly push their children into the arms of an offender. In all these cases, the parent should never abdicate control over their child's movements, friends, extracurricular activities, and mentors. If you don't stay actively involved in your child's life, your blind trust could easily be betrayed and your child mentally traumatized for the rest of his or her life.

Typology of Child Molesters

According to Lanning, offenders can be broken down into two primary groups, each with subcategories of behaviors. That said, he also states that offenders can also change behaviors over time, so they don't always fit neatly into these boxes; instead, they should be viewed on a flexible continuum.

SITUATIONAL CHILD MOLESTERS do not fit the psychiatric definition of a pedophile, an individual only sexually attracted to children. The situational offender is an opportunist and will abuse anyone, whether it's a child in a daycare center, a patient in a hospital, or an elderly adult in a retirement home. He does so for a variety of complex reasons, including stress or insecurity. This man targets victims who are within his reach and vulnerable. Most of these offenders are members of a lower socioeconomic group. Within this type there are four behavior patterns.

The **Regressed** offender seeks any victim who is easily available to him. He also very likely keeps photo or video evidence of his abuse to fuel his memories and fantasies. He can be the easiest to catch and convict if investigators look for this evidence in his possession.

Morally Indiscriminate offenders are experimental sociopaths without a conscience. They will lie, steal, cheat, and attempt any crime simply because they believe he can get away with it, including sexually traumatizing a child. This man is capable of abducting strangers as well as members of his own family, typically doing so using lures, manipulation, and even force if need be. He likes to collect adult pornography and may possess some child pornography. In the latter case, the porn is most likely of pubescent children. It is also not unusual to find a collection of detective magazines.

Sexually Indiscriminate offenders may be particular about certain facets of their lives, but when it comes to sex, they will try almost anything. Lanning calls them "try-sexuals." This behavior includes practicing bondage or even sadomasochism. This offender is not necessarily sexually attracted to children, but if he does molest a child, he probably does so out of boredom. The most important aspect of his behavior is that each of his victims be new and different to the previous victim. He may also traumatize his own children or even share them with like-minded adults who practice group sex or sex rituals. This offender is usually from a higher socioeconomic background, collects lots of pornography, although mostly of adults, and has more victims than other types of situational child molesters.

Inadequate offenders are men with eccentric personalities. They may be senile, be mentally retarded, or have a mental illness. While most individuals with those personalities are harmless, the few that do become interested in children do so because they don't feel threatened by them, making it easier for them to try out a sexual fantasy on the child. These individuals act out after a buildup of sexual impulses, and their behavior may include sexual torture. Anyone who appears vulnerable to them, including children or even the elderly, may become their victim. In a worst-case situation, they may kill the victim.

As seen from this discussion, not all situational child molesters are pedophiles, but the harm they do is no less traumatic. In the second typography, Lanning describes true pedophile behavior.

PREFERENTIAL CHILD MOLESTERS are true pedophiles. All their sexual fantasies, behaviors, and urges are focused on children, primarily in the prepubescent age group. This offender has gender and age preferences, and most of his victims are boys. The preferential child molester tends to belong to a higher socioeconomic group and abuses the greatest number of children relative to the other types of offenders.

Long-term behavior indicators:

(1) Even though a sexual offender may have suffered sexual abuse by someone, not all sexual abuse victims become pedophiles. This type of molester typically was groomed and abused as an early

adolescent, as a result of which he shows little or no sexual interest in his peers.

(2) If an offender who is enlisted in the military gets caught molesting children, he may be kicked out of the force. The military is usually more interested in getting rid of that individual than prosecuting him, so he may be dishonorably discharged with no specific reason given and released into the community.

(3) Preferential child molesters frequently move from place to place. He may hold a job for many years and then suddenly leave town. This often means he was caught but not prosecuted. He was probably told to leave town or else.

(4) While no single behavior proves an individual is a pedophile, if many of the following indicators are combined, there is a greater probability that this is the case. These behaviors include:

a) He is over twenty-five, single, and never married.

b) He lives alone or with parents.

c) He has limited dating experience.

d) He has an excessive interest in children.

e) He has a circle of friends who are young, and they hang around playgrounds, malls, or anywhere children gather.

f) He has a close adult friend (who may become his partner in crime).

g) He seems focused on children of a certain age or sex. Lanning says, "The older the age preference of the pedophile, the more exclusive the gender preference. Pedophiles attracted to toddlers are more likely to molest boys and girls indiscriminately."

h) He refers to children with endearing terms like "imps," "innocent," "pure," or "clean."

i) He has hobbies that appeal to prepubescent children, which includes toys, dolls, model airplanes and trains; if he is interested in older children, he has "hobbies" like pornography, alcohol, and drugs, or other interests that generally appeal to pubescent children.

j) If the individual is interested in a particular gender, he might decorate his home or his yard in a way that appeals to his favorite type of victim, including turning his home into a theater or an amusement park.

k) With smart phones being so ubiquitous, pedophiles have ample opportunities to photograph compliant children; alternatively, they will surreptitiously focus their lens on them. The pedophile will do so whether the children are clothed or unclothed, because in either case, the images fuel his fantasies. Anyone who takes an inordinate number of pictures of children, whether in his home or at public events, including sports, cheerleading, gymnastics, and playgrounds, is suspect and needs to be watched. Especially if other behavioral indicators align with this "hobby," parents should ensure their child is never in contact with the individual and should consider reporting suspicious behavior to appropriate authorities.

l) Not surprisingly, these offenders collect a lot of child pornography.

Lanning tells us that preferential child molesters have three behavior patterns:

Seduction offenders seduce children just as men and women seduce each other. He is willing to slowly groom a child to gain his or her trust, or an entire group of children, as in scout troops, Sunday school, daycare centers, the classroom, and in the neighborhood. As an adult he is automatically an authority figure. The seduction offender also has good interpersonal skills that make him a pied piper. He is a magnet to children because he makes them feel as if he understands their needs better than anyone else; plus he offers lures that appeal to them. These types of offenders have a knack for spotting children who are neglected or emotionally troubled. They are his easiest victims. He is one of the nice, cool guys to hang out with. Consequently, many naive children become compliant with the offender's increasingly sexual behavior. After he wins their trust, they think whatever he does to them must be okay. So long as the children are prepubescent, they may not be inclined to divulge what's happening to them. However, if the abuse goes on until the child becomes pubescent, the child will experience normal sexual urges. After that life change, a child may think he or she is in love with the sexual offender. This is a huge problem for the molester because his sexual preference is for prepubescent children. When the offender attempts to end the "friendship" with the now-adolescent, the abused victim may threaten to divulge what has been happening. The pubescent child may follow through with his threat in any case, but often the offender counter-threatens the child with violence to himself, his family, or anyone he cares about.

Introverted offenders are not pied pipers. This man uses few or no words. He does not have interpersonal skills to seduce his desired victims, so he turns to other means to access children. Lacking words to entice a child, he usually turns to very young children he knows for gratification because they lack awareness and the verbal skills to defend themselves. They are totally vulnerable. He may hang out wherever little children play and expose himself or opportunistically fondle anyone he can get his hands on, especially if he works with small children. Failing those opportunities, he will befriend a family or a single mother and become an unofficial uncle or offer to babysit. If that fails, he will develop a sexual relationship with a single mother so that she trusts him around her children. If he is truly desperate, he will marry a woman and impregnate her so that he will have direct access to their children and may begin his abuse when each child is a tiny infant. This type of marriage arrangement typically results in sexual difficulties because his fantasies are focused on his child rather than his wife. If the woman gives birth to a child that does not fit his gender preference, he may continue impregnating her until he gets the child of choice. However, these pedophiles will sexually abuse both genders of children, sometimes simultaneously. Were it possible to investigate this man's background, we would likely discover he had already abused other victims, who could include his own siblings or friends.

Sadistic offenders are extremely dangerous. The good news is that they are fewer in number than the other types of offenders. This man achieves sexual gratification by causing bodily harm or emotional pain. He uses lures or force to capture his victim and is quite willing to abduct and kill the child.

What Type of Offender Was Leo Purtha?

Our grandfather fits into the typology of a preferential child molester with introverted behavior, but first, how did his pedophilia originate? It likely didn't develop in a vacuum, so we are left to surmise using circumstantial evidence. We know that Leo's parents were disciplinarians and that the family were Roman Catholics. Corporal punishment, with the body partially disrobed, was common in homes, schools, and churches. We also are aware of the Catholic church's documented history of child sexual abuse around the world. In 2021 a report revealed that 330,000 children in the French Catholic Church were abused over a seventy-year period, so the problem continues. We know that abuse occurs in other denominations as well, but at a minimum, sexual abuse has been ongoing in the Catholic church for decades, if not centuries. Priests have always served a paternalistic role, and as such, have enforced corporal punishment on children, as well as native peoples who the church considered to be children. What we don't know is whether Leo's father, John, was himself a pedophile because of his upbringing.

Leo fits the preferential child molester with introverted behavior type for several reasons. First, he was a quiet man who used few words. He never spoke to me during his molestations. He snuck up on me when I was sleeping. I suspect he behaved similarly with Gil. Second, he began molesting Gil at the age of two and a half and me at the age of three and a half. He knew Gil and I were fatherless and vulnerable, especially when Elsye went to work and left us in her parent's care. His abuse of me ended after about three years or so. The victimization of Gil continued off and on for at least ten years. He also molested Elsye, beginning at age three, and continued doing so for ten years. Third, even though they were raised as Catholics, Leo and May only had three children in ten years, suggesting that intimacy may have been an infrequent event, which would be typical for this type of offender. There was a gap of three years between Jack and Elsye and a gap of six years between Elsye and Neil. Thus, we believe he married May for the purpose of fathering children he could abuse. As he was a father, his children were required to obey him because he was the authority figure in the home. Although Leo had a quiet nature, he always got the last word. Fourth, the Purthas moved with great frequency, as did our mother when she needed to run away from a problem.

Knowing with certainty that Leo sexually abused his daughter and his two grandchildren, it isn't a stretch to believe that he also abused his two sons. However, the only circumstantial evidence that he might have molested Jack lies in the fact that Jack's two adopted boys did not live with him and Anna very long. Elsye's behavior is fully described in the chapter "It's a Mad, Mad World." What that chapter does not reveal is that our mother married three additional times; two of those times to the same man. She also became an alcoholic, although we never saw her drunk. I learned of her problem when she told me she had joined AA. Thankfully, she remained sober for the last ten years of her life. Neil, on the other hand, was a child who acted out as a young man and an adult. I don't know what he was like in school, but for starters he was dishonorably discharged from the military, supposedly for going AWOL. Neil was also involved in a suspicious fatal car accident, he was unfaithful to his wife numerous times, he stole from his parents, and he died an alcoholic at the age of forty-two. Sexual trauma manifests itself in many ways, one of which is the type of behavior displayed by Neil.

On the surface, the Purthas were cordial with their neighbors, their home was well maintained, a garden was always growing in the back yard, and May was devoutly religious. Behind that facade, though, family life was not normal. The lesson here is that even though a family may seem nice on the surface, it tells you nothing about what is going on behind closed doors. However, one might look at the behavior of the children for warning signs.

CHAPTER 10
WARNING SIGNS
OF SEXUAL ABUSE

(As told by Jeanne)

> *Your child is at serious psychological risk if she does not feel you believe her. Your belief is crucial in supporting your child and the most important predictor of your child's recovery.*
>
> **Mel Langston**, *PhD*

Whether you discover sexual abuse of your child on your own or your child divulges the abuse, you will be angry, in shock, and possibly in denial. Some offenders lie to their victims, saying that their mother or father knows and are okay with what is being done. Alternatively, the offender might say that no one will believe the charge because he or she is too important and trusted in the community. If your child finds the courage to divulge abuse perpetrated by anyone—including a parent, grandparent, uncle, teacher, pastor, nun, close friend, or older sibling—and you fail to believe him, the offender will know he has carte blanche to continue. So, it is critically important for you to believe your child whether she hints at, or openly reveals, her abuse. This is true even if your child suddenly recants. Unfortunately, many children do this out of embarrassment, guilt, or fear, so the initial revelation should be taken as gospel. Either way, you will feel guilty, especially if your child blames you for not preventing the abuse. Once you know one of your children has been abused, you should also regard your other children as potential victims of the same offender, regardless of the children's gender differences.

In the previous chapter, based on the investigative knowledge of Kenneth Lanning, we discussed the different types and behaviors of sexual offenders so that you will be forearmed with information that could help you prevent sexual abuse of your child before it happens. Remember also that the greatest number of sexual offenders are *known* to the child and the family, and too often the offender is very close to home. Stranger danger is a real threat, but nearly all sexual trauma is perpetrated by people you know, so don't give blind trust to every person who is near your child. Recall that anyone whom your child spends more time with than you do is a potential candidate for being a sexual offender. Keep your eyes and ears open. Listen to and communicate with your child daily.

According to Mel Langston in *What Should I Do Now?*, kids respond to sexual abuse in many different and sometimes contradictory ways. To begin with, each child is unique in character based on their DNA. Additional factors that will affect the child's mental and physical responses include the age when abuse begins, the duration and frequency of abuse, the child's relationship with the abuser, and the ways in which the abuser traumatizes the child.

Toddlers and preschool children don't have the vocabulary to verbalize what is being done to them, although there are other ways to discern potential abuse, whether by their behavior or physical signs. Very young victims also do not know right from wrong, so they may think what is being done to them is normal and a sign of affection. For example, in "Gentling: A Practical Guide to Treating PTSD in Abused Children," William Krill Jr. writes,

> Children are fully "wired" sexually. While their wiring lies largely dormant until developmental progress reaches a point where full sexual awakening occurs, it surely can be "powered up" when an older child or adult decides to perpetrate a sexual crime against a child. Once the psychosexual system is powered up, it is not easy to simply switch off. This leads to a second, rather uncomfortable fact to confront: the sexual contact that the child had may have been, at least in part, or at an initial stage of the abuse, pleasant to the child. As a parent myself, and as someone who has worked with countless innocent and precious small children, this is a very difficult fact indeed to absorb. Sexual perpetrators of children will often use the existing level of intimacy in the relationship to press for sexual

contact, leading the child to believe that the contact is an expression of affection and love. The perpetrator is lying to the child. The sexual behavior has nothing to do with love or affection. The child, as a sexual being, may respond sexually to the overtures. It is only at a later time, possibly as early as during the abusive act itself, or perhaps many abuse episodes later that the child begins to experience the crushingly negative effect of the abuse.

In "Sexual Abuse in Male Children and Adolescents: Indicators, Effects, and Treatments," Cheryl Black and Richard DeBlassie describe the warning signs in very young, preverbal children. These include aggressive or withdrawn behavior, sex play with other children, especially if force is used, excessive or compulsive masturbation, and treating toys as sex objects. Small children who play passively alone may also be showing signs of withdrawal. Physical signs include red or swollen genitals, bruising, and fissures in the anus. The child might also exhibit a sudden fear of an individual known to him or cry and fuss during diapering, baths, and dressing. Children beyond the potty-training stage may start wetting the bed or manipulating their own feces.

Older children do have the vocabulary to divulge abuse but for many reasons may be reluctant to do so. This could be due to fear, particularly if an abuser threatens the child, his loved ones, his friends, or even his pets. The child may also feel embarrassed, think that it is her fault, or consider that no one would believe her since everyone likes and respects the individual who is abusing her. Black and DeBlassie state that this group of victims also displays signs of aggression or withdrawal and can appear excessively dependent on, or fearful of, specific people. Some children develop a school phobia because the abuser is there or, in contrast, may want to go to school early and stay late to avoid someone at home. Importantly, they write, "It is the suddenness of onset and the degree to which they are exhibited by these young victims that are the critical factors in early detection."

Lanning adds to the indicators by including sudden signs of inexplicable fear triggered by a person, place, or thing. The child's sensory memories can be set off by taste, smell, sight, hearing, and touch. Because the child is highly stressed, she may exhibit contradictory behaviors. Lanning states she "may fear all men, or approach all men. She may dislike being touched, or may inappropriately touch others. Extreme responses suggest difficulty in self-regulation. Fear is biochemical, not just a 'feeling.' Cortisol, a stress hormone released when fearful, causes cascading bodily effects. With repeated fear, neurochemical processes adapt, and the brain is hardwired to over-respond."

Lanning and Langston both suggest that prepubescent and pubescent children may become depressed, cry, have trouble sleeping, have nightmares, become irritable, lose interest in a favorite activity, vaguely complain of illnesses, cause self-harm, and even attempt suicide. Self-esteem is also at risk, particularly if your child has few friends and negatively compares herself to her peers. Another sign of potential abuse is present when a child loses self-control and hits out at peers, disrespects adults, steals, harms pets, sets fires, gets involved in adolescent prostitution, and/or runs away. If your child is constantly angry, it could be because he may be angry with his abuser, angry with himself, and/or angry with you because, in his mind, you didn't protect him.

Some signs that indicated our brother Gil was abused include a string of illnesses, bed wetting, being withdrawn in the company of adults, and playing alone most of the time. The first summer we arrived in Texas to stay with our cousins, Gil was afraid of everything. He got over those fears once he had an opportunity to play and run free with children his own age; furthermore, because of the weeks of physical distance between Gil and our grandfather, Gil didn't have to think about being touched by him. His stress levels changed when we returned home.

An abused child, regardless of the age at which the abuse happened, loses a great deal of self-control, healthy ego development, childish innocence, and trust through betrayal. Added to this toxic mix, Peter T. Dimock, author of "Adult Males Sexually Abused as Children," reports that these children can suffer from gender identity confusion, sexual orientation confusion, and chronic post-traumatic stress disorder.

Lanning tells us it is important in the healing process to grieve these losses with your child so that he doesn't feel like he's carrying the entire burden on his young shoulders. Even though you will feel your own sense of grief for not knowing about the abuse, or because you ignored the signs, you must put your child's mental health first and then grieve privately later.

Above all else, this cannot be repeated often enough: believe your child!

In the next section we discuss resources to help parents protect their children from abuse and, failing that, help you and your child heal.

CHAPTER 11

HELPFUL RESOURCES

(As told by Jeanne)

PREVENTION AND EARLY INTERVENTION
Silly Gillee™ Card Game

The genesis of this book began many years ago. My personal goal was not simply to tell a sad story about my brother: I also hoped this book would open the eyes of parents and caregivers in ways that might prevent another child from experiencing similar abuse and then suffering lifelong consequences as my brother did. While in the process of writing, and remembering how young we were when our abuses started, I asked myself a question: "Is there a way we could get a preschool or elementary-age child to reveal when someone is grooming or actively abusing him?" In answer to that question, I created a card game that asks simple, silly, open-ended W-questions that serve multiple purposes, not just eliciting signs of abuse. Yet the game has the potential to do exactly that if parents or caregivers supervise the game. The card game is called Silly Gillee™ and is dedicated in memory of my brother Gilbert Lee Johnson. (Gillee is an amalgamation of Gil's first and middle names.)

If this game serves no higher purpose, at the very least it inculcates the habit of one-on-one communication between parent and child before technology becomes a distraction. Since the questions have no wrong answers, children can use their creative imaginations to provide answers. The only rule of the game is that in addition to answering the question, the child is also expected to explain why he/she gave that answer. "Why" is the key to revealing potential trouble. Simultaneously, the child may draw on his or her own experiences and feelings. The supervising adult should be able to discern between imagination and truth and, in either case, show pleasure at the child's response. This will encourage your child to keep playing the game. In a more mundane way, Silly Gillee™ can also be used as an icebreaker at children's parties, to entertain children while traveling, or in any group setting. If the adult participating in the game has read previous chapters of this book, he or she should also be able to discern potential signs of bullying, inappropriate behaviors, sexual grooming, sexual abuse, depression, and suicidal ideation from the way the child answers questions.

If children are old enough to read, they can play Silly Gillee™ on their own. In that case, it is still important for the parent or caregiver to pay attention to the answers given by the children and follow up if necessary. If the children are too young or untrained to read, then an adult will have to play the leading role. For example, the cards would be placed in a pile between all players. Any child can pick up a card and hand it to the adult to read aloud. Then the child answers the question and explains why she gave that answer. This might also be an opportunity to teach children how to read, since the questions use very few words.

Silly Gillee™ offers the best of two worlds: it can be a fun game to pass the time with your children, and it can elicit signs of serious troubles if they exist. The card game can be found by searching the internet.

National Center for Missing and Exploited Children

www.missingkids.org

The NCMEC is a private, nonprofit organization specializing in helping find missing children, preventing child abuse, and reducing sexual exploitation. To that end they offer a wealth of free supporting materials, including downloadable publications, videos, tip sheets, games, and education kits to teach children about personal safety. These can be found on their KidSmartz page. Another page, called NetSmartz, teaches kids through videos and free resources how to recognize cyberbullying, online exploitation, sexting, as well as providing peer education and mentoring kits for upper elementary and middle school students. Both of those pages are located by clicking "Education" in the menu bar. NCMEC also offers legal resources for families, legislators, law enforcement, and more.

BOOKS

What Do I Do Now? A Survival Guide for Mothers of Sexually Abused Children (MOSAC), by Mel Langston, PhD with Leona Puma, 2021.

Mel Langston, a mother of six children, learned when she was six months pregnant with her sixth child that her husband had been abusing one of their daughters for some time. She also learned that her twelve-year-old daughter wasn't the only child traumatized. She went into emotional shock. When speaking to a friend about her daughter's disclosure, Mel said, "Give me a book. Give me something with a list of what to do when this happens to you." In 1980 no such book existed, nor did the internet or smart phones. She couldn't google for help. Mel spent years learning all she could about child sexual trauma, eventually earning a master's degree in psychology. She wanted to make a difference, and she has done so by becoming a therapist specializing in trauma and family work. Mel's survival guide will hold your hand as you and your child walk the path to healing. Her appendix includes twenty-four pages of additional resources, including resources by state. Very importantly, she includes six resources for legal advocacy.

The Connected Parent, by Karyn Purvis, PhD and Lisa Qualls with Emmelie Picket, 2020.

In the forward to this book, David R. Cross, PhD, writes, "This book is a celebration of the creative genius of the late Dr. Karyn Purvis. Dr. Purvis qualifies as a genius for two reasons. The first is that she synthesized a wide range of information and created something entirely new—that which we now call Trust-Based Relational Intervention (TBRI). Dr. Purvis synthesized information from the deep roots of her faith, from her scientific understanding of children's development, and from the rich web of her own caregiving experiences as parent, foster parent, and minister's wife. She blended all of this into a seamless whole that teaches us all how to be better parents and caregivers."

While *Wounded Wings* deals with sexual abuse within the family, *The Connected Parent* deals in large part with children "from hard places," typically children forced into child protective services because of neglect, sexual, and/or physical trauma.

If you adopt or foster one of these children, you will face challenges regardless of the sincerity and depth of your love for the child, because these children no longer trust anyone, and believe it or not, this can also be true with infants from hard places. In some cases, the child will reject the foster parent outright. Many of these children have sensory triggers that cause severe stress, which results in behavioral issues that seem inexplicable and insurmountable. In some situations, adoptive parents simply give up and return the child to protective services, but this doesn't have to happen to you and your child. Dr. Purvis and Lisa Qualls's solutions provide hope for both children and parents using scientifically proven techniques.

These methods have been so successful that Texas Christian University established the Karyn Purvis Institute of Child Development, a program of the Department of Psychology. Their mission is "research, education, training, and outreach to improve the lives of children who have experienced abuse, neglect, and/or trauma." The TBRI methods they teach are now being implemented across the United States and around the world. Not only do they train professionals to use their trademarked techniques; they also make abundant resources available to parents who are struggling to raise a difficult child. You will find information on their website (https://child.tcu.edu/).

Technological Red Flags

The National Center for Missing and Exploited Children offers excellent advice about the dangers your child may encounter using smart phones and computers, so I refer you back to them for extensive advice on this topic. However, there is something you can do today to protect your child from online predators, as well as peers who attempt to involve your child in sexual activities or drugs.

You may not be aware that children use coded language while texting or participating in social media groups. It is both a convenient shorthand and a way to keep parents clueless about the content of their conversations. Below is a sample list of some of the acronyms and emojis that are commonly used and the websites where I found them. I combined the sources into an alphabetical list to help parents find each symbol. Because these links may have already expired, and because kids' imaginations are always evolving, it would be wise to periodically search the internet for the latest acronyms and emojis to stay up-to-date on coded conversations. Then follow up by examining your child's phone and computer on a regular basis. Exercise your parental authority.

Internet Acronyms All Parents Need to Know

8	Oral sex
99	Parent gone
143 or 459	I love you
182	I hate you
1174	Nude club
CD9	Code 9 (meaning parents are around)
FYEO	For your eyes only
GNOC	Get naked on camera
GYPO	Get your pants off
HAK	Hugs and kisses
IWSN	I want sex now
J/O	Jerking off
KFY	Kiss for you
KPC	Keeping parents clueless
MIRL	Meet in real life
MOS	Mom over shoulder
NIFOC	Nude in front of computer
NSFW	Not safe for work
P911	Parent alert
PAW	Parents are watching
PAL	Parents are listening
PIR	Parent in room
POS	Parent over shoulder
PRON	Porn

RUMORF	Are you male or female?
RUH	Are you horny?
SWAK	Sealed with a kiss
TDTM	Talk dirty to me
WTTP	Want to trade pictures?

(https://www.verywellfamily.com/the-secret-language-of-teens-100-social-media
-acronyms-2609651)

ASL	Age/sex/location / "Ass h—"
FWB	Friends with benefits (friends who occasionally have casual sex)
FYEO or 4YEO	For your eyes only (may indicate explicit photos)
GYPO	Get your pants off
KPC	Keeping parents clueless
LMIRL	Let's meet in real life
NIFOC	Naked in front of computer
NSFW	Not safe for work
OC	Open crib (no parents will be home) / (may also stand for Original character, a unique character in fan art or fanfiction not found in the original property)

(from https://www.bark.us/blog/teen-text-speak-codes-every-parent-should-know/)

Daddy	An attractive man, usually older, who conveys a sense of power and dominance
FBOI	F**k boy; a guy just looking for sex
Hentai	Graphic anime pornography
KMS	Kill myself
KYS	Kill yourself
Netflix and chill	Getting together and hooking up
Plug	Term used to refer to someone who can "connect" you with drugs; a drug dealer.

Skeet	To ejaculate
Smash	Means to have casual sex
Thirsty	Desperate for attention, usually sexual attention
Turnt	Excited and having a good time, often with the help of drugs or alcohol
WAP	Wet ass p*ssy
Zaddy	A well-dressed, attractive man of any age

(Older-teen slang terms)

Chad	A hypersexual young man
Coney	Slang for "penis"
Dabbing	Refers to concentrated doses of cannabis; also a dance craze
Dongle	Slang for "penis"
ILY	I love you
School Bus	A 2mg Xanax bar, which is yellow
WUF	Where you from?

Popular Emoji Slang

	Penis
	Used to express drunkenness, sexual arousal, or a grimace
	Butt
	"Dump truck," which refers to a large and/or shapely bottom
	Vagina
	Used when getting caught in a mistake or when feeling like a fraud
	Indicates being "ghosted" (dumped with no explanation)
	Symbolizes a lie, which could also be called a "cap"
	Shy, nervous (usually in the context of flirting)
	Oral sex
	Ejaculation

May indicate sexual activity, especially oral sex

Used when someone has an "hourglass" body shape

Feeling frisky or naughty

A response that means, "It is what it is"

Can be used in comments to denote a sarcastic, mean-spirited tone

Marijuana/weed

Desiring someone sexually (often used in response to nudes)

Breasts/testicles/virginity

Represents nudes, which are often called "noods"

Used when sending or receiving nudes

A stamp of approval; "I agree"

Used to refer to sexual activity

Indicates "spiciness," i.e., inappropriate or risqué content

(https://www.bark.us/blog/emoji-slang-guide/)

CHAPTER 12

HANDWRITING ANALYSIS OF GILBERT JOHNSON AND ELSYE PURTHA

Graphology deals with the study of the physiological and psychological
mechanics that create the handwriting, and the cognitive and
behavioral aspects that it reveals.

AAHA FAQs

Readers might wonder why I have included a handwriting analysis of Gil's and Elsye's handwriting in this book. Because of my childhood experiences, I have been interested in psychology for some time; I have often wondered why people behave as they do, especially those who cause harm or heartbreak to others. When I discovered graphology in the early 1970s, I thought I had finally found a source that would give me insights into people around me and help me identify people I should avoid. It's difficult to avoid family, but choosing friends and life mates is another matter, so when I came across two used books, *Handwriting* by Klara G. Roman and *Handwriting Tells* by Nadya Olyanova, I became a student of handwriting analysis and have maintained my interest over the decades. To that end I became a hobby member of the American Association of Handwriting Analysts, which is how I became acquainted with Sally Mosko, a certified graphologist in Wisconsin. I asked Sally if she would be willing to do an analysis on my brother and my mother, to which she agreed. Sally was aware that Gil had died a tragic death at a young age and that he once said he wished he had studied ballet. I also told her that mom had been sexually abused by her father, but beyond that she knew nothing else about my family. I gave Gil's journal entries from 1975 and 1984 to Sally because I could see a drastic change in the style of his writing between those two samples. When a person changes his or her writing so dramatically, it means something has altered in that person's life, whether physical or mental or both. The questions are, what and why?

After Gil's and mom's analyses were completed, I sent Sally my memoir, part of which appears in this book, so she could compare it to her analyses. I believe she hit the mark on Gil. What she did not know beforehand is that Gil had two primary "father figures": Leo pre-1968 and then Marlin post-1968. Gil described Leo as "gentle"; Marlin was authoritative. Sally was also correct in her analysis of Elsye's handwriting. In addition, she pointed out some of mom's good characteristics that I had been too blind to see because of my emotional involvement and attachment issues with my mother.

Jeanne Donovan

Sally Mosko

Sally Mosko is a certified cursive coach and conducts the Northern Illinois Handwriting Analysis Study Group, which meets quarterly. She is a life member of the American Association of Handwriting Analysts since 1987, is a member of the American Handwriting Analysis Foundation (AHAF) since 2012, and served as a board member and secretary of AHAF. Sally keeps her skills current by participating in the AHAF Online Chapter and AHAF's weekly educational sessions. She has given presentations on graphology to community groups and to the online chapter. Sally received the Member of Distinction Award at the 2021 AHAF Conference for going above and beyond in her work promoting graphology.

Gilbert L. Johnson
Right-handed male, age 24 in 1975
by Sally Mosko, CG - 9/23/2020

Handwriting is often referred to as "brain writing" as it provides a map of the mind, a visible record of the brain impulses that govern one's behavior. These impulses not only dictate how we write but are an expression of our whole personality. Our handwriting is as unique to us as our physical features, speech, and mannerisms. I consider it an honor and privilege to be asked to analyze the handwriting of Jeanne Donovan's brother, the late Gilbert Lee Johnson.

Self-Image:

In graphology we look to the personal pronoun I (PPI) to assess how a person views the relationship between (and with) their mother (main nurturer) and father (or dominant male). The PPI also tells us how the writer views himself. Gil's PPI deviates from the school form PPI that he was taught and is quite distorted. The initial stroke that represents the mother forms a small hook to the left. It appears that Gil did not perceive his mother as having as great an impact on him as his father, yet the hook formation shows he was still clinging to his mother in his thoughts. The stroke representing father forms a large circle that goes in a centripetal direction instead of moving to the right. Gil did not perceive his father as propelling him forward toward the future. The father stroke curls into itself, much like the lower zone y and g loops that Gil has incorporated into his handwriting and signature. This could be interpreted as a turning into or absorption with self.

Gil's PPI is slightly larger than the other capital letters which may be his way of compensating for some feelings of insecurity. His PPI is not resting on a firm foundation. It has a "rocker" bottom which means Gil was not firmly rooted or confident about who he was at age 24. Other[s'] opinions could easily sway him; too much stress could make it difficult for him to cope. Five out of six of his PPIs have a phallic-like shape pointing to the past in the area of the mind/intellect. Perhaps at the time of the writing Gil's thoughts were preoccupied with a sexual event(s) from the past or he was preoccupied with thoughts of sex at the time of the writing.

Gil's signature on his passport application shows that he took more pride in himself and his accomplishments, than from his family name. The G in Gilbert appears larger than the J in Johnson. The J had a retraced tip in the upper zone (UZ) which indicates an adversarial relationship with the father, one he would like to repress rather than think about. The G in Gilbert has an ending stroke that curls back over the G as if protecting himself. The very tall upper zone would indicate that he viewed his father as an authoritarian figure. The smaller middle zone (MZ) in contrast to the tall UZ and long LZ

Gilbert Johnson's signature on his passport application, 1982. *Courtesy of the Author's Collection.*

may indicate Gil was not as confident as he appeared on the surface. Fearful he may not get the affirmation and praise he needed from others, he affirmed himself through a pride that could sometimes border on vanity.

One of the biggest contradictions in Gil's writing is the contrast between his right slant that reaches out toward others and his wide word spacing which says, "Don't get too close." This disparity created a lot of inner tension and anxiety for him. At the time of the journal entry, Gil was feeling down but was trying to pull himself up. Gil also has what graphologists call "rivers" in his writing. These are signs that the writer had emotional hurdles he had not overcome. He felt emotionally isolated as if he had a hole in his ego. This presented yet another conflict for Gil as he had the highly connected writing of an extrovert. While he needed those human connections, he found forming healthy relationships difficult.

Relationships/Social Skills:

When anyone met Gil, no doubt their first impression was of a friendly, outgoing extrovert. He would be the "fun guy" at the party, suggesting some spontaneous and unconventional activities. Gil relished the limelight as he needed the affirmation the attention gave him. He might even embellish or exaggerate a story or accomplishment to ensure people would like him. He was sensitive about his appearance and liked to present himself well which made him vulnerable to criticism.

Gil could get very emotional about topics near and dear to his heart and would not hold back on giving you his strong, frank, and blunt opinion. Unfortunately, Gil's excitability and enthusiasm would cause him to act impulsively and not thoroughly think things through. His emotions would color his logic and allowed others to easily sway him.

While Gil could impress others as a demonstrative and friendly guy, he had a hard time forming lasting personal relationships. Unresolved issues from the past made it hard for him to trust. If anyone got too close, he would put up a wall. The very friends that were attracted to him, he could just as easily walk away from before they had a chance to hurt him. Gil's tendency to be absorbed with himself also made it hard for him to maintain close relationships. He judged people subjectively in relationship to his own values and standards. He impressed others as thinking he was more important and more knowledgeable than they were. Boredom and a desire for change made him restless. All these factors could have made Gil susceptible to abusing drugs or alcohol in his penchant for pleasure, relief from anxiety, and search for himself.

Thinking Style/Intellect:
Gil would have been considered a cumulative thinker, a mental process that involves carefully gathering and assembling proven facts to draw a conclusion (like a bricklayer builds a wall brick by brick). It is a slower process of thinking but one that yields accurate conclusions. Gil also had some analytical ability. If he had to assemble something, he would follow the instructions one step at a time, not intuitively. Gil had average to above average intelligence and the ability to grasp abstract concepts and envision new concepts and theories.

Talents:
Gil mentions Ray Bradbury in his journal entry; it sounded like he had a desire to be a writer. This would have been a good choice considering his talents. He was good at expressing his emotions and was a clear, verbally articulate communicator. He had a taste for the aesthetic and cultural and could be very creative with an abstract imagination for storytelling and an ability to produce new ideas involving people, places, objects, and activities.

His cumulative thinking style meant he could build his stories in a logical sequence for the readers. His writing shows indicators of being poetic and sensitive. Writing could have served as a great outlet for Gil's strong mental energy. He might have been drawn to spiritual and philosophical topics. Gil's writing also shows he might have made a good composer and performer of music. Jeanne mentioned he considered becoming a ballet dancer. This would have been an ideal pursuit for him with his creativity, aesthetic nature, and love of physical activity.

Work Habits:

Oftentimes there was a big difference in what Gil *wished* to accomplish and what he was actually able to accomplish. He had lots of pent up mental and physical energy that he had a difficult time translating into action. He would get enthusiastic about a project, but the effort in his follow through would be inconsistent or he would lose steam as the project progressed. If he was "on a role" telling a story or working on a project, he did not like to be interrupted; it was difficult for him to be flexible if he was asked to suddenly switch gears.

Gil did show some signs of initiative. He had fairly good planning and organizational skills but was better at organizing himself than being responsible for others. He could be a good listener but was selective about what he was going to absorb and/or ignore. Gil would have worked best in an environment that was not too stressful. It was hard for him to cope under too much pressure. Any disciplined approach he took to a project was oftentimes undermined by his impulsivity and strong instinctual drives. He had a tendency not to see things as they actually were, as if he was not firmly rooted in reality. Gil was motivated by ambition. He had big dreams and wanted to acquire the nicer things of life that he thought could bring him pleasure.

Conclusion:

Gilbert Lee Johnson, at age 24, was an intelligent, creative, sensitive, emotional, and ambitious man blessed with many talents and much potential. At the time of the writing, the challenges that may have held him back from his full potential were his impulsiveness, need to satisfy his instinctual drives, and the emotional hurdles from the past he had not fully confronted. Felix Klein, the Father of American Graphology, used to say that if everything went wrong in a person's life but their use of space on the page was good, they could survive life's hardships. Gil's use of space on the page was very good at age 24. He was doing his best to deal with the cards he was dealt.

5/17/75
2:45 a.m.

I scared Ray Bradbury tonight. I asked him if he had ever gotten trapped into a 9-5 job.

"No," he said, "don't ever do that; it's a trap that will allow you to stop writing." I vowed to quit my 9-5 job, and thanked him for the encouragement. I suppose it's frightening to think that you may have influenced someone to do something inheritantly dangerous, especially without knowing whether that person has the abilities necessary to pull it off. I, however, never would have put myself in the position to take

Journal entry from 1975, recording Gilbert Johnson's conversation with science fiction author Ray Bradbury. *Courtesy of the Author's Collection.*

Comparative Analysis of Gilbert L. Johnson's
Handwriting from 1975 to 1984
Right-handed male, age 33 in 1984
By Sally Mosko, CG - 10/7/2020

Having previously analyzed the handwriting of Gilbert Johnson from 1975, I will now point out the graphological differences in his writing from a journal entry written nine years later in 1984.

Self-Image:
One of the most notable differences in Gil's personal pronoun I (PPI) from 1975 is its simplification. Almost all the mother strokes are shortened and simplified, and the father stroke (or dominant male) has been eliminated altogether. Gil's self-image had evolved a great deal in nine years; he had a better sense of who he was. His mother still maintained an influence in his thoughts and perhaps his life, but father's dominant presence was no longer represented in the PPI. Only the early authoritarian influence remained.

The downstroke of the PPI is straight and firm. Gone is the "rocker bottom" of the PPI which showed how unrooted and susceptible Gil was to the influence of others. The elimination of the large centripetal circles in both the PPI and text, also points to a new, less egocentric, and self-absorbed person. This is affirmed also by the reduction in relative size of the PPI. He no longer had to compensate as much for feelings of insecurity. While Gil still looked for affirmation, his sensitivity and vulnerability to criticism was less pronounced. He no longer had the need to draw attention to himself and had moved away from the self-indulgence of nine years ago. The phallic type of symbolism is all but eliminated except in one PPI. It appears that Gil had chosen to block any memories of past sexual events.

"Rivers" remain in the writing, showing that Gil had not fully overcome the emotional hurdles of his past; he still had that unfilled hole in his ego. The bouncy and free writing of nine years ago had been replaced with a certain rigidity. He seemed to be trying hard to keep it together, forging ahead and fighting off despondency. As Ruth Holmes, a certified graphologist, often says, "The more control you see in a handwriting, the more the writer is trying hard not to lose control!"

The main contradiction in Gil's personality remained. He wanted to connect with others and his surroundings yet was still guarded about who he would allow to get close. While Gil had eliminated the elaborate t-bar whip from his writing in 1984, he had kept it in his signature of 1982. Only this time, the dramatic stroke now reaches back cutting through his first name and middle initial as if crossing himself out.

Relationships/Social Skills:

Gil's handwriting in 1984 showed he no longer craved the limelight or needed to exaggerate and embellish his stories for attention. He was far less the self-indulgent and spontaneous "fun guy" at the party. He could concentrate better and had less need for constant variety. He even showed more diplomacy in his writing. These changes should have enhanced his ability to form new friendships; however, Gil in 1984 became a more tense, anxious, and rigid person. He was less open to new ideas, more stubborn and assertive and still felt his opinions were the right ones. His new inhibitions may have had a negative impact on forming close relationships and enjoying a healthy sex life.

Thinking Style/Intellect:

By 1984 Gil was thinking faster with more mental clarity. He had greater powers of concentration and more control over his impulses and distractions. His planning and organizational skills had improved.

Gil had also added another type of thinking style to his cumulative one, an investigative/analytical method. This means that sometimes he preferred to do his own research and then analyze his findings. He didn't like to take someone else's word that the fresh paint on the bench was wet; he had to touch it himself. Another noticeable difference from his 1975 writing is that, while he could still grasp abstract concepts, his ability to imagine new concepts and theories was diminished. Emotions still played a greater part in his decision making than logic.

Talents:

In 1975 Gil expressed a desire to be a writer in his journal entry referencing Ray Bradbury. By 1984, he had less abstract and material imagination and a more restricted range of ideas to draw from for creating stories. This is further reinforced by the fact that he was unlikely to accept ideas that differed greatly from his own. Perhaps with his intelligence and mental clarity he could have found satisfaction reporting on cultural, spiritual, or philosophical topics. Technical writing or travel-related narratives that pursue facts might also have been rewarding for him.

Gil's writing shows a gift for manual dexterity that was not present before. With his attention to detail and greater ability to concentrate, that may have been a good route to pursue. He had expressed a desire at one time to be a ballet dancer. With the rhythm of his 1975 writing, I would have encouraged that career for him. But dancing would not have been a good fit for him in 1984 with the rigidity, tension, and emotional inhibition he was experiencing.

Work Habits:

By 1984 there was still a difference in what Gil wished to accomplish and what he was able to accomplish, but the gap had narrowed in those nine years. Gone were the strong instinctual drives that distracted him and his constant need for change. They were replaced with a greater ability to concentrate, more mental acuity and stronger determination than before. He was more efficient with his time, took more initiative and was better at planning and organizing his work than before.

Gil showed a strong desire for perfection in 1984. This could have worked to an employer's advantage in that he would have made sure the job was done correctly. But it would also have slowed his work pace and increased his tension due to compulsively checking and rechecking his work. One strives for perfectionism to avoid criticism, but this positive trait would have been an added source of tension and anxiety for Gil. He would have been better suited to working alone in 1984 than as a team player where it required a lot of give and take. While he could be diplomatic with people when it suited the occasion, he was now less interested in listening to others' viewpoints, more set in his thinking and more likely to push for his own agenda.

Nine years before, Gil had a lot of pent up mental and physical energy he needed to release. By 1984, he no longer had the high ambitions as before. He was utilizing more mental than physical energy and his writing seemed to be losing its healthy rhythm. I would have advised Gil to see a doctor to rule out any medical problems that could have been contributing to his displaced energy and physical weakness. As was true nine years ago, he would have thrived better by seeking a work position that was not too stressful.

Conclusion:

Gil had matured a great deal in nine years; he was less egocentric, self-indulgent and attention seeking with a better sense of who he was. He could focus better, think faster and clearer, and plan and organize more efficiently. But instead of maturity making him a more relaxed person, Gil had grown more anxious and tense, impeding his creativity and impacting his relationships. The "rivers" that remained in his writing reveal that he still had not been able to fill that hole in his ego created by trauma from the past. In 1984, Gil was trying very hard to mentally forge ahead and fight against the pessimism and despondency he felt. Constant anxiety and tension could have been wearing him down and impacting his health, or he may have had an underlying medical issue. Either way, I would have suggested he see his doctor for a medical check-up.

24 Feb 84

This may be one of those strange letters. I'm sitting in my jeep with my dog, who's asleep, & a falcon, overlooking the hills of a municipal dump, smokey – like a battlefield, facing a setting sun. It's a lonely place, but I'm not lonely, not at the moment. I'm trying to trap an eagle & the trap is on a small hill about 500 yards away. Packs of wild dogs are scaring the eagles away, & playing by the trap. They are fighting & barking at one another, calling each other from back & forth across the hills. They are — home.

Have you ever closed your eyes, or stared at one space on an empty wall & felt the people around you. Not people in the same room, but people, souls, minds, thoughts, living beings within, say, a quarter of a mile. Happens to me all the time. In a quiet moment, if I listen, feel, I get the impression that I can hear, know everything going on around me — how many people are fighting, praying, having sex, sitting alone, crying, laughing — I suppose that's strange, my imagination — but it feels real, as if ... I could almost hear their conversations, like the pack of dogs who don't even know I'm here.

Journal entry from 1984, written by Gilbert Johnson while in Saudi Arabia. *Courtesy of the Author's Collection.*

Elsye Purtha Johnson
Right-handed female, age 25 in 1957
by Sally Mosko, CG - 11/2020

Handwriting is often referred to as "brain writing" as it provides a map of the mind, a visible record of the brain impulses that govern one's behavior. These impulses not only dictate how we write but are an expression of our whole personality. Our handwriting is as unique to us as our physical features, speech, and mannerisms. I consider it an honor and privilege to be asked to analyze the handwriting of Jeanne Donovan's mother, the late Elsye Purtha Johnson.

Intellect/Thinking Style:
Elsye's method of thinking would be considered cumulative-analytical. She had a creative mind that gathered established facts then analyzed the information. Elsye's ideas flowed easily from one to another; she solved problems associatively. She would attempt clarification if she felt her ideas were not understood.

Elsye had a probing mind and an innate ability to grasp abstract concepts. She had a good abstract imagination, but she placed limits on the ideas she would consider and accept largely due to her strong need for security. This limited her objectivity and problem-solving. It was difficult for Elsye to be objective as she allowed her feelings to play a big part in her thinking. People and events were evaluated subjectively. This emotional impulsivity was often the cause of mistakes in judgement.

Elsye was blessed with a creative imagination when it came to the area of everyday life involving people, places, objects, and activities. The immediate concerns of family, home, friends, and community were the areas that dominated her interests and where she focused her creative gifts. Elsye was a doer with a tendency to become overly involved in too many things at once. As a result, she was not always efficient with her time. She accomplished more when a project had structured steps to follow, few distractions and well-defined goals where she could control the outcome. She might have dragged her feet getting started but once she got going, she did not want to stop until completed. Asking her to change course halfway through would have been upsetting for her.

Social Skills/Relationships:

When Elsye entered the room, it was hard not to notice; she would light it up with her presence. She could draw a shy person out of the corner and make complete strangers feel perfectly comfortable. She had a gift for relating to many different types of people on their level. Elsye no doubt dressed smartly and spent time on make-up and hair as personal appearance was important to her. She was excitable, demonstrative, and quick to react with elation or discouragement. Elsye cried and laughed easily, and her emotions were on display for all to see in her voice, gestures, facial expression, gait and even in her silence. It was almost impossible for her to conceal her feelings. She could stir others' emotions and be stirred by their emotions. Elsye could be very affectionate, amiable, and quick to respond with compassion for a good cause. She did not care for it when someone interrupted her emotional displays and was easily hurt by coldness, or slights.

Elsye had a strong need to be accepted by others, so much so that she could be indiscriminate in her relationships. This set her up for disappointment as she would be hurt over and over from choosing poorly. She could get entangled in other people's lives whether intending to or not. She might even have put her own opinions aside to conform to others just to gain acceptance. Elsye avoided friction. She may have had a lot of conflict in her past and just did not want to deal with it anymore. The path of least resistance was easier.

Elsye could become quite possessive in a friendship once established, sometimes making unrealistic demands of a person's time and resources. She wanted others to give her space, yet she crowded them with her dependency. She was clever in manipulating a situation to her advantage. Regardless of the amount of attention she received, she still experienced a sense of deprivation. Others saw her as outgoing, but inside she was insecure and in a constant state of anxiety and dejection. Sometimes it was hard for her to recognize herself as worthy and adequate. I sense that Elsye felt a void inside that she tried to fill with material things. Indicators in the writing show that she had a taste for the finer things in life with her dreams and ambitions set on acquiring nice things, symbols of prestige, just for the sake of owning them and the feelings of security it gave her.

Self-Image:
We look to the personal pronoun I (PPI) to assess a person's self-concept and the impact of the parents (or dominant nurturer and dominant father figure) on an individual. Elsye's PPI showed she did not always view her parents as seeing eye to eye on parenting or as a unified team. Father appears to have had a greater impact on Elsye. The return stroke of the PPI, which represents the father, should move to the right or the future, but 36% of the time the end stroke plunges into the lower zone, the area representing the past, unconscious drives, and memory. Like her son Gilbert, many of Elsye's PPIs have a "rocker bottom," which means at age 25 she was not anchored firmly in the knowledge of who she was and could be easily influenced.

Since I had prior knowledge of Elsye's father sexually abusing her as a child, I looked for indicators in the writing that might support that possibility. While graphology can never confirm a particular past event or predict a future one, we can still look for marks in the writing that could collectively demonstrate the *likelihood* of sexual trauma in the past.

- Most of the PPI's have a leftward (father) emphasis that goes far beyond what Palmer copybook handwriting taught. This leftward movement represents a preoccupation with the past, someone who lives in their memories and relates everything happening now to what happened then. (Graphologist Erika Karohs, PhD, author of *Handwriting Analysts' Companion*)
- The father stroke of the PPI points downward toward the LZ 36% of the time, an area representing the past, unconscious drives and memories. Possibly, memories of abuse by her father could be what she was pushing into her unconscious.
- Many oval letters have circles inside which often point to past sexual problems, conditions, or situations. (Pat Peterson, CG, author of *Fast Facts*, volumes 1 & 2)

- Dots made in some of the initial strokes of oval letters can represent a "dark spot" in a writer's past, as observed by Jean-Hippolyte Michon, a 19th century French graphologist and founder of graphology.
- Angles inside ovals can represent humiliating childhood experiences which the person has not been able to overcome. Sometimes it is no longer in the conscious memory. (Graphologist Erika Karohs, PhD, author of *Handwriting Analysts' Companion*)
- While this is not an indicator of abuse, it does point to possible conflict with the father, the pinched triangular shape on the capital letter D at the left base. Dor Gauthier, a Canadian graphologist, sees this part of the D as a symbol of the father figure. Many flattened letter a's indicate anxiety caused by superiors or persons that have authority over her. Could her father have been the root of that anxiety?
- In 8% of the PPIs, the father stroke has a phallic-like shape.

Other indicators in the writing point to a dysfunctional upbringing. Elsye's constant search for love and approval shows she didn't get the nourishment she needed as a child. Parents were probably slow to praise and quick to criticize which left emotional scars and a lasting sensitivity to criticism for Elsye. Fortunately, this sensitivity gave her the ability to empathize with others.

Elsye's writing shows many marks of inner sadness, dejection, and a negative attitude. She felt pressure from superiors or anyone in authority which caused her constant anxiety. Financial worries may have plagued her. She feared that her dreams might never materialize yet wanted others to believe she was happier than she was. All these stressors could have set Elsye up for self-destructive behavior.

So how did Elsye learn to cope with stress, anxiety, and the despondency she felt? Her first instinct was to protect herself from situations that caused her stress. Stress made her behave in a way that helped take the pressure off herself such as employing one or more avoidance techniques like procrastination, evasion, excuses and even withdrawal. This does not mean she was deceitful; these behaviors just helped her cope in the face of what she felt was an overwhelming threat.

Elsye mentioned her Christian faith in her letter to Marlin. Her handwriting indicates religion and spirituality were important in her life. Turning to her faith in times of stress may have carried her through many tough moments.

Work Habits:

Elsye possessed many fine qualities that employers would have found desirable. She shows indicators of being a reliable and productive employee. She approached a job with enthusiasm and a willingness to please her supervisor or manager. She strived for accuracy and persisted until each assigned job was completed. Elsye's enthusiasm and willingness to please might have driven her to take on too many projects at once; she had to be cautious as she did not possess an endless supply of physical energy. Her desire to be thorough sometimes hampered her efficiency if she was under a tight deadline. She would have worked best with a supervisor that structured an assignment with clear cut steps and expectations.

Elsye had many good qualities that would enable her to work well with other people, be it supervisors, employees, or customers. She was diplomatic and tactful and if things were not going her way, she knew how to maneuver a situation for the outcome she wanted. She had a sensitivity that made her empathetic towards others.

Elsye's daughter Jeanne had mentioned Elsye worked as a bookkeeper. Before knowing this, I guessed from the handwriting she might have made a good accountant; that's fairly close! With her good mind, analytical skills and attention to detail, a bookkeeper position would have been a good fit for her.

Conclusion:

Elsye was an intelligent, creative, productive, and outgoing 25-year-old woman who was hard to keep up with. She wore her heart on her sleeve and was never afraid to express her emotions. For a woman who had endured years of sexual abuse in childhood, Elsye had developed the coping skills to survive and persevere. However, her early trauma came with an expensive psychological price tag that affected her feelings of self-worth and her personal relationships. She had to learn to look after herself. Elsye hid her emotional scars, secrets and inner sadness behind a smile and leaned on her faith to get through life's challenges. She truly was a survivor.

Additional Remarks

A graphologist's best measure of accuracy in analyzing a handwriting is the feedback from the writer or the person submitting the handwriting for analysis that knows the writer well. To test my skills, I analyzed Elsye's letter first then read her daughter Jeanne's memoir in addition to receiving written feedback from Jeanne. Below are some additional comments.

I had stated that Elsye's sensitivity might have made her an empathetic person toward others. She was empathetic, but it seems she showered this empathy on the many pets that were taken into the household. Jeanne said she was also very empathetic toward her son Gil later in his life.

I stated that the many angles in Elsye's oval formations could represent her humiliating childhood experience of sexual abuse. This was true, but Elsye then repeated the pattern of humiliating her own children when angry by making Gil eat soap, beating Jeanne with a bristle brush or belt, and striking two-year-old David causing bruises and burning him with a match to teach him a lesson for playing with matches.

Jeanne mentioned Elsye had a nervous breakdown shortly after writing the letter to Marlin. Her overall writing pressure was light, indicative of a person that does not have unlimited physical energy; she was easily taxed from the stress of two small children and limited finances. Elsye not only had light pressure but had t-bar crossings that were quite faint. T bars represent how much will power one puts into their goals. Clearly, Elsye was depleted of energy.

Handwriting sample from a letter written by Elsye Johnson to Marlin Johnson during their **separation.** *Courtesy of the Author's Collection.*

REFERENCES

"330,000 Children Abused in French Catholic Church over 70 Years, Landmark Report Estimates." Catholic News Agency. October 11, 2021. https://www .catholicnewsagency.com/news/249185/330000-children-abused-in-french -catholic-church-over-70-years-says-landmark-report.

"2004 Khobar Massacre." Wikipedia. Accessed September 19, 2024. https://en.wikipedia .org/wiki/2004_Khobar_massacre.

Advincula, A. "The Mysteries of Isshin-Ryu Karate." *Black Belt Magazine*, April 1986, 26.

Apple, R. W., Jr. "Airport Is Closed." *New York Times*, January 25, 1979.

Bennett, C. T. *Our Roots Grow Deep: A History of Cottle County*. Floydada, TX: Blanco Offset Printing, 1970.

The Bible. King James Version. Oxford University Press.

Black, C. A., and R. R. Deblassie. "Sexual Abuse in Male Children and Adolescents: Indicators, Effects, and Treatments." *Adolescence* 28, no. 109 (Spring 1993): 123–33.

"Borger, Texas." Wikipedia. Accessed September 27, 2024. https://en.wikipedia.org /wiki/Borger_Texas.

Burns, K., dir. *The Vietnam War*. 2017; BBC.

Cadwell, L. L. "Recollections of Jeet Kune Do Project." Interviewed by R. I. Johnson, August 11, 2021.

"Catholic Church Sexual Abuse Cases by Country." Wikipedia. Accessed October 1, 2021. https://en.wikipedia.org/wiki/Catholic_Church_sexual_abuse_cases_by _country.

Centers for Disease Control and Prevention. "A Timeline of HIV/AIDS." HIV.gov, 2016. https://www.hiv.gov/sites/default/files/aidsgov-timeline.pdf.

Citron, A., and V. Merina. "'Cleaned Up' Gay Baths Fight to Survive Closure Threats." *Los Angeles Times*, January 26, 1988.

Collection of personal correspondance between M. E. Johnson and E. Johnson. August 1947–October 1951.

"Dharan." Wikipedia. Accessed December 27, 2021. https://en.wikipedia.org/wiki /Dhahran.

Dimock, P. "Adult Males Sexually Abused as Children: Characteristics and Implications for Treatment." *Journal of Interpersonal Violence* 3, no. 2 (1988): 203–21.

Fell, B. *Chalk History*. Special report, Cottle County Historical Commission, 1995.

"Flagstaff, Arizona." Wikipedia. Accessed September 16, 2021. https://en.wikipedia.org /wiki/Flagstaff,_Arizona.

France, M. Letters and emails, 2011–21.

France, M. *The Mystery of Loving Men.* Unpublished screenplay, 1994.

France, M. "Recollections of Gilbert L. Johnson." Interviewed by J. Donovan, February 22, 2011.

"History of Isshin-Ryu Karate." United States Isshinryu Karate Association. Accessed September 17, 2021. https://usika.com/history/.

"History of the Catholic Church." Wikipedia. Accessed September 27, 2024. https: //en.wikipedia.org/wiki/History_of_the_Catholic_Church.

Inosanto, D. L., dir. *The Sensei.* 2019; KDMG.

Johnson, D. "Family Lore." Interviewed by R. Johnson, April 1, 2018.

Johnson, G. L. "After Report of the Iranian Revolution." Unpublished manuscript, written in 1980.

Johnson, G. L. Personal journals, 1969–71.

Johnson, G. L. Personal letters of GLJ, 1972–84.

Jones, S. "Polish Americans." Wikipedia, September 16, 2021. https://en.wikipedia/wiki /Polish_Americans.

Kaplan, T. "Group Calls for AIDS Unit at County Hospital." *Los Angeles Times*, July 10, 1988.

Kent, C. "Recollections of GLJ." Interviewed by R. Johnson, September 14, 2021.

"Khobar." Wikipedia. Accessed December 27, 2021. https://en.wikipedia.org/wiki /Khobar.

Kolnegari, M., M. Jamali, M. Naserifard, K. Ghous, M. Hazra ., C. T. Panter, and J. Dwyer. "Falconry Petroglyphs in Iran." *European Journal f Wildlife Research* 67, no. 3 (2021).

Kondourajian, L. "Could an Iconic Abandoned Hospital Ea e LA's Housing Crisis?" *Design and Architecture*, December 17, 2019.

Lanning, K. V. *Child Molesters: A Behavioral Analysis for Law Enforcement Officers Investigating Cases of Child Sexual Exploitation.* Quan co, VA: National Center for Missing and Exploited Children, 1992.

Lanning, K. V. *Child Molesters: A Behavioral Analysis or Professionals Investigating Cases of Child Sexual Exploitation.* Quantico, VA: National Center for Missing and Exploited Children, 2010.

Lee, B. *Tao of Jeet Kune Do.* Valencia, CA: Ohara, 1975

Longely, K. "The Grunt's War." *New York Times*, February 17, 2017.

Maloney, S., and K. Razipour. "The Iranian Revolution—A Timeline of Events." Brookings Institution, January 24, 2019. https://www.brookings.edu/blog/order -from-chaos/2019/01/24/the-iranian-revolution-a-timeline-of-events/.

"Mohamad Reza Pahlavi." Wikipedia. Accessed September 27, 2024. https://en.wikipedia .org/wiki/Mohammad_Reza_Pahlavi.

"Muqurin bin Abdulaziz." Wikipedia, December 27, 2021. https://en.wikipedia.org /wiki/Muqrin_bin_Abdulaziz.

National Center for Victims of Crime. "Child Sexual Abuse Statistics." Victimsofcrime .org. Accessed October 2021. https://victimsofcrime.org/child-sexual-abuse -statistics/.

National Institute of Justice. *Youth Victimization: Prevalence and Implications.* Washington, DC: US Department of Justice, 2003.

Neugebauer, J. M. *Plain Farmer: The Diary of William G. DeLoach, 1914–1964.* College Station: Texas A&M University Press, 1991.

"Prohibition in the United States." Wikipedia. Accessed September 27, 2024. https: //en.wikipedia.org/wiki/Prohibition_in_the_United_States.

Ryan, H. "Farming and Family Lore." Interviewed by R. I. Johnson, May 21, 2017.

Ryan, M. J. "The Johnson Family History." Personal memoirs of Mildred Johnson Ryan. Unpublished manuscript, 2002.

"Saudia Arabia." Wikipedia. Accessed December 27, 2021. https://en.wikipedia.org/wiki /Saudi_Arabia.

"Super Chief." Wikipedia. Accessed August 5, 2021. https://en.wikipedia.org/wiki /Super_Chief.

Thomas, C. "The Isshin-Ryu Karate System." *Black Belt Magazine*, January 1996, 60.

Tommaney, S. "True Texas Tales of Prostitution, Cocaine, Gambling, Violence and Murder." *HoustonPress*, September 19, 2021. https://www.houstonpress.com/arts /true-texas-tales-of-prostitution-cocaine-gambling-violence-and-murder-8154965.

Wanted advertisement. *Los Angeles Daily News*, November 14, 1945, 16.

"What Is Immune Thrombocytopenia." *Healio*, September 19, 2016. https://www.healio .com/news/hematology-oncology/20160919/what-is-immune-thrombocytopenia.

INDEX

ABOUT THE AUTHORS

JEANNE DONOVAN, sister of Gil Johnson, and simultaneous child sexual abuse survivor. After a rollercoaster childhood, she determined never to repeat her Mother's mistakes, and succeeded. As an endcap to her life, she resolved to reveal Gil's story so that other victims, especially males, would not feel alone. In this book she offers insight and resources that will help.

RONALD I. JOHNSON is a mechanical engineer within the Department of Energy and holds a Professional Engineering license. He has also served as a forensic expert witness in accident reconstruction litigation throughout the state of Texas. He resides in Amarillo with his wife, Suparaht, and their Australian Sheperd – Thunder.